Follow Your Heart

By

Eva Hoffmann

ISBN: 978-0692093634

I dedicate this book to anyone who wants to follow their heart and transform their life.

Grief can be the garden of compassion. If you keep your heart open through everything, your pain can become your greatest ally in your life's search for love and wisdom.

Rumi

Your pain is the breaking of the shell that encloses your understanding.

Khalil Gibran

My biggest *Thank You!* goes to my dearest husband, who has always stood by my side and encouraged me to write my story down, as well as helping me to finally find the person who could write the story with me. He knew that in doing that I could heal from it and move on. He was so right.

I want to thank my wonderful kids, who helped their mom and respected not to talk to me when I had my writers head on.

A big thank you to Linda Mary Smith, who had the patience to listen to my story and convert it into a novel. Without her help, it would be nowhere near as much fun to read. And also to Joanne Sale, who helped me to edit the book and put it in the format you are reading now.

And last but not least, my life, which gave me the gift of transformation, the virtue I am the most grateful for. This is how I started my new career as a holistic coach for life and nutrition.

After all, what I learned from my years in Egypt was:

If you are not happy, then you must change!

Eva Hoffmann

Chapter 1

A Daring Adventure

I always love the cocooned feeling of being in an airplane, assured of some peaceful moments while flying high above the world's shadows. Back then, those regular escapes from my hectic career in the fashion industry were important and going on holiday with my father was an extra bonus. He gently shook my shoulder as I dozed against the headrest. "Ella, Ella. Wake up. The plane's about to land. We need to get ready." I opened my bleary eyes to gaze out the window onto a brilliant, blue sea. It took me a few seconds to recall where we were flying to - South Sinai, Egypt.

The aircraft's wheels whirred into position, as we descended over expansive coral reefs with dive boats bobbing at the water's edge. I squinted and was sure I could make out huge shoals of fish just below the water's glittering surface. "Wow, look! The reef looks so clear, even from here."

My father however, was looking the other way, craning to see out the other side of the plane. I followed his gaze and gasped as I saw the Sinai Mountains bubbling up from the sand in their ancient volcanic way, streaks of black basalt cutting jagged lines through the softer red granite; layers of peaks stretching far into the distance. Strangely beautiful.

It seemed impossible that there was enough land between mountains and sea to accommodate the sprawling, thriving tourist town of Sharm el Sheikh with its low rise resorts crowding every stretch of beach front. Gusts of wind caught the side of the airplane a couple of times and as our landing speed became more obvious the closer we got to the tarmac, a tense silence settled over the passengers. A few seconds later as the wheels made jolting contact, some passengers broke into spontaneous applause. Whispered words echoed around the cabin as veiled women and lightly bearded men, sighed with relief that our turbulent journey from Cairo was over. I had, in fact, slept through most of it.

The passengers (who were a mix of locals, package tourists, backpackers, divers and sun seekers) stuffed their now obsolete jackets into carry-on bags and readied their designer sunglasses. We stood at the head of the plane, eager and impatient in the aisle as the stewards swung open the fuselage doors. Regardless of the amount of time I had spent in hot countries, the wall of heat that momentarily engulfed me took my breath away. We rattled down the aircraft's metal steps, clanking all the way and shuffled into the shuttle bus waiting at the bottom.

It was sweltering. "Ooof, I don't recall it being this hot the last time we came to Egypt" groaned Papa. "I forget just how intense this desert heat can be." His rapidly reddening face was already glistening but he grinned and winked at me, "Now I understand why our flights were so cheap at this time of year!"

I pulled a fan from the top of my bag, a beautiful, detailed piece and one of my favourites, which I had recently added to my collection after finding it in a Bali bazaar. I enjoyed its cooling breeze. Two Egyptian children stared at me solemnly through wide eyes. I hid my face behind the fan for a moment, then whispered "Boo!" around the side of it. They giggled with surprise then smiled shyly, reaching out for their mother whose serious expression softened. I wondered if I would ever be taking a holiday with children of my own, just as I was going away with my father.

A Daring Adventure

We entered the airport and descended into noisy chaos. There were no queues, only clamouring tourists pushing and shoving in throngs around the desks of uniformed officials, who showed their distinct disinterest by slouching and scowling (with what appeared to be an obligatory cigarette, either in one hand or hanging out the side of their mouth). Everything seemed so random. Some tourists were ushered through, others detained. Some sent through one door and others through another. There were few signs in Arabic and even less in English.

I glanced at Papa and together we began to thread our way through the mob towards a desk. "Visa, visa!" the official shouted at us once we were in front of him. We handed over our passports.

The official looked at the pages and looked back at us blankly, "Visa visa?"

"Here!" I said, opening my passport and pointing at the stickered page, "Here it is".

"No visa!", the official repeated, shaking his head and gesticulating roughly at the page. "This no visa. Need visa."

I insisted, resorting to pigeon English. "YES visa. This visa Germany!"

The official shook his head with conviction and tried to hand the passports back, "You need visa. Over there", pointing to the melee in front of other desks.

I was just as determined, "What's the problem? We got this visa from the Egyptian embassy in Germany. It is a valid visa!" We had both purchased visas prior to departure in Germany, just as the travel guides had advised we should.

A smartly dressed Egyptian man in the crowd stepped up to the desk. I couldn't understand a word of their rapid conversation in

Arabic but the official looked at the visa again while the business man pointed at the German text. The official shrugged, nodded vacantly over our shoulders and handed the stamped and now approved passports back to me saying in a flat tone "Okay visa, okay visa" as he waved us through. I rolled my eyes at Papa.

We hesitantly followed other tourists to try to locate the baggage carousel where we could find our bags. The chaos continued, as I firmly grasped onto a metal luggage carrier that sported a wonky wheel despite being the best I could find (at least it had four wheels!). "There! There's our luggage! Quickly, before it disappears through the flaps again!" My father offered a polite "Excuse me. Excuse me" at first to the people crowding round the carousel, but in the end he just battled through to reach our bags.

As we walked outside the building directly into blinding sunshine, we were faced with a barrage of local taxi drivers who stood boisterously touting for business. Regardless of our shaking heads and telling them we were going to Dahab, not Sharm el Sheikh, they still persisted on hounding my father as the man in our party, "Taxi! Taxi!", "Hey, you need taxi?", "Sir, where you want go? Hadaba? Na'ama Bay? Nabq? Marriot?" "Hey, taxi! Taxi ... taxi!" We pushed through while ignoring them, clutching at our luggage as drivers grappled to lift it off the trolley. The contrast to our tranquil flight was astounding and instantly exhausting.

"Look for a sign for the hotel, Ella... there must be one somewhere. There should be hotel transport waiting for us." We spotted the sign for the Daniela Hotel and waved at the rotund Egyptian man holding it. He quickly responded, "Mr Hartmann? This way, please." Rescued at last. Papa and I exchanged relieved glances, feeling frayed from the intense heat and the mob. As our driver reached out for our bags, the crowd of disappointed drivers fell away. "Come Mr Hartmann, Madam Hartmann. The car is ready. We can move straight away to Dahab."

Inside the minibus two other couples waited, wafting themselves with makeshift fans - leaflets, brochures, landing cards. They occupied all the seats in the shaded part of the bus. But that didn't bother me as our smiling driver hopped behind the wheel, I was now in full holiday mode! I worked incredibly hard in my professional life but on the flip side, I knew how to holiday extremely well!

When my father had asked me where I wanted to dive that year (2002), I had immediately opted again for the Red Sea. On a previous trip to Egypt we I had flown to Marsa Alam in the far south, where the diving had been so superb that I was keen to relive the magical, underwater experience. We had spent most days there on a launch and only ventured into the local village to make phone calls or other urgent errands. It was an eye opening and hugely fun experience.

This time (after some research) I had chosen Dahab in South Sinai on the western shores of the Gulf of Aqaba. Papa had suggested we stay at the Sheraton in Sharm el Sheikh but I had pouted cheekily saying, "But for work I always stay in five star hotels. I don't want to think about work." I talked him into the smaller, more intimate German operated Daniela further north in Dahab hoping for a more personal experience.

My head was already spinning with a thousand questions to ask the driver but first, we had to find a way to squeeze ourselves into the back of the Daniela mini bus. I soon saw that this was a blessing in disguise. Our driver continued to chain smoke stiflingly coarse, acrid cigarettes and involuntary memories as an ex smoker flooded my brain. On other occasions whilst on holiday with friends I had fallen for the lure of cheap, truly awful cigarettes. Despite being in my mid thirties, this time under Papa's protective eye, I had to resist the temptation.

It wasn't long before we left the airport mayhem and the Sharm el Sheikh resorts (which are modern yet of dubious taste) far behind us and were driving through rubbish strewn desert towards the rough, jagged mountains. The rubbish was something I would never get used to but my eyes were anyway drawn away, to the strangely stunning mountains. "Papa," I whispered, pointing out of the car at the strange, jutting rock formations. "Aren't they beautiful?" He stared out of the window before replying with "Hmmm, the Alps are beautiful. The Himalayas are beautiful. These are ..." and he took some time to think before adding pointedly: "...not beautiful." I laughed. "You are always so brutally honest, Papa. OK, I agree they aren't conventionally beautiful but there is something very special about them. They are the biblical mountains of Moses after all, where he received the Ten Commandments." I instantly felt in awe of those mountains, ancient and austere, as if laying bare the geological skeletal bones of the earth for us.

We all dozed as that dreary heat lulled us into lethargy. The warm air was flowing through the open window with little cooling effect, more like the air from a hair dryer than anything else. I lay my head against my father's shoulder and watched the scenery float by. I wondered at the ramshackle settlements we passed; the crude concrete block huts surrounded by patchwork fences, with goats and camels wandering about picking at sparse, scrubby

6

bushes. This wasn't the desert I had imagined of flowing sand dunes and Arabian Nights. This was harsh and rude and seemingly, of little grace. How could people live here? Where did their water come from and what did the animals survive on?

My ears popped as they had in the airplane, so I sensed we were very gradually climbing up a pass in a northern direction, winding our way up wide, rocky valleys where rivers must have flowed before. When does rain fall in these mountains? There was certainly no sign of water. Everything was so dry and dusty.

"Why are we stopping?" my father asked. I shrugged and tried to peer forward out of the van window. A large, colourful mosaic boasting 'Welcome to Dahab' was directly in front of us. In the centre of it sat a picture of President Mubarak, like a bay leaf framed Roman Caesar. He was surrounded by a mountain scene, of a Bedouin woman seated in front of a tent, a camel and a horse nearby, along with a sparkling blue sea full of fish, a diver and wind surfers. I replied to the mosaic's greeting with a silent 'Thank you!'

"There's a policeman talking to the driver. I wonder what's wrong." My father shrugged, "Oh.... Probably just another of these checks they have in Egypt. Nothing to worry about." All I could see where some casually dressed men and black uniformed police with rifles slung over their shoulders milling about but it wasn't long before they waved us through. I have to admit, the nozzle of the rifle poking out of the concrete watch tower did seem slightly ominous but other than that, I didn't find it too menacing.

There were still no real signs of any habitation, just more towering peaks rising out of the flat, sandy valley. The centre of the road had tall palm trees placed at regular intervals along it and free standing bougainvillea, blazed with stunning red and white blooms. The valley widened and I caught glimpses of the sparkling sea. "We're here! I can see the sea again. Dahab must be close," I proclaimed excitedly, my enthusiasm for new places clearly showing. "Not much to see." Papa said without enthusiasm. He was tired. He wasn't usually so surly.

We drove along rough, narrow streets past low, single or two storey buildings made of concrete. Everything seemed so untidy, with rubble and rough edges everywhere. The van slowed for a small herd of multi-coloured goats and straggly sheep crossing the road to a rusty, overflowing dumpster. I frowned, "Oh look, one of those sheep has such long hooves! That must be so difficult. It's limping. Why doesn't someone do something to help it? I wonder if anyone owns them." Papa looked indignant, "If someone does, they certainly don't take much care of them. They could easily be run over." Our driver impatiently honked the horn as we wound our way through them but the animals ignored us, meandering along at their own pace.

As we drove down a slope towards the sparkling sea, I looked across the gulf to see Saudi Arabia's mountains rising in the hazy light. The Gulf of Aqaba reaches north from the Red Sea with Egypt to the West and Saudi Arabia to the East, to a point in the north where Israel and Jordan touch its waters at established ports. At that moment, I truly felt I was right in the epicentre of the Middle East with its history and modern conflict, none of which I was to find in Dahab.

The Bay, Dahab

It was late afternoon by then with long shadows streaking across the sandy slopes and the shadows etched into the mountain's ruggedness. Their dusty colours had changed from beige to Paris pink, with grey ridges and striations. "Wow!! I thought, "What sort of place has Paris pink mountains!" And the sea! Bright aqua coloured patches like swimming pools inside the reef, with gentle white breakers rippling at the reef edge. I was mesmerised by the colours that seemed to change before my eyes.

The van bumped over a ridge and we were crunching along a gravel road, or a track, more like. I wondered exactly where our hotel was. Perhaps my father had been right and we should have chosen the Sharm el Sheikh Sheraton. The only other vehicles on the road were a few battered old Jeeps bouncing along, passing us by with tourists crammed in, holding on to the metal frames covered in tatty canvas. They were laughing and in good spirits as they got jolted along. I smiled at their joyous freedom. We finally turned into the gates at the Daniela Hotel, with its white painted walls and cooling domes on the water's edge, overlooking the Gulf to Saudi. The granite cliffs to the west gave a protective feeling.

We checked in and I was delighted to find my room looked

down on a clear blue pool with views to the sea as well. But Papa was tired, "Ella, you go along and enjoy the last rays of sun. I am a little fatigued. I think I will just have a short rest before we dress for dinner." So I wandered out to the water's edge, dipping my toes into the lapping waves and watching the setting sun paint the hazy mountains of Saudi Arabia; first pink, then violet, before fading away. I would learn over time how that view changed every day. Sometimes you couldn't even see those mountains, yet at others, it felt like you could touch them.

There were a few tourists still stretched out in the fading light, beach towels covering their loungers under the woven cane sun shades. The temperature had cooled to a very pleasant 24°C, with a light breeze wafting along the shore. I could smell jasmine releasing its beautiful perfume into the evening air.

That evening, we ate in the hotel dining room and retired early. The night air was warm but I didn't use the air conditioning and fell asleep to the whirling fan and the faint sound of waves lapping on the coral shore. Bliss.

The next day, I woke gently to the sound of those same waves but already felt the heat of the sun as it rose over Saudi. I had missed the first sunrise of our holiday but I thought to myself, "It doesn't matter, there will be others. Every sunrise here must be so beautiful."

I knocked gently on Papa's door. "Yes, Ella. I'm coming." He knew I would already be keen to have breakfast and head to the diving centre to get kitted out. That's what we were there for after all! The diving centre came well recommended in the hotel's information and as it was German - Egyptian owned, we figured they would operate to international standards. No fly by night cowboy operation that you hear some travellers complain about! My father had been diving for many years and yet he was still as excited as I was, anticipating the always changing vista that one sees underwater. Scuba diving might take place on our planet but it feels like another world. I had done my first dive when I was fourteen years old and had many diving holidays all over the world since then.

"Hi, I'm Steffi. Welcome to the Daniela diving centre. I hope you both slept well," said the instructor as she greeted us brightly, with an obvious German accent. We replied in English but it wasn't long before we slipped into our native language and felt at ease as we discussed the diving plan for the day. She explained we would be required to do a 'check dive' as it was longer than six months since our last one. We would spend some time demonstrating safety skills and then commence with a familiarisation dive in the area.

A German guy rocked up and confidently introduced himself. "Hi, I'm Kurt and I'm the manager here so if there's anything you need or want please feel free to ask me. Steffi will kit you out and I will be your guide for the check dive this morning." Kurt excused himself and disappeared into an office while we went to get fitted for our equipment. I always travelled with my own mask and fins but the weight and bulk of the other gear made it impossible to carry them with me. Which was another reason why we always chose reputable diving centres, to ensure they had modern, well-maintained equipment.

By nine thirty by we were being bundled into one of the small pickup trucks, like the ones we had seen when driving through the township. Papa opted to sit inside the cab but I scrambled into the back with a couple of the other divers. I wasn't going to miss a minute of this fresh air and sunshine. It felt glorious to be sun kissed in the gentle sea breeze while wearing my bikini. I was eager to enjoy the early rays of sunshine, as I knew within an hour or so the sun would be too strong too bear, even for my easily tanned skin.

We carried our gear to the shore, in the large plastic crates provided by the diving centre. The temperature was already in the high twenties even though it was before ten in the morning.

I stayed close to my father as we were buddies on the dive, a scuba system that ensures that there are always two people looking out for each other underwater. "Papa, do you need help with that weight belt?" I could see sweat gathering across his brow and that he was struggling with all the equipment in the heat. We had opted for full suits and I realised that perhaps this was making him far too warm. The extra neoprene in them meant we would be carrying even more lead weight in this buoyant sea, although this would protect us from any scrapes from coral or (heaven forbid) touching a deadly poisonous scorpion fish. All our dives were to be shore dives, rather than stepping off boats, which we were more used to in other diving centres in the world. Kurt looked over and seemed to take in the situation very quickly. "Before we put on the equipment, let's wade into the water and get our suits wet. It makes them fit easier and keeps us cool while we gear up." It was indeed a relief to get wet but it felt funny to be floating so high in the extra salty water. I giggled as my feet kept floating to the surface, encased in dive booties. It was as if I was sitting in a chair in the water. We finished gearing up and waded in up to waist level to finish putting on our fins and masks, before slowly slipping below the surface to sit on our knees and go through the skill routine that Kurt briefed us with. It wasn't long before he gave us the "OK" signal with his circled thumb and finger, indicating we were about to start the dive.

We were immediately surrounded by fish and I revelled in the amazing visibility and easy floating sensation that I always love when diving. I signalled "OK" to Papa and he returned the gesture. He seemed back to his own self now, under the water in the buoyant 25°C waters and was obviously enjoying the dive too.

Kurt called our attention to look at something, so we followed his pointing hand to a coral outcrop. At first I wondered if I was looking at the right place as I couldn't see anything but the coral. With a flash of colour the coral suddenly moved and I realised there was an octopus mimicking its surroundings, perfectly camouflaged! Watching us warily as we kept a respectful distance from its territory, it quietly slithered his tentacles into a small hole and squeezed completely inside. Such a wonderland! Lionfish fluttered around under ledges resembling strange aquatic birds or insects (I couldn't quite decide which). I did however, know their poisonous reputation and to be aware of their confidence, even if they were not overtly aggressive with us. It was a wonderful first dive seeing so many healthy fish just cruising around the reef and it seemed too soon that we had to return to the entrance.

"Hold my shoulders Papa. Steady yourself before removing your fins." He gripped my shoulder but the difference between being weightless while diving and finding his feet in the slight waves was too much and he stumbled awkwardly backwards. Kurt was there in a second and helped him regain balance and remove his fins. As we emerged from the water we felt the true weight of our equipment as made our way to the mat area. Kurt took over as Papa's buddy so I could easily remove my own equipment.

Later Kurt came over to me and quietly said, "Your father is finding the shore diving in the heat a little taxing, which is not unusual; it has its advantages and disadvantages. We'll take it easy, at your father's pace until we are in the water. We'll both be his dive buddies on the surface to make sure he is feeling comfortable. OK?"

I felt relieved, "Yes, please. I can see he is fine under water, he is very experienced. But gearing up and walking in the water isn't so easy. I guess we are all getting older without realising it."

Kurt smiled, "It'll be fine. We just need to plan around it. I want your father to enjoy the diving without struggling."

"Thank you. You're very kind," I appreciated him taking the time for us to be comfortable. So between Kurt and I, we subtly organized to help each other keep my father safe and I was grateful for his efforts. If Papa noticed, he never mentioned it.

On our third day, I woke to see great piles of fluffy clouds building over the mountains, tumbling and billowing upwards into the open blue. The massive thunderheads, heavy and announcing a storm, nonetheless shone brilliantly in the ever present sun that dominated the normally clear sky. "Will it rain today?" everyone was asking Kurt. "Probably, yes. Rain is forecast and if not in Dahab, most likely in the mountains. We'll do one dive this morning at the Lighthouse and see what happens."

Divers in the Bay

The sun was still shining and the water flat and calm, as we submerged into the clear water. About thirty minutes into the dive, the light suddenly dulled giving an ominous feeling like a partial eclipse under water. We had become so used to brilliant colours and easy visibility it took us a moment to realise the clouds had blotted out the sun. How spoilt for diving we were!

As we remained at five metres doing our diving safety stop, we could see the raindrops pelting onto the surface of the water. Emerging from the water into the rain was a bit weird, although I felt elated to be walking in it in a wetsuit, as thunder and lightning crashed around the now hidden peaks. "We'll take all equipment off, leave it in the boxes and find somewhere to shelter," said Kurt.

My sarong was wet but I didn't mind. It was still warm as about twenty of us crammed into the closest restaurant to shelter from the downpour. "Rain in the desert! How cool is this!" someone remarked. "Yes, very special. It only rains once or twice a year in Dahab, if we are lucky!" laughed Kurt. "Do you think we will be able to do a second dive?" someone else asked. "We'll have to wait and see. Sometimes the water comes down under the bridge and ruins the visibility for a few days here. There are other places but anywhere the fresh waters break through will take a little while to settle down. That's why there is less coral there; the fresh water and silt kills some of it."

We sat drinking tea and chatting in groups. "Who's going to the Halloween party at Tota tonight?" asked one of the local dive masters. Many people chimed in saying they were going. "What about you, Ella? Are you coming to the party?" asked Kurt sitting nearby.

"I didn't know there was a party. Will you be going?"

Kurt smiled and said, "Yeah, sure. Quite a few of us from the diving centre are going. You're welcome to join us and your father too, of course. Tota parties are always great fun." I looked at Papa wondering if he would want to go or how he would feel if I left him alone this evening.

He read my thoughts, "Ella, of course you should go if you want to. I am perfectly able to entertain myself in the evening," smiling at me. I might have been thirty-five but I always felt like his little girl.

"The party won't really start until late," added Kurt. "We probably won't go before ten or even later."

"Ok. I'll go!," I heard myself saying, wondering what a party would be like in an Arab-Muslim country.

"Great," said Kurt, "Do you want us to organize a taxi to pick you up from Daniela?"

"How about we eat in one of the restaurants in the bay tonight, Ella?" suggested Papa. "Then you can go off to the party after. Where is this Tota?"

"Just on the other side of the bridge from here. You can't miss the place, it looks like an old sailing ship plonked on the side of the path!" Kurt laughed, "There'll be lots of people there since it is Halloween tonight. But any night is a good night for a party".

"What should I wear? Do I have to dress in a costume?" I asked.

"Anything you like. Some people will dress up but in Dahab it doesn't matter. Dahab is casual"

It stopped raining as quickly as it had begun and the sun shone brightly once again, making everything steam with vapour. Staff were busy sluicing off the water from the pavement and the carpets and cushions were shaken before being hung out to dry. We decided to walk along to the bridge area to check out the situation. It quickly became obvious that there was a reason for the hump back bridge with concrete embankments, as a swift torrent of clay coloured water was raging into the bay.

The Bridge, Dahab

At the wider opening upriver where the water flowed over the road, a few of the higher sprung 4WDs were slowly wading cautiously across. A red saloon car was skewed across the swirling waters, rammed up against some metal poles where it had come to a halt after been swept away. Without those poles it would probably have floated under and out to sea. Other vehicles wisely waited, stacked up on either side of the clay coloured water. Bedouin children slithered and splashed like eels. They practically lived in the sea, so the currents were nothing to them. "I think that's it for our diving today. Visibility will be shot," explained Kurt. "We may as well pack up and head back to the diving centre. Everything will have settled down again by tomorrow."

Papa and I decided to spend a lazy afternoon at the hotel, as holidays were also a time for us to reconnect as father and daughter. My family lived in the small German town of Kaiserslautern and although I also was based there in my own apartment, I was an inveterate traveller for my career and not often around at home. Fashion was my passion and at that point in my life, I felt I had reached a pinnacle, truly feeling that the world was my oyster. I had negotiated a management position for a very successful fashion house that entailed working for three weeks at a time leading a team of buyers all over the world. Then I had a whole week free to do as I wished, which was usually also spent travelling (airports and hotels were like a second home to me). When working I stayed in five-star hotels but for personal travel I backpacked. That particular holiday to Dahab was ten days of annual leave after which I would return to work for one week before having my normal week off. Life was not only good, it was great.

A Daring Adventure

As the evening approached I wondered what I should wear to the Halloween party. I hadn't brought anything suitable for fancy dress, so in the end I just chose pants and a strappy top, pretty much my usual summer style. I left my long, blonde hair loose around my shoulders and placed my colourful bindi in the centre of my forehead. bindis had become something of a trade mark of my style, as I loved their minute, colourful intricacy. I also appreciated how they encouraged people to look into my eyes, especially when travelling in male dominated societies where men could stare with impunity.

The taxi delivered us to the Lighthouse entrance and we walked to the beach past the Bedouin Son restaurant where we had sheltered that morning, which was now closed for the evening. "Wow. Everything looks different by night! So many foreigners walking about." I said as I took in the busy local area. "Yes, it seems to be a popular night spot," agreed Papa. "Let's explore a little before we choose a restaurant." I slipped my arm through his and we sauntered along, perusing the menu boards in front of the various restaurants. Workers were cajoling, pushy with questions and demands, trying to entice us into each restaurant. We eventually chose one on the water's edge with bright hanging scarves and carpets all over the floor. Within seconds, waiters had delivered our menus and complimentary mixed *mezze* dishes of hummus, tahina, tzatziki and fresh flat bread for us to taste. No doubt it was also a ploy to make sure we stayed seated, as it meant we had already sampled their food for free.

There were lots of options for me to eat with my vegetarian diet and it was a delicious meal in comfortable surroundings. I was pleasantly surprised. Between courses we could see lionfish and others hunting under the restaurant spotlights. "Ok Papa? Best du satt?"

The Butcher's shop

"I am full to the brim! That was a great meal." He sat back and smiled. "So my princess … shall I walk you to the ball?" I laughed.

"Of course! And if I don't like the look of it, we shall just keep walking! Easy … I was surprised you could order beer with your meal. I wonder what a party in an Arab country is like."

We paid for the inexpensive meal (leaving a generous tip) and wandered along the gaily lit promenade. It seemed to come alive at night and there were tourists everywhere, haggling for items in the small garage like shops opposite the restaurants. I was an old hand at that game from my job as a fashion buyer and my regular trips to third world countries like India and the Philippines. Ideally, if the customer starts low and the seller high, they theoretically meet in the middle. The middle ground is where the fun starts, always trying to stay on either side of the midpoint. I always try to know the reasonable price before starting the negotiation. If the seller is asking way too much straight off the bat, then I know it's not even worth bothering.

I could also see that many of the tourist souvenirs were produced in China or India and not Egypt, as the shop assistants were claiming. "Kashmir, madam. Made in Egypt", "Real Egyptian cotton. Best in the world" The last part is true (I smiled to myself) but I have seen those tops being made in India. "Come in to my shop. Look for free." Always trying to guess where I was from, speaking first in Dutch, in Russian then German, "Shai? Would you like to drink tea?" with outstretched arms, trying to usher us in. I didn't reply. If they get you to engage in conversation you are lost! The shops seemed to be selling a lot of the same goods and I wondered where the novelty was - scarves, shoes, sunglasses, poor reproductions of Ancient Egyptian statues, light shades, dresses, and jewellery - all mostly junk.

An old lady sat on a low stone wall wearing a black *abaya,* a light full length coat, and black head scarf. Her goods looked more authentic and I noticed she had small blue black tattoos on her face, chin and forehead. She quickly noticed that I was curious and started her spiel, "Real Bedouin decoration. Cheap price for you. Where you from?" The beaded tassels and fringes were colourful. Ever the magpie, I bought a couple of pretty tasselled key rings and a beautiful, intricately beaded bag to hang over my shoulder.

It wasn't long before we were walking over the small, humped bridge where we had witnessed the flood. The water had subsided but there were thick and sticky streaks of fine clay, stretching all the way back up over the road. The road itself was ripped up, with the tarmac carved out leaving rough stones and gravel exposed. The sea on our left was quietly lapping the sandy shore but I couldn't see in the reflected light if the water had cleared for our dives in the morning.

"There's your boat," indicated Papa. "Looks like an odd place for a party."

"Yep! Pretty obvious that's where it is!" I said, as the music blared out from a large structure (that looked like an old sailing ship with masts and rigging) looming to our right. There were even round port holes facing the pavement and the entrance was sideways through the hull. A small crowd of young Egyptian men jostled in front of security personal who were stopping most of them from entering. At first I wondered if there were only men there, before seeing a couple of foreign women being ushered inside without hesitation.

When we were right in front of the doorway I could see the place was packed for the Halloween party. It was lit well enough to make out a bar along the left and a low seating area just inside the door and I could see a number of pool tables crowded with players. The music was loud, modern and club like, cigarette smoke coiling its way through the whirling fans. A totally crazy mix of activity compared to the sleepy promenade.

"So what do you think, Ella? Do you want to stay?"

I smiled and said "Yes, I think so. It looks like fun. I am surprised to see so many people and they seem to be having a great time. Will you be OK to go back on your own?"

Papa touched my shoulder gently and said "Of course Ella. We just passed a guy on the bridge asking if we needed a taxi so I will just go directly from here to Daniela. Have a lovely time and I'll see you at breakfast."

"Ok, *gute Nacht*," I said, kissing him on the cheek before heading off towards the entrance.

"Ella! You're here! Come inside!" It was Steffi from the diving centre. She was leaning over the top deck where people were sitting in the open air, drinking and smoking together at tables. She came down to greet me.

"What would you like to drink? The wine is terrible and the cocktails lethal, so beer is the safest," she explained grinning.

"Beer it is then!" I replied.

"I'll get you a Heineken. OK?"

I was surprised, "Sure. Wow ...but ... Heineken? Here? ... In Egypt? Well this place is full of surprises.

She handed me an open bottle. "Let's go upstairs and I'll introduce you to some of the others." The table was full of people coming and going and of course I couldn't remember so many names but I saw Kurt and recognised a couple of others who had been sheltering from the rain earlier in the day. It turned out many of the foreigners were there for scuba diving, that being one of the main tourist attractions in Dahab. A lot of the instructors and dive masters were foreigners too, bringing their expertise and experience to the dives here.

Steffi was clearly a party girl in her free time and it wasn't long before she announced " Let's dance! Who's coming with me? Ella?" We trooped down the stairs off the boat and threaded our way through to the back area past the bar. I was amazed to see such a mix of people of all ages and ethnicities including Egyptians, even a few Bedouin men in their white *jalabiya's* and chequered head scarves. The bar opened out with more tables and a disco at the back with an area for dancing. The dance floor was crammed with people enjoying themselves, just like in any club in Europe. The music was so loud I didn't even attempt to talk, just danced and swayed to the rhythm of the music. I relaxed and realised that I felt safe to be myself among the throng. A few men approached to dance with me but I wasn't in the mood to , so just stayed dancing in the group. The dance floor was in the open air yet the body heat was so oppressive that after a while I needed a break and pushed my way back to our tables on the boat deck to rest.

Kurt was still there, in an animated discussion with some other divers and he motioned I could take the empty seat beside him. I sat and relaxed while sipping my beer, looking out over the twinkling lights circling the Lighthouse bay. It looked so pretty and inviting with gentle waves lapping around the restaurants. Despite the lights I could even make out the stars above, so I knew the sky was clear of the days rain.

Eventually the discussion died down and Kurt turned to me asking, "So how are you enjoying the party, Ella?"

I smiled and said "It's great! I must say I'm surprised to see so many people and they all seem to be having a great time. Are parties like this normal here?"

"Yes, often. Although this is a bit special because of Halloween and the fancy dress but there are parties every week for sure - more than one per week actually. Dahab is a relaxed place. People come to dive and enjoy their holiday."

I added curiously, "I'm surprised too that local people drink. I would have thought alcohol was difficult to get in Egypt. Not that I can't live without it."

Kurt shrugged, smiled and said "Foreign tourists and diving - it's to be expected. The Bedouin who had lived here for years enjoying the fishing and the dates, started camps for the Israelis who holidayed here after the 1967 war. South Sinai was an Israeli party place – Sharm el Sheikh, Dahab, Nuweiba. The beaches were packed. Israelis still come here on holiday but so do a lot of other nationalities too now ... as you can see." He paused and then added "Cheers!" while raising his beer to mine. "Would you like to dance again?"

I didn't have to think twice, replying "Sure. I've cooled off now. Let's go!"

We found the group again and danced until the crush on the dance floor became too much. "I think I'll take another break," I mouthed to Kurt, pointing to where our group had seats. He followed me. "Would you like another beer?" I nodded. "Ok, I'll bring them up to the seats."

"So how are you enjoying the diving?" He asked, as he returned and handed me a cold beer.

"Oh, it's wonderful. I went diving with Papa in Marsa Alam once and was really keen to come back to the Red Sea after that experience. Red Sea diving is amazing! Dahab doesn't seem to have as many large fish but I enjoy the coral and being so close to town is a bonus."

Kurt grinned. "Yes, that's one of the reasons I love this place. Boat diving is different - more accessible to great sites but also more involved and somehow more intense with such close quarters. At least here you can spread out and relax easily during the day and at the end of it too. When I finish work I just get on my bike and let the wind blow problems out of my head. Don't even need to wear a helmet!" he quipped.

"How long have you lived in Dahab?" I asked.

"Only a couple of years. I came here to do my instructor's course then decided to stay to teach scuba diving. I fell in love with Dahab, it's perfect for me. I would never choose to live back in Germany."

I understood his adventurous spirit. "That's great. I'm thinking of going to live in Bali. Have you been there?"

"No, but I hear it is a nice place too."

"It's amazing! Ideally I would love to live half the year in Bali and the other half travelling and visiting family and friends."

"Did I hear you say that you work in fashion? That must be a high flying lifestyle!"

"It is. I absolutely love it. I have a great life," I hesitated. "But sometimes I want more in my life than just working. I want a sense of life, not just a career. Someday I want to have a family and children." In fact, that 'someday' was often nagging me when I discussed my life. I couldn't imagine living my whole life without having children. My biological clock was more than ticking, it was chiming loud and clear.

"I have two children back in Germany. They were born when I was very young. Melanie is almost twenty now. They still live in Munich." He sounded a little wistful.

"Don't you miss them?"

"Yes, of course. But I was so young when they were born. I missed the freedom I have now. It is too difficult for me to live in Germany so they come to visit me here."

"Oh, that's great." But I felt a slight twinge in my throat wondering if I would ever get to say the same thing. I had separated from my husband just a year earlier. A timeless story; somehow we had been so busy working and setting up our lives that starting a family hadn't been a priority. I'd always imagined my life with children and despite not having used contraception, I still hadn't managed to fall pregnant.

The conversation drifted back to diving, the middle ground for all foreigners in Dahab. Suddenly I realised what the time was.

"Oh my! I am sure I have missed the bus back to the hotel! Do you think it will be easy to get a taxi?"

"Don't worry. There are always taxis in Dahab, any time of day or night. But I can take you to the hotel if you like, on the back of my bike."

The look on my face must have revealed my horror. "What? You don't like bikes?"

"No. I've never liked motorbikes. They are not safe at all!"

"Oh!" Kurt looked amused, adding with a wry smile "Well we can find you a taxi when you want to leave. You want to go now or have another dance?"

"Dance!" We headed back to the crowded dance area. I looked at Kurt, thinking that he was quite attractive in a punk sort of way; with his Mohawk hairstyle, a slight, wiry frame and physically fit. He was confident and comfortable in his own skin. I liked that.

The party was still going strong in the early morning hours so it would seem Kurt was right about it being a party town. However, despite having a great time my energy was fading so I told Kurt I was ready to go back to Daniela.

"OK. Shall I find you a taxi? The offer of a ride back on my bike still stands." He was challenging me with a cheeky grin.

I hesitated, mulling over my options. I thought to myself "I *am* on holiday, maybe I should try something different. Kurt seems very sensible. A different country - different customs..?"

"Well, OK. As long as you promise to look after me and not go too fast."

"Sure. I've only had a couple of beers. I have work tomorrow - today actually!" His bike was parked in an alleyway close by. I knew nothing about bikes but noticed it had high small seats and knobbly tires.

"It's a trail bike," he said, as if that explanation meant anything to me. "Better for when I go off road."

"Oh" was all I could say, feeling the nerves in my tummy. I was terrified of falling off with nothing to protect me against the road. "Do you wear a helmet?"

"No, they aren't required here. Look, I promise I won't go fast and if you are really scared I can still find you a taxi."

"No, no. I'll be fine," I said, with bravado on the outside that I didn't feel on the inside.

Kurt started the bike with little effort and then told me to put my leg over the small seat behind him. I was very glad I had chosen to wear stretchy pants and managed without too much contortion (I felt grateful for my regular running and yoga sessions!). It felt quite strange to be almost intimate with him in such a practical way, legs astride and our bodies touching. I remembered the Egyptian woman I had seen earlier on the back of a bike, sitting side-saddle with her ankles crossed, long skirts close to the wheel. That had looked demure but definitely not safe.

"Ok. Now put your arms around me and hold on. Ready?" I was as ready as I would ever be and closed my eyes tightly as he revved the engine and we moved off. It was some minutes before I trusted he was telling the truth and started to enjoy the feeling of the warm wind flowing by. I tensed at every bump in the road gripping involuntarily around Kurt's midriff, especially when the road changed from tarmac to rough gravel. The sound was entirely different as the bike crunched over stones and we rode through pitch black with no buildings or traffic to light the way.

The Sinai night skies with their stars shining brilliantly in the inky velvet, were working their magic on me. My nervousness dissipated into elation on the back of that dreadful motorbike, with my arms around a man I hardly knew. The cool night air fluttered and swirled my blonde hair over my bare shoulders in a caressing touch. I realised that with the warm air blowing over me, I felt part of the world that I was moving through, not a cocooned spectator inside a vehicle. It all started to feel easy, somehow.

By the time we pulled up outside the entrance to Daniela with its bright lights drowning out the sparkling stars, I was actually wishing we had further to go. I managed to climb off more gracefully than I had climbed on.

"Kurt, thank you for the ride back. It was lovely, really lovely on this beautiful night."

"You are welcome Ella."

There was a moment when we looked into each other's eyes, and I questioned myself, "Is something happening here?

"It really was a lovely evening. Will you be our guide tomorrow morning for diving?"

"Yes, for sure! Shall we start a little later? Say 10am?"

"Great." I hesitated then quickly lent closer to kiss him on the cheek. "*Gute Nacht. Bis Morgen.*"

"*Bis Morgen dann.*"

I skipped up the steps to the entrance where the night porter was standing to greet me, before turning to watched Kurt ride off onto the road. I noticed he was riding somewhat faster than when I was on the back and it felt comforting that he had cared about my fears. I was tired but happy to be feeling so relaxed about where I was; meeting someone I was interested in, overcoming my fear of riding a motorbike, being under the stars, the dancing. I wasn't drunk on alcohol but on life at that very moment. Life was good, extremely good, as I sunk into my pillows and drifted off into sweet dreams.

I never manage to sleep late and hardly ever wake to an alarm, so only a few hours sleep, I woke up and decided to go for a swim in the pool. It was another beautiful day.

"You're up bright and early this morning, Ella" Papa had come down to join me. "How was the party?"

"Great! I had a really nice time. Lots of people of all nationalities, dancing and partying. Kurt bought me back on his bike."

My father's raised his eyebrows. "On the back of his bike? Were you drunk?"

"No, no!" I laughed. "The Hotel taxi had long gone and Kurt offered to bring me or organise a taxi. I decided to live dangerously for once in my life. But don't worry. He drove very carefully and I was fine."

"Glad to hear it. Are you up for diving today?"

"Of course! You know I never drink very much and I'm fit as a fiddle. But we're starting a little later though. Meeting Kurt at ten."

Kurt seemed none the worse for wear either, as he gave us our briefing for the day. "We are diving at the Islands," he explained. "Can I have a brief word, Ella?" My heart skipped a beat when he said my name and pulled me aside. 'Don't be ridiculous' I told myself. Kurt explained, "I just want to explain the dive entrance so we can make it easy for your father. There is quite a long walk over the reef before the reef drops off and I know he finds walking on the rough coral difficult, especially at low tide, which it will be. If it's OK with you, you will walk close to him in case he needs a shoulder to steady himself and I will take his gear out. I will help him put it on just before we enter the dive." That was it?

"Of course, thank you", I replied. My heart had hoped for some other recognition.

But then he added, "I hope you had a good time last night. I did," smiling directly at me. My eyes met his, "Yes, absolutely. I had a really nice time." This time, my heart did skip a beat.

When I saw the width of the reef at low tide I realised why Kurt had given me the extra briefing concerning Papa. Carrying the twenty or so kilograms of equipment over the rough, pocked coral to a depth where one can at least snorkel easily, could be fraught with problems. Professional divers learn to cope but recreational divers in such heat could easily have problems.

Everything went according to plan and we were kitted up ready to enter the dive site through a large hole in the coral. It looked far too small to fit through, even in single file but in reality it proved simple enough (although I felt my tank clang on the coral roof a couple of times). It was breath taking to swim through the hole into a beautiful sandy-bottomed pool, surrounded by stunning ancient corals. A giant moray glided over the coral, poking his head inside the crevices looking for food, while a blue spotted ray skimmed over the sandy bottom, nine meters below.

As there were only four of us on the dive with Kurt as our guide, it was easy to keep each other within sight. I was in awe of the natural beauty; by far the best coral dive with myriads of fish. Kurt drew us quietly into a swirling mass of baby yellow fin tuna and I stayed in the centre of their vortex as long as I could, watching mesmerized, as they swirled around me. At times we had to fin high over the massive porite corals to drop down into the next pool. We rounded one pinnacle to see a turtle gracefully flipping his fins around the corals, nipping off seaweed. He turned and swam directly at Kurt. I gasped inside my suit, "Oh my, what is it doing?!" Kurt just pushed it gently away each time it came back towards him and it eventually trundled off over the coral. I was astounded and asked using my hand, "What was it doing?" He signalled that everything was OK and that he would explain later at the surface. Eventually we were in more open water and I could feel a strong current take hold of me. I glanced at Papa but he was right beside me, calm and beaming. We no longer needed to fin, just remain buoyant as we glided over the forest of table corals with no effort. It really was like flying! Not long after that, a huge napoleon wrasse glided by hardly moving a fin, yet keeping a wary eye on us as it swept past.

All too soon the dive came to an end as we exited via the original entrance in single file. I popped out on the reef proper and removed my fins in order to walk.

"How was that Papa!" I was so excited. "Did you see those corals? Wasn't that brain coral huge? And that Napoleon!" Of course he saw them. "Kurt, what was that turtle trying to do?"

"Sometimes they go for regulators and hoses. Not sure why,

maybe they look like food to them. It isn't a problem as long as you see them coming and just push them away. They might do some damage to hoses otherwise."

"Well it looked frightening to me. I will be a bit more cautious around turtles from now on. But the corals were amazing. That was my best dive so far."

"Glad you liked it. The Islands is always an interesting dive - never the same twice. Sometimes lots of fish, sometimes not so many, but always beautiful coral. The currents can be strong too, as they were today. Always be ready for a challenge!" He looked directly at me and winked. I laughed but again felt my heart skip. He did feel attracted to me! And that is where it started, the romance between Kurt and I, as joking and fun under the hot Sinai sun.

He joined Papa and I for dinner that night and we talked about life in Dahab. I was fascinated how someone could leave clean, orderly, efficient Germany to live in beautiful chaos, especially as I was considering moving to Bali. He seemed to have pulled it all together in the desert, life between the barren mountains and the deep blue sea. He had followed his dream despite a tough beginning. He hadn't gone to university because his first child had been born when he was nineteen and he had needed to support his wife. His German business fell through, he eventually broke up with his wife, left his family and found his way to Dahab, where he found his calling as a scuba diving instructor. He said diving in Dahab was the perfect way to make money doing something he loved in a place he felt at home. I realised that here was a man who was unafraid of following his dreams in order to be successful. Like me. I had been following dreams all my life. From the time I decided to work in the fashion world at the age of fourteen, setting my sights on success.

I started scheming and dreaming of what life must really be like living in Dahab. How did this compare to Bali, which was clean and warm and tropical and much more industrious? Balinese people are friendly and open, not closed like Arabs. I was dreaming of making a life for myself buying and selling Balinese goods and dividing my time between living there for six months, with another six months selling orders overseas. But I could feel myself drifting off, beginning to dream of other possibilities. It felt so easy to be with Kurt, we seemed to speak the same language literally. I had had many cross cultural relationships including some Muslim men, a Bosnian and a Turk, but things always became too difficult and we always parted. I had eventually married a German man from my home town but he hadn't liked my international lifestyle. With Kurt it felt comfortable to be able to speak German in a foreign country.

On the afternoon of our last diving day, Papa told me, "Ella – I know it is our last night here but those two deep dives today at the Canyon and Blue Hole have left me a little shattered. Do you mind if I have an early night?"

"Sure, will you be OK? I am a little tired too but I promised to meet Kurt for a goodbye drink in town."

"Go ahead. I'll just grab a snack here at the hotel and see you tomorrow for breakfast. We have an easy morning anyway as our flight doesn't leave until late afternoon. Have fun!"

I met Kurt at The Three Fishes, one of the better Italian restaurants in Dahab and we sat out in the open air, by the water's edge under a half moon, drinking red wine. I loved that he enjoyed good food as much as I did. I had in fact, been mulling something over in my mind and in the spur of the moment blurted it out without too much thought. "What if I came back to Dahab next week?"

Kurt looked surprised and cocked his head questioning, "Next week? You can come back *next week*?"

"Well, yes. You know how I said I work for three weeks then I get one week off and often spend it travelling. When I go back I will travel to Istanbul in Turkey for a week's work. I can easily fly back from there to Egypt."

Kurt looked stunned but smiled, "Of course. If that is what you want to do."

"I haven't really thought about it much but, why not? I don't have plans, other than perhaps staying a few extra days with friends in Istanbul. They aren't expecting me though."

"Wow great. That's ... great." He seemed hesitant but then added, "You can stay at my house if you like. I have to work so I can't spend all the day with you but we'll have the evenings."

"Really, I can stay at your house? That would be awesome! I have work I can catch up on and I'm always happy spending some time reading and relaxing. A holiday after the holiday!", I laughed enthusiastically. I also detected a gentle warning that he was responsible to his work commitments and I would be expected to entertain myself. I respected that, as that's how I am too. So it was settled. I would book flights back to Sharm el Sheikh from Istanbul at the end of my working week.

I was excited to return to see Kurt so soon. On one hand, I kept telling myself to look at how things work out if you let them. At the same time, another voice inside me screeched, 'What am you doing? You've only known this guy for ten days and you're planning to stay at his house?' But I ended my interior pep talk abruptly, Nothing ventured, nothing gained! This was to be my next new adventure. I was prepared to go with the flow of it and see what would happen next ...

Chapter 2

I See Blue

I felt excitement as we drove back through the mountains towards Sharm el Sheikh, knowing that I would be returning to Dahab in less than a week. The mountains even seemed to look brighter since the deluge had washed away much of the dust, or maybe it was only their reflection in my enchanted eyes. The road had been badly affected in a few places but it was still passable with care. We arrived back in our German hometown of Kaiserslautern late that night and as I sunk into my luxuriously comfortable bed, I let out a huge sigh while drifting off into my dreams.

Always an early riser, I woke early and went for a jog around the sleepy city, following my favourite route through one of the nearby parks. The oak leaves were thick on the ground after a breezy autumn night and as I ran, my breath billowed out into the cool frosty air. The grey contrast against Dahab's warm sunny skies made me shiver, more than the temperature difference could explain.

Returning to my apartment where I had lived for nearly ten years, I packed quickly and piled my suitcase into my red Mazda MX5, heading for the company office in Nuremberg. I loved driving that car, especially with the top down (although November in Germany is far too chilly for that!). I usually spent time during the journey mentally shifting from my personal life to work mode but as I drove along that particular morning, I reflected on just how far I had come in making my dreams come true. My job as

Head of Purchasing and Design at *Unique Jeans,* seemed the pinnacle of a career I had been planning since I was fourteen years old.

When I was thirteen, my mother wouldn't buy me the clothes I liked, so I asked for a sewing machine for my upcoming birthday present. From that moment on, I took myself off to the laundry room in the basement of our home and set myself the challenge of learning to sew. I have always had an independent attitude and my parents constantly fretted at what I would want to try next in comparison to my more sedate brother. Using sheets I 'borrowed' from my mother's linen cupboard, I experimented with cutting patterns, teaching myself the rudiments of sewing. The more I learned, the more I loved it and fashion truly became my passion.

I decided to study fashion as a career and my life became totally focused on it. Not long afterwards, I was selling my design items to local boutiques for pocket money. I did school holiday internships with Adidas and the local theatre and also worked part time for a local tailor, always continuing to hone my design and sewing skills. I even learned Italian at school so I would be able to study in Rome, as I felt that city was one of the best centres for fashion alongside Paris and New York.

I come from a successful, middle class German family, but my parents weren't wealthy enough to pay for my studies. So I started to finance those by working as a guide and translator for American soldiers touring Italy by bus, as well as sewing clothing samples for small companies. Unlike most of the Italian students who lived at home with their families, I shared a cheap apartment with two other young women. Lea from southern Italy still remains a great friend today. After four years of studying, I graduated in Fashion

Design, Pattern Making and Clothing Technology.

One of my teachers offered me a job in a company on the outskirts of Rome. I loved the job but despite being paid a higher salary than most, I still didn't earn enough money to cover my living expenses (companies in Italy usually employed students who were able to live at home). The decision about what to do was taken out of my hands when the company burned down one weekend (under suspicious circumstances) and I was left without a job. In those days, Italian job offers often circulated by word of mouth, or even from bed to bed (and despite loving Italy and my work, I wasn't prepared to do that for a job!). Only similar jobs with similar pay were available and as I sometimes found Italian work ethics and reliability difficult to accept, I decided it was time to look elsewhere.

It was the mid nineties when I said goodbye to my steady Italian boyfriend and went back north to Germany. But before I even had a chance to look for work I started suffering from serious abdominal pains, which turned out to be caused by a spinal tumour. Suffice to say, it was a frightening time but after a successful surgery, I moved back to Kaiserslautern and into an apartment owned by my family to recover. I discovered that illness can be a time when reflection is forced upon you and can bring about change for the better.

On taking a friend's advice, I decided to look for work in German companies where the design and production systems were completely different to the Italian ones I knew. Production took place in local areas in Italy, whereas in Germany, companies outsourced the manufacturing to other countries all over the world. This meant that designers had to travel regularly to ensure design quality was up to standard. And so I discovered that through working I could combine two of my greatest loves; travel and fashion.

I found a job with a company in Cologne quite some distance north, so each week I would travel and base myself there, returning most weekends to Kaiserslautern My experienced colleague had previously worked for a very successful company that produced twelve collections a year. She taught me how to manage my work and showed me how to coordinate designs that would pass from production to sales within four to six weeks, rolling out on a monthly basis. It was a hectic and fun job. Part of our duties were to fly to London, Paris and New York for a day or two and check as many shops as possible, as well as purchase suitable samples. It felt very decadent to be young women in our twenties travelling business class, living in five star hotels and eating restaurant food as a matter of habit.

The company worked with production suppliers in Turkey and Italy. Because of my knowledge of Italian, I was responsible for the designs and production there, conversing with and organising the Italian suppliers (as many of them only spoke Italian). However, after a few months I realised all was not as it seemed. I discovered the company had severe cash flow problems and I was in a difficult situation because the suppliers trusted me (as if any unpaid debts might have reflected on me personally). Fashion can be a very small world if things go wrong! So I quit my job after five months rather than risk losing the good reputation I had built.

Not long after returning to Kaiserslautern I met Stefan, who would later become my husband. His parents were friends of my parents. We got married one week before I started a new job in

Bremen and had a whirlwind honeymoon in Thailand. Every week I travelled five hundred kilometres to work before returning home to spend weekends in Kaiserslautern with Stefan. The company was well established with over twenty years experience in the fashion industry but my first task, was to facilitate their modernisation to rapid delivery, from design through to sales. I was working together with three other designers and life just got better and better. I enjoyed my life in fashion, where travelling and living out of suitcases became second nature.

It was just one year later when I got a surprise phone call. It was from an employment agency, head hunting me and offering a position in a fashion group close to Stuttgart. I was to be the only designer and would have sole responsibility for the whole collection. They were offering a much higher income than I was earning and it seemed a fantastic opportunity. I took the job and worked for *Jeanstreff* for five years. Based in Stuttgart, I travelled regularly to Turkey, Greece, Italy and Hong Kong to check on our production, visiting the former two the most often. I was also responsible for reviewing all of our two hundred and fifty stores throughout Germany and Austria. Life was full-on. I was working seventy hours most weeks. I would spend quiet weekends at home with Stefan, take the 6am train on Monday morning to Stuttgart (where I lived in a small hotel) work two days in the office and then fly to Istanbul or Thessaloniki.

But it wasn't all work and no play. My suppliers became my friends. Despite working late many evenings, after work we sought out hip restaurants and bars to hang out in or would party hard, often dancing until the early morning hours. Frequent fliers get all sorts of benefits and I took full advantage of them. I learnt how to catch up on lost sleep while travelling business class and made the most of airport lounge facilities. There is some irony that the more successful one becomes, the more gratuitous privileges one receives.

I worked hard but with such a lot of passion because I simply loved my job. But truth be told, I wasn't completely happy. Stefan (who was at home in Kaiserslautern) couldn't understand my world at all and it seemed to me that he wouldn't try which of course, caused some problems. At the same time, I had made a very successful career for myself but I still wanted a family and children. When I tried to talk to Stefan about it, his answer was always, "Later, later." Eventually, I stopped using contraception in that hope that nature would intervene and make the changes for me. Nothing happened. We did tests because I feared the spinal tumour had made it impossible for me to conceive; the tests proved normal for both of us. My gynaecologist just said I never made enough time to get pregnant. I suggested to Stefan that we consider adoption but he got upset and refused to discuss it. I felt cheated, because at the beginning of our marriage we had both decided that kids were important for us and yet, time was ticking by and nothing changed.

We had also both agreed that we would eventually move to live in a hot country, so when a Turkish friend offered me the chance to open up a fashion agency with her, I was really keen. Moving to Izmir and working in fashion would have been a great opportunity but Stefan wouldn't entertain the idea. He was so firmly rooted inside Germany's four walls that he wouldn't even consider trying my international lifestyle. I still loved him but I wasn't living the life I needed, in order to feel truly fulfilled.

I continued to work a heavy schedule and partied hard in my free time. In the evenings, I would usually be taken out for dinner by one of the companies. It was inevitable that I made close friendships outside Germany as I literally spent more of my life outside its borders than within them. One such friendship developed into a full blown affair with a successful musician in Istanbul who showed me even more of Istanbul's amazing nightlife in the two years we were together. I'm not proud of myself looking back on that time and I could never reconcile my conscience with the double life I led. Sometimes it felt like I had a split personality, leading two completely separate lives, loving two different men in two different countries. But neither the exciting life in the fashion world, nor the quiet life at home, were wholly fulfilling me.

After five years I decided that I needed to change my way of working, in order to make more time for myself. Developing monthly collections required long hours, week after week and I knew I was burning out. I suggested to my boss that I needed an assistant and I would work three weeks with every fourth week off. He said he "would think about it."

Then serendipity stepped in when I got a call from a company with a large chain of retail shops. They had heard I would be the perfect match to be their central buyer. I told them I was too busy to even go for an interview but they were very persistent. Two weeks later, I found myself flying to Nuremberg for what turned out to be the strangest interview ever. I had no idea why they wanted me as I was a designer and told them I had no real experience in purchasing. Apparently, my suppliers in Turkey had recommended me so highly, that the General Manager wanted me at any cost. If I took the job I would double my income, with a package deal that included a sports car, the latest laptop and mobile phone and anything else I would need. When I still hesitated, they offered an annual bonus. It was just too good to be true!

Upon accepting their offer, I had my dream job with a personal assistant, the latest business equipment and a convertible sports car, while working three weeks out of four on a super high salary. It was an added bonus that I was still able to work with my friends all over the world. The company planned to increase sales and I was in a personal heaven, purchasing the latest fashion items as well as leading a team of designers. I wouldn't have believed work could be even more fun than before. In my increased free time, I travelled to fantastic places such as Bali, Hawaii, Tuscany and of course, Dahab.

After my Dahab holiday, I arrived in the Nuremberg office of *Unique Jeans* where my right hand 'man' Brigitte greeted me enthusiastically, "Ella! Great to see you back. Wow, what a tan. You are positively glowing! How was it?" I loved Brigitte's energy. In fact, she was more than an assistant to me, she was a good friend too.

"Oh it was amazing. I had such a wonderful time ... diving, relaxing, a few parties, time in the sunshine. I've decided I'm going back next week."

"You *what*? Really? Oh...who is he? He must be good!"

"Ha-ha, cheeky. I'll tell you all about it later but we better get this week's work organised first, then we can catch up," I winked at her. "I'm off to Istanbul, right?"

"Yes. You have to prepare for the February collection so I have arranged meetings with Teks-Tim, Marineks ... the list is here.

Your flight is booked for tomorrow evening to Ataturk, leaving at nine pm."

"Great, thanks. Can you also look for flights from Istanbul to Sharm el Sheikh on Saturday, returning to Frankfurt on the following Sunday?"

"So you really mean it? You're going back to Egypt next week. Wow! They say there is something about the water there," Brigitte looked amazed.

I laughed, "Well, I think it is said that once you've drunk from the waters of the Nile, you're under its spell and always want to go back. Dahab is quite a way from the Nile, but yes ... I want to go back."

I spent the morning catching myself drifting off into daydreams of sea, sand and sunshine, finding it difficult to concentrate on my preparations for leaving the next day. I quietly avoided Herr Schneider (my boss) as I didn't want his lecherous manner to spoil my reverie. There was an uneasy truce between us by then. When I first started at the company I found his behaviour towards women repulsive and was shocked that many succumbed to his sleazy manner. It didn't take him long before he was trying his charms on me and I found it difficult to keep my revulsion in check. I refused his advances as politely as I could. I was worried that he might fire me but there was no way I was giving in (to what essentially amounted to sexual harassment). Luckily for me, it seemed my skills were too important so he eventually ceased trying. However, once I was onto his game, I wouldn't mix with him socially except for work related events and when we had to travel together for business, I always made sure I stayed at a different hotel.

I flew to Istanbul late the following evening, going directly to the Hyatt Regency close to the airport rather than city centre. Like all large hotels it was impersonal but the regular staff all knew me so treated me with a relaxed, friendly manner.

"Good evening! You have your usual room, Miss Hartmann. Organ will carry your bags." I preferred to have a room on the tenth floor, high enough to enjoy a wonderful view of the Marmara Sea, where the blue horizon calmed me after a frenetic day.

I tipped Orkan at the door. He was new and I wanted to stay on his good side, but not too much. I closed the door recalling a bell boy at another hotel. He had instantly developed a crazy crush on me, regularly leaving roses on my bed with lovesick notes. He had even found out how to get hold of my phone number, calling to profess his undying love and devotion. In the end I had to be blunt to the point of rudeness, to make it clear that I would never go out with him let alone have any kind of relationship with him. From that day on, neither he nor any of the other bell boys would carry my bags to my room for the three months I stayed there. When I eventually did change hotel, the manager of that one banged on my door in the middle of the night to see if I was lonely and needed his company! Honestly ... the audacity of men is astounding if they think that a women alone must always need the company of men. Maybe they have been treated as princes surrounded by sycophantic females, unable to understand that some women don't actually *need* men to validate their own existence. I eventually gave up being too polite to these men.

I was used to burning the candle at both ends, staying out late and getting up early, especially in Istanbul where the night life is fabulous. However, that night I didn't even phone any of my Turkish friends, just prepared for the suppliers I was scheduled to meet, had a relaxing bath and went to bed.

Days in Turkey were always full of appointments which were scheduled one after the other, every few hours, to make sure I saw four to five companies each day. I visited the showrooms, checking on the current production for quality and progress. There might be minor or major things to deal with, such as a zipper that didn't sit correctly or a faulty fabric. I had to be constantly resourceful and clever to make sure everything kept on track.

One potential supplier had been desperate for me to visit their out of town showroom. I had refused on a number of occasions because the long drive to their showroom was too difficult to schedule into my manic day. They eventually organised a private helicopter to whisk me to their showroom and back. I had never ridden in a helicopter before and I loved it! I felt like I was in a James Bond movie skimming over the sea, snow fields and forest. Because of my enthusiasm I rode in the cockpit on the return journey, contemplating what it might be like to learn to fly a helicopter. We worked with that company for a while but even with the use of private jets on latter occasions, I couldn't justify the disruptions to my normal week in Istanbul: their product was good but not exceptional.

That week in Istanbul seemed to drag, which was so unusual. Even dining in my favourite restaurants couldn't satisfy my craving to get back to Dahab. I finally saw the last of my suppliers and retreated to the hotel ready to fly back to Egypt the following morning.

AsOmar Beach

The flight landed in Sharm el Sheikh late morning and unusually for me, I hadn't slept during the flight. When we crossing over the Sinai mountains, I felt my skin prickle with elation and excitement at how events might unfold. How would I feel seeing Kurt again? Would Dahab still weave its magic? What was going to happen?

I knew that Kurt would be busy working but he told me I would recognise Ahmed from the diving centre, who would be at the airport to meet me. This time I would actually have to purchase a visa at the airport, as the previous one was invalidated when we exited the country. I joined the now familiar jostling crowds and got my visa, before bursting out of the airport into the brilliant sunshine.

"Hi Ella! Welcome back!," Ahmed was waiting beside a driver.

"Hi Ahmed," I grinned "It is nice to be back."

"*Yallah?* Let's go. I'll carry that for you."

The journey to Dahab was uneventful and we arrived early in the afternoon. The November sun was still bright as we drove to Kurt's rented house. I had only seen the house once briefly at night, so the daytime reality was somewhat more revealing without Kurt there to distract me. I didn't remember it being so tiny and so frugal. He certainly lived with the bare minimum; hardly any amenities and certainly no luxury. It was hot inside, without fans and not one sprig of green to alleviate the dusty brown and grey. He hardly had any furniture, apart from a double bed, a small coffee table and some cushions on the floor for sitting on. I had about four hours before he would return, so I tried to make myself as comfortable as possible.

I climbed the stairs up the side onto a small roof terrace. From there I could see a sandy football pitch, directly in front of the house towards the west. There were open sandy spaces all around and a few houses behind his, towards the eastern water's edge. I could make out the coastline of Saudi Arabia behind buildings, which was hardly visible in the haze. People obviously gravitated to living on the water's edge as that was where it was more built up.

I decided to have a shower to freshen up and turned on the taps, trying to find out which one was the hot water. They were both the same. There was no hot water! I discovered there wasn't even a hot water cylinder. The water temperature was pleasant anyway but I was surprised to find Kurt lived with no running hot water! I was a little shocked at that. 'Surely it must get colder than this in winter and he showers in cold water?', I thought to myself. The kitchen wasn't really a kitchen either - just a stainless steel sink on a stand and an open gas burner on a tiny bench. I could see that Kurt didn't do much cooking and certainly no entertaining. At least there was a fridge with some cool water. I settled myself down in the only shaded part of the house, the bedroom. The kitchen had no roof at all.

I was actually a little afraid to venture out alone. I didn't exactly know where I was in relation to the Lighthouse where we had been diving and had no idea how safe the streets were for a lone woman. I harboured a fear of Arabic and North African men, due to a horrific experience when I first went to Morocco with my Italian boyfriend. Essaouira on the coast had been fine but when we went to explore the amazing *souq* in Marrakesh I was subjected to sexual harassment, with men manhandling me almost every step of the way. We were crushed and pushed seemingly ever deeper into the *souq* and my boyfriend was powerless to help. I started to panic, with wild thoughts that if I couldn't escape they would eventually rape and murder me. It was truly horrific. By a stroke of luck we found a café that only admitted foreigners and I sat shaking on the roof terrace until we could safely get a taxi back to our *riyadh*. After that (rightly or wrongly) I had never trusted North African or Arab men. Even when I went to Morocco for work where the supplier was an Indian man, I dressed in *shalwar kameez* with my bindi like an Indian and most people thought I was married to the supplier.

I huddled inside Kurt's tiny house with no fan, finding what shade I could. Air conditioning was obviously way down on the list of his priorities and the hot, dusty, stifling heat was pushing me to the edge of my comfort zone. I mused that not twelve hours before, I was leaving a modicum of comfort from the 5 star Regency.

Kurt's home was very basic for sure and I did wonder if I was just a little bit crazy to be there.

However, by the time Kurt returned I was so eager to see him that my discomfort was quickly forgotten in the cooler evening air.

"Hi! Welcome back! ," Kurt breezed in. I learned that this expression is used regardless of whether one has actually been away or not, it doesn't matter. "Did you have a good week?"

"Hi to you too!" I stood up and we hugged and kissed like long lost lovers, despite that being the first moment we had really been alone. We were happy to be in the moment and we had a whole week to look forward to. We fell into each other's arms and into bed. Where else could we relax in that house?

"So this is your plan for having no real furniture?" I teased.

"Yep, you've caught me out," laughed Kurt. Our lovemaking had the urgency of new love, happy to discover each other and enjoying the moments of being together in private at last.

"Welcome back," he tenderly, brushing the hair from my face.

"Glad to be back," I smiled.

"Are you hungry? I never have much to eat here."

"I can see that. And yes, I'm famished. Shall we get something to cook or go out?"

"Out." He said. "We can go to Eel Garden Stars. It's an easy walk from here."

That was a relief. I love to cook but I could see I would need to stock up before I would be able to produce anything in that kitchen.

"We can have a shower first. You first, or me, or together?"

"You don't have hot water! How come you always shower in cold water? I'll freeze."

"Nonsense! Cold showers are good for you. Anyway, in summer it's more difficult to keep the water cold. I often shower at the diving centre after work."

"OK, I'll go first to get any warm water left in the pipes – since you're so tough!" The banter flowed easily between us.

We walked the dirt track directly down towards the beach and settled in a small restaurant on the waters' edge. We sat on upholstered mattresses and cushions on the ground with thick, old palm trunks to rest our backs against, with a low wooden table in the centre. The lapping water covered the reef table about five meters away, rhythmical and relaxing. The moon over Saudi Arabia so clear and light, that not many stars were visible.

We sat close together, at ease, with Kurt's arm around my shoulders and talked about anything and everything that came into our heads. First, about our week at work; him telling me about the odd customers he had taken for courses and I, about fashion in hustling Istanbul, time pressures and crazy schedules. We were worlds apart in both life and work so it felt slightly unreal to be back in Dahab, sitting there under a clear moon on the water's edge in comparison to the smelly, noisy, crazy world I had been tangling with just the day before.

The food was fine but I could have eaten pig slops and been happy in that restaurant that night. We walked home with our arms around each other, passing few people on streets.

"Is it OK to walk around here at night?" I asked remembering my Moroccan experience.

"Yes, of course! Nothing to fear in Dahab."

"But there are hardly any street lights. Are women safe here?"

"Sure. I've never heard of any problems. A lot of the foreign women live in Assala." That was the local residential area of Dahab for Bedouins.

"OK." But I wasn't convinced and was glad there was bright moonlight that night.

As soon as we had closed the door, Kurt wrapped his arms around me as we kissed. I felt safe and calmed, so comfortable to fall asleep beside him. We both woke early and made love in the cooler dawn. Kurt climbed out of bed for a cold shower, "I have to start work at 7.30 like I said, so will leave in half an hour."

"Yes. I know. I'll be fine. I can just walk back down to Eel Garden Stars right? It is just straight down the track from here?"

"Yes, out the front gate and keep walking straight to the sea. I don't get home until about six but I will try to be a little earlier tonight."

Kids and Camels

I read books and lazed about, not really trusting to explore far by myself. Crazy really looking back on it but that is how badly experiences can cloud your judgment. I spent most days snorkelling directly from the shore over the reef at high tide. The extra salty water ensures that you float so high in it, I could snorkel in thirty centimetres of water, kicking out the twenty meters to the reef drop off. I spent hours just hovering over the corals, watching and getting to know the fish. I would even feel slightly wobbly on shore finding my land legs again. The rest of the time, I was camped at Eel Garden Stars, relaxing and reading books. The restaurant owner, Mohamed, spoke English very well and told me about Dahab and its growth. His restaurant was one of the last before the more local area of Assala beach and while not known to so many tourists, Eel Garden Stars was a haven for me.

Kurt would come home and we would go out for dinner and a drink exploring a few of his favourite restaurants and bars. I realised that Dahab was small place but very attractive to independent travellers rather than large tour groups. Diving was the main tourist industry, supported by camel safaris and wind surfing. It was a younger person's town, a destination for a few adventure tour companies that bought groups regularly down through Syria, Jordan and Israel. Backpackers and independent travellers made their way there by word of mouth and some of them ended up staying for diving, just as Kurt had.

Dahab was a vibrant, fun place but without all the pseudo glitz and polish of new Egyptian resorts like Sharm el Sheikh and Hurghada. Also more authentic due to the indigenous Bedouin, who had originally come for the fishing and dates but were now living and catering for tourists. I didn't mix with a lot Bedouins, except for one evening when Kurt arranged that we go for a dinner in the desert mountains close by.

This time round I was more relaxed about riding on the back of his bike, so proud I had overcome my pathological fear of them. He had come home and announced, "I have a surprise arranged tonight. We are going for a short ride on the bike. Get some jeans on."

"Oh I love surprises! Where are we going?"

"Well if I told you, it wouldn't be a surprise would it? *Yallah!*"

I was getting used to that word, '*Yallah!*' which is Arabic for 'let's go'. At first it had sounded like a command but I soon understood it was usually meant as 'shall we do it?'

We headed out of town up the gravel road and then turned towards the mountains. The sandy track wound through rocky slopes that were closed in by the rapidly darkening night. A Bedouin jeep was parked on a levelled out area, where a couple of Bedouin men stood around a small rock edged fire, preparing food for us. Kurt introduced me, then they quietly returned to chatting between themselves, leaving Kurt and I to our own conversation. Cushions had been laid out on a rug for us to relax on and they offered us the ubiquitous Bedouin tea; black, hot sweet tea mixed with local herbs (in this case *marmaraya* which has a sage flavour, served in tiny glasses).

"Come, let's climb to the peak behind us," suggested Kurt. He picked up one of the smaller rugs.

"OK. It's not too dark?"

"I have a torch and it's an easy climb." He had obviously been here before. I wondered with whom.

We picked our way over the crunchy granite, following a route to a peak and sat under the stars that increased in number as our eyes adjusted to the inky blackness.

"Oh wow! This is so beautiful. I feel I can touch the stars," I sighed.

"Yes, I never get tired of these mountains or these skies." We sat close together on the rug with our shoulders touching, just looking, not saying much.

"I just saw a shooting star! Did you see it?" I said.

"Yes, I saw it. But you have to make a wish and not tell anyone or it won't come true" he teased.

"OK then. Next one I won't say anything."

I lay back and just watched the skies, watching for my shooting star. It wasn't long before I saw more and I wished and wished. Please let me have children. Please let me have children soon. I want a family.

"Look!" said Kurt" You have to watch now. It happens so fast!"

I sat up and looked to the East across the gulf. A thin orange strip was glowing behind the mountains of Saudi Arabia and at first I couldn't understand what I was seeing. However within seconds I realised it was the moon rising, a great orange ball that was climbing into the sky.

"Oh My God! That is amazing. It is so orange! And it looks huge!"

We sat in silence for a few minutes, just watching the fabulous, one of a kind spectacle. Little did I know then, the moon rises like that, amazing and miraculous, every month in Dahab.

Kurt let out a deep breath. "Let's go eat! I'm starving."

In the moonlight we could see without the torch to find our way back down. The Bedouins had laid out dinner on the rug and it smelled delicious. Special Bedouin bread, rolled thin with slightly charred bubbles chewy and tasty. I broke off pieces to dip in the *tahina*. There was rice mixed with thin noodles (they fry the noodles first and then cook them with the rice so it has a tasty flavour), vegetables, potatoes, tomatoes, onion and peppers (with slight flavours but not too hot or spicy). There was also some chicken which I didn't eat. I was following a vegan diet as much as possible but I realised that this wasn't practical in Egypt and quite a difficult discipline to follow. Egyptians don't even have a concept of vegetarianism. When I told waiters I was vegetarian, they asked, "Would you like chicken instead?" It has something to with the translation for meat only describing red meat from mammals. Anyhow, Kurt had also arranged for a bottle of local wine that evening and it tasted like vintage champagne. I was so happy and floating on cloud nine. I was falling in love.

As luck would have it, Kurt was already booked to fly to Germany for a three week holiday on the same day I returned for work. We drove to the airport together, he to catch a flight to Munich, I to Frankfurt. I kept telling myself, this is meant to be. How could everything be working out so perfectly?

I walked in to work on Monday and Brigitte was all over me with questions about my week in Egypt, "How was it? Did you have fun? Did you spend time with Kurt?" I gave her a bland run down but my sparkling eyes were a giveaway.

"You're in love!" she said.

"Just a little..." I admitted. "Smitten" I added.

"Oh My God! Have you told Peter?"

"Yes, I broke it off with him last week before I left for Turkey. You know we were nothing more than friends with benefits anyway. It was never going to be more than that."

"Oh, wow. I'm so happy for you Ella. You are positively glowing."

"Thank you. I'll tell you about what happened in more detail later. Always the same, I have to get some work done now." I disappeared into my office and fell into the weekly routine I had built up over ten years of working in the fashion industry.

Life is for sure too short for boring clothes but constantly finding trends and supposed new ideas is more about sales and merchandising, than originality and cleverness. One can truly be original and fashionable without succumbing to buying new clothes every week but that does not make the fashion industry money. It needs new items and collections every month.

I spoke with Brigitte later, telling her about my week in Dahab with Kurt, trying to explain how it felt to be so far away from all this stress and fuss over fashion, both literally and metaphorically. She looked at me a little dumbfounded, this did not sound like the usual passionate Ella.

"We also need to discuss what we will do about the Christmas holidays now. Will we still go to Bali since they cancelled our flights? Have you given it any thought?" I asked Brigitte. We had been planning our Christmas holiday in Bali for some months when bombs began going off, killing patrons in the bars and on the streets.

"I looked at flights the other day. A lot of airlines have completely cancelled flights. Those that are still flying are charging a lot more money too."

"Oh, not good. I'm having second thoughts for sure although it is probably the safest time to go there. Now there have already been bombs. So sad for the Balinese."

"Yes, I know."

"Actually Brigitte, I'm thinking of going back to Dahab for Christmas. I haven't said anything to Kurt but would you mind if I did?"

"Oh Ella, of course not. I wouldn't mind. You look so happy and since the flights to Bali are cancelled anyway. Whatever is best for you."

"Thanks Brigitte. I'll decide before next week, OK?"

The week went pretty much as usual but it seemed to drag more because I had arranged to travel to Munich at the weekend to meet Kurt and his children. I liked Martina a lot from the first moment I met her. She was a composed, confident young woman who had got used to her independence from her mid teenage years. Franz was a couple of years younger, more reserved and shy, hiding behind his overweight features.

Kurt didn't have anywhere private for us to stay so I booked us into a hotel in Munich. I joked, "At least we have running hot water here!" We had a luxurious sexy night making the most of the hotel room next to the English Garden with its beautiful trees and meandering paths beside the Isar river.

"Kurt, you know how I said Brigitte and I had booked to fly to Bali for *Weihnachten* but the flights were cancelled after the bombings?"

"Yes. You did mention it."

"We are having trouble rebooking now and the prices are so expensive. I was thinking maybe I could go back to Dahab for those weeks. How would that be? Shall I do it?"

"Well, yes of course, if you want to. I would love you to. But you know I'll be busy at the diving centre. It's high season from the week before Christmas until mid January."

"Yes, I understand. I could do more diving and help around the diving centre. Sort of a working holiday?" I was so keen now to get back to sunshine and sea. I questioned why I should be doing this when I had been quietly planning on living in Bali but it seemed the universe was closing doors and opening others. I just had to step through them to find out where they would lead.

"You can stay with me again if you like," he grinned. "But no complaining about cold water!"

"Ok. I'll install a water heater anyway. But just for me! You say you don't need it!"

On the last weekend before flying back, Kurt and I drove in my Mazda from Nuremberg to Kaiserslautern to stay in my apartment. Funnily, my father came round to discuss something about the other tenants (my family owned the building). I kept information about my life from my family on a sort of 'need to know' basis and I hadn't seen any need to tell Papa I was having a relationship with Kurt at that point. He looked nonplussed at seeing Kurt there though. He looked at me questioningly but nothing more was said. After all, I had been separated from Stefan for almost two years and I was an adult.

Kurt returned to Dahab after that weekend and I had a couple of days at home before flying back to Egypt too. It seemed so perfect how everything was working out without seemingly making any effort.

That was my third time back in Dahab in a short space of time and everything was quickly becoming familiar to me; the flight, the airport and its hustle, the drive through the barren red granite mountains, Kurt's quirky house, the rough grey buildings, the clear cerulean sky and the aqua tinted sea.

I fell into the rhythm of Kurt's day, waking up with him and working alongside him, to learn more about diving and cover the syllabus of being a dive master, even though I had no intention of sitting the exams. I helped the students and tagged along on dives, spending hours under water over the four weeks I was there. I was in blue heaven and it was feeling like home.

As it was winter, the days were still warm but the nights much cooler, making snuggling under blankets even more fun. It got dark by six o'clock, so we didn't take so many motorbike rides into the mountains unless Kurt managed to take a rare day off. My fear of bikes disappeared completely, replaced with an appreciation for the feeling of freedom and excitement riding them with Kurt gave me.

Living in the moment, I was fully focused on my time in Dahab: scuba diving, cooking meals for us and partying a few nights in the local night spots like Tota, Rush or Tree Bar which wouldn't close before 4am if there was a good party going. Christmas in the sunshine in an essentially Islamic country didn't seem real, so we didn't bother celebrating it.

When I flew back to Germany in mid January 2003, I felt like I was flying to a very foreign land and a very foreign life. For four weeks I hadn't had one thought about fashion or my job. I felt like I had walked through the looking glass and now (not unlike Alice) I was finding it very difficult to be going back to the 'real world'. I kept asking myself, 'How can this be? How can this life look so different to me now after such a short time away?' My staff were asking me what I envisaged for the new collection and all I could say was, "I see everything blue." My eyes and my heart could see nothing but blue skies and blue water, deep blue water. I knew I was in trouble.

As Head of Purchasing and Design, one my first tasks for the New Year was to arrange design and production for the following season's winter coats, planning almost a year ahead. These were less trendy with cheaper production in China, so I had to fly to Hong Kong with my boss and a couple of other staff to organise everything.

We set off on our trip, but as the flight went on, I started to feel very uncomfortable. My abdomen was tight and wondered if I my period was coming early. By the time I got to the Peninsula Hotel I couldn't sit at all, only stand or lie straight and was starting to feel excruciating pain. I knew something was terribly wrong. Unable to bear the rapidly increasing pain, I arranged an emergency appointment with a gynaecologist who diagnosed a blocked vaginal cyst. It would require lancing he said, a simple procedure to cut open the cyst so it could drain. He could give me an anaesthetic but advised that it was just as painful to administer as the procedure itself, so I could choose do it without the meds. I was terrified but went ahead without anaesthetic and screamed out loud at the initial incision. It was such a shock. I quivered uncontrollably but once the cyst was draining the pain subsided. I managed to recover enough to return to the hotel.

By the time I got back to the hotel room I could feel wet seeping through my clothes. I checked to see my clothes stained scarlet as I realised I was haemorrhaging massively. I raced into the bathroom grabbing towels to absorb the blood. I called the doctor but by then he was on duty at another hospital and couldn't come to the hotel. He suggested I get a private car to the Matilda Hospital where he was working, so he could attend to me. I hobbled through the hotel lobby with a blood soaked towel tucked under my clothes, too worried to be embarrassed and collapsed into a private taxi. It was the stuff of nightmares in a foreign land.

A blood vessel had inadvertently been nicked when the cyst was lanced and that was continuing to bleed so the doctor had to stitch it closed. With all the stress and adrenaline from the pain I was a total nervous wreck, so he insisted I stay overnight at the Matilda Hospital for observation. I eventually fell into a deep, post adrenalin sleep. By morning the bleeding had ceased and I had recovered enough to eat breakfast. I ate thoughtfully in my room high up overlooking Hong Kong Bay with its view over crowded skyscrapers. 'Is this the kind of view I really want in my life?', I wondered.

Over the following days, doped up on pain killers and antibiotics and walking very cautiously, I managed to see all our suppliers, set out the production schedule and complete my tasks. I fidgeted constantly, uncomfortable in any position. Sitting was difficult, yet my boss was still expecting me to fly to Bangladesh in two days time for more factory visits.

I said "Two days ago I felt I was bleeding to death, I still can't sit or walk properly and you expect me to take an eight hour flight to Bangladesh. Are you crazy?"

He looked at *me* like I was crazy.

"Well, I'm not going. I won't be going to Bangladesh nor will I fly straight home. I need a few days to recover from this."

At that point I felt used and abused, feeling that no one in that industry really cared about me. Money was the bottom line. Alone in my hotel room I burst into tears and wondered why I felt so lost. It was a bitter pill to swallow after so many years dedicated to the industry. Had I sold my soul to the devil?

After a few days I had recovered enough to get on a flight back to Germany. I was still weak and angry at the lack of empathy my boss had shown. I went to see my personal doctor and told him what had happened. He decided to give me a medical certificate allowing me more time off to recover. I sat at the window of my Kaiserslautern apartment looking out at the typical late winter weather - dark, cold, raining and grey. I was miserable with my parents out of town, no work to distract me and no close friends in my home town. What was I to do? ... I picked up the phone and booked a flight back to Egypt. Better to recover in guaranteed sunshine!

During those two weeks of recuperation and while I regained my health in Dahab, I knew my life had taken an irrevocable change of direction. Fashion and trends, pressure, constant travelling and cold Europe, faded in comparison to sunshine and sea. Never underestimate the power of a beautiful day and every day in Dahab, seemed *so* beautiful. And just like that, I was finished with my old life, it was over. I couldn't actually believe how simple it was. I had decided to go to live in Dahab with Kurt.

He never pushed me or even really encouraged me but we were in love and it felt so easy together. He was happy when I told him I had decided to leave my job and move to Dahab. We went to our favourite restaurant *Ramez and Paola* to celebrate with the good Italian wine I had brought with me.

"Here's to us! Here's to living in Dahab."

Once I had made the decision, things became clearer and focused. I told Kurt we would need a larger house for the two of us. Even though I had bought the small water heater and we had hot running water, I wanted a proper kitchen so I could cook and some decent furniture to relax on. I wanted an outside garden area too with space to breathe. I had enough money to make a comfortable life for both of us. I wasn't expecting him to be the traditional male provider.

We went looking for places together and eventually found a newly built house in a large sandy garden of date palms. I was ecstatic! It was basic Bedouin style, with walls of coarse, hand-made, concrete bricks roughly grouted together and no plaster outside. Inside however, was plastered smooth and brightly painted, ceramic tiles on the floor making it clean and serviceable. I could finish the kitchen and organise furniture as I wished. I thought it was perfect for us. It wasn't on the beach front but only minutes walk from the water's edge.

"Shall we take it?" I asked Kurt

"Sure, it looks great. If it's what you want," he agreed. There were no window frames or doors at that stage but as I had to give six months notice to leave my job, there would plenty of time to finish it before I could actually move to Dahab permanently. I was so excited, we arranged to formalise the rental agreement within a couple of days.

The day before we were to meet with the Bedouin owner Kurt casually said, "I think you should take the house on your own. I will stay in this house."

I was stunned. I felt like he had slapped me in the face. I could think of nothing to say, just sat trying to make sense of what he had just said to me. "Why do you say that now? Are you getting cold feet? Don't you love me? Do you want me to come to Dahab?" Confused, I couldn't really comprehend anything.

"No, no! Of course I still love you. I still want you to come to Dahab. But I guess I am still wary of jumping into living together. Maybe I don't want to give up my place just yet. I'm mixed up I know, but I want to be honest with you."

"Well I appreciate that but I am feeling a bit lost now. Everything has been fine and you never said anything when we were looking for properties. You know I haven't handed in my notice yet. I love you and I want to see where this love takes us but it will be a big step for me."

That night I felt wary of Kurt but I could also see his point. I didn't even know if I was really ready to be living with someone so soon after my marriage. In my heart, I knew I had already left my job and I wanted to live a different life. I was feeling happy in Dahab. I decided to go ahead with it anyway and signed up for the house in my name. I had already planned how I would finish the interior decoration and the garden outside, my garden of sixty, beautiful old date palms. I kept pinching myself, 'I have a garden with sixty date palms and the beach is within a hundred metres of my door! I will be in heaven!'

I finally went back to work in Nuremberg and had to face up to my boss to hand in my resignation. I hadn't seen him since Hong Kong. "I've decided I need to change my life. I'm leaving Germany and going to live in Egypt. Here is my resignation." No point beating around the bush.

He was dumbfounded, "You can't be serious! Where are you going?"

"Dahab, Egypt. I want to go live on the coast of the Sinai desert. It's the right thing for me."

"Are you sure? Do you want to think about this?"

"I have thought about it. I've thought about it a lot and this is something I want to do," I wouldn't admit to any doubt, not even to myself.

He was silent for a moment. "I find this difficult to believe. How you be so successful and have everything we offer you and just chuck it in? Just like that? You have been offered another job with I think … NEW YORKER ….they have offered you more money! Do you want more money? A new sports car? "

"No. No! This is for real. I need to make a change in my life. I am going to live in Sinai, Egypt. I know I have to give six months notice so I will be leaving in August. That should give the company plenty of time to replace me and for me to train the new person."

He was still shaking his head in disbelief when I left the office.

"Brigitte! I've done it! I just resigned from my job!"

"Oh my God! Ella! I knew you were pissed off after how you felt in Hong Kong. But leaving? Really? Wow. When will you finish?"

"I have to give six months notice so August. Wish it was tomorrow. No offence, I will miss you."

"And I'll miss you. This Kurt must be some guy!"

"I do love him but it is not only about Kurt. I've been working in the fashion industry now for over fifteen years and dreaming about fashion for over twenty but something inside me has changed. Completely. I want to find a new passion. I need to get away from this life. When I was in Dahab over Christmas I never once thought about fashion or trends or clothes or anything. I didn't miss it at all. It was then that I realised this dream is over."

"Well, I hope you are doing the right thing. It's not something I could do." Brigitte said.

"Maybe Dahab is not forever but right now it is where I want to be."

"Oh, I will miss you Ella! I'm in shock," said Brigitte.

"Me too" I said. "But it is the right thing for me to do and we have months before I leave."

I had the same conversation over and over with friends and family. They were all doubtful as to why I was doing it, chucking in my job, moving to Egypt. They all thought I had lost my mind. Didn't I want to take some time to think about it? "I have thought about it!" I kept explaining.

So from that point on I had a focus, finishing my life in fashion and in Germany, starting my life in Egypt and moving to Dahab. I had a whole room full of fashion clothes that I had been given throughout my career. There were still hundreds of items despite giving many away to friends throughout the years. I sold as much as I could on eBay and gave the rest away. There were fifty pairs of high heeled shoes alone that had to go! There would be no chance of wearing those on rough Dahab streets (unless I wanted to risk breaking my neck). It was difficult to choose which favourites to keep but eventually I narrowed it down to three pairs. The racks of clothes disappeared and in some ways it was liberating to be getting rid of so much stuff. Gone from my life.

Nobody approved of what I was doing. They really thought I was being stupid, even if they didn't say so, or at least in so many words. This was breaking too many of the rules; throwing away an amazing job, a successful career built up over years and moving to Egypt to no job and no planned future. Too much for most Germans. But I followed my plans. Every three weeks I went to Dahab, filling my luggage with as many kilos as possible of things for the house and living life there. I lived with Kurt while my house was being completed. Despite him not wanting us to live together, we got on absolutely great. I didn't push any more for us to live together, I guess I thought it would just happen naturally anyway. All in good time. I was doing all the cooking, playing mother and enjoying my role. I have always loved to cook when I have enough time. My grandmother had a bakery and when I was younger, I spent many an hour with her baking cakes and learning to bake bread.

I had always been into health and fitness and was training and running marathons for fun. I had one planned for May but didn't feel so well. I still ran but something just didn't feel right. I ignored the signs. I had already had to deal with the spinal tumour and I was burying my head in the sand thinking that nothing was going to stop my move to Dahab. I figured with all the stress and changes with moving, my body was telling me to slow down, so I just let it go. There would be time for marathons later.

About a week before I was to leave Germany in June a friend came to visit from Turkey.

"Ella. You look so pregnant!" she exclaimed.

I blinked, "What do you mean?" But I knew perfectly well what she meant. The penny dropped.

"Well, look at you! Your boobs are so much bigger, your tummy isn't flat anymore and you're positively glowing! Have you had any other symptoms?"

I hesitated, "Well, yes, I guess so. I have felt a bit unwell and uncomfortable running. Do you really think so?"

"God, yes. You look pregnant! You need to get a test done. Let's go to the pharmacy now."

My head was spinning. Pregnant! Just what I wanted, but now? A week before I leave for Dahab with no income and a partner who wants to live in a separate house.

I went to see my doctor and it was confirmed. I was about 8 weeks pregnant and I started to get scared. A bit late for that, one might think. My doctor was happy and even laughing though. He said, "Ella, women have children all over the world. It's what you have wanted for years and now you are lucky. I said it would happen as soon as you decided to change your manic fashion lifestyle." He was right, of course.

At least I didn't have to worry about why I was feeling ill and thinking maybe I was heading for another tumour scare. I was pregnant! I couldn't wait to tell Kurt but decided to wait until I saw him the following week rather than tell him over the phone. We had discussed children, how I really wanted to have them in my life and how I had been desperately trying to get pregnant when I was with Stefan with no success. Kurt had quipped "Well I know I can! The problem doesn't lie with me!" I took that as tacit approval that us having children would be OK. He knew I was not using any contraception and he never mentioned it either.

Finally, I touched down in Sinai for what would be the last time for many months. I was there to stay, no more racing back to work at the end of the week. It felt so great to be free in my life. Now had time to breathe and enjoy the fact I was now pregnant too. My life was changing in so many ways, all at once.

Of course Kurt was working, so Ahmed was again there to drive me to Dahab. I had a few hours to spare before Kurt would finish so I waited at his house, sitting up on the deck contemplating what the future might hold. When he came home I could contain myself no longer and after the *hellos* and *how are you's*, I blurted out "Kurt, I'm pregnant! We are going to be parents!" I was beaming.

He looked shocked, "Really? You're pregnant? Oh, wow."

I couldn't work out if he was happy or just shocked. I was in disbelief when I'd found out, so I figured he was just going through the same process. "After all my trying it has finally happened. I'm so happy. Are you happy?"

"Well yes, but I didn't expect it to happen just like this. With no warning." He was silent and looked away.

Then I was really scared but anger crept into my voice, "So what's this? You knew I wasn't using contraception, you never used contraception. You even boasted that you were obviously fertile with two children. Now you're telling me you are not sure you want children with me when I have told you all along I want children more than anything in the world! Oh god, I'm not even here for a day and we are arguing about something I thought we agreed on!"

"Ella, this is all just a shock that's all. I thought we would have more time to get to know each other before having children together." He hesitated, "And I just chucked in my job."

"You what?" How could I be such a hypocrite considering how I had chucked in my job? But he had given no warning that he was even unhappy with his job and I guess I thought everything was OK. What a way to start my life in Dahab. The walls were crashing inside my head and I burst into tears. Tears of shock, of fear, of pregnancy, tears of anger. Kurt wasn't comforting but I probably would have shoved him away anyway, I just needed to work this out for myself. It wasn't long before I fell back into my resourceful mode and reflected on my situation. I had money saved and living in Dahab was cheap. I had a house all ready for me to move into. I had sunshine and water and I was healthy and pregnant with the child I had craved for so long. I was determined I would be happy ... no matter what!

Me and a camel in my backyard

Chapter 3

Beautiful Luna

Kurt made an excuse about having to meet some friends and left the house. It was late afternoon and the air was starting to cool, so I went up on to the roof and sat watching the sun dip behind the ragged peaks to the West. The dry cooling air, the clear sky and the colours of Sinai with their pinks, mauves and soft violets, calmed me. The waters of the Gulf of Aqaba looked like liquid silver reflecting the lilac sky. It really was such a beautiful place. Only humans were sullying its beauty at that moment in time.

I knew the house I had rented was still not quite finished to the point where I could live in it, so I had planned to stay with Kurt for the first few weeks. I was confused as to whether I should consider him as the father of this child, even though of course there was no doubt that he was, physically speaking. He didn't want us to live together and I felt he was abandoning me because I was pregnant.

However, physical needs blotted out the emotional turmoil - my body needed food. I went back downstairs and raided the fridge. It had food in it so at least he had planned for my arrival, even if he wasn't expecting me to be expecting! I laughed at my own joke. Dahab didn't offer much variety of fruit and vegetables back then, but some of them were fine, especially the small, sweet local bananas that were best eaten when their skins were still looked green. I made myself a sandwich as well as fruit *lassi* with the bananas and yoghurt.

I had no idea if or when Kurt would return, so I made myself comfortable on the bed we had shared on my previous visits, returning every three weeks out of four as my work schedule allowed. The work on my rented house had been painfully slow but without me being there continuously, I wasn't there to push them along. They had been going off to do other construction jobs they were concurrently being hassled to finish.

I heard Kurt come home late but he made no attempt to come near me, sleeping on the cushions in his living area. It was some time before I managed to go back to sleep. He hardly spoke to me in the morning either and mumbled something about having some people to see early as he was looking for a new job. I felt hurt and confused but refused to show my feelings and quietly made plans for my day. At least Dahab was familiar to me by then and I knew how to get about, not worrying about dealing with Arabic men. I hardly ever saw Arabic women, although I hoped that as I was now going to be there for longer, I might get to know some.

I had already bought myself a twenty year old Wrangler Jeep for getting around in. I didn't want to rely on dubious taxi drivers all the time and wanted the freedom a 4WD drive would give us. When I was looking for one, I realised that it could be so easy just to make a mistake and buy a heap of junk. The prices of vehicles in Egypt are ridiculously high in comparison to a normal person's income. Most of them were all old and rattling so when a friend of Kurt's found one he recommended, I bought it straight away. That Jeep cost me the equivalent of what I had sold my beautiful Mazda convertible for in Germany! I kept shaking my head whenever I considered it. I had bought it for 'us', but I was beginning to doubt there would ever be an 'us'. However, I also figured I could also hire it out for tourist and diver transportation. My Jeep was white with a permanent metal cover over the rear, unlike many that had open frames with a fabric cover. It may have been less cool in the summer heat but it also was less dusty and well cared for considering its age. It had '4 x 4' proudly painted in large black numbers down the side. It still wasn't registered in my name, so I knew that I would have to get that sorted over the initial few weeks. But not today.

After Kurt had left for wherever-he-was-going-determined-not-to-tell-me, I climbed into my Jeep and drove to my house at the north end of Assala, just as determined to make things happen there for myself.

Assala Street

The house was a basic construction favoured by the Bedouin at that time - a single storey, rough concrete block, wooden frame windows with double windows opening out, that were small to keep the heat out. No such thing as double glazing or hermetically sealed windows there. There were slatted wooden shutters to close across which also helped to keep the rooms cool. All the interior walls were painted pink, a colour chosen by Said, the Bedouin male owner (they are obviously not hung up on assigning colours to specific genders!). The floor was smooth cement and the roof made of beautiful, slatted, dark wood. Unusual, as wood is an expensive commodity in Egypt and most ceilings are just plastered concrete. I had a large central living area and a small kitchen which I organised as I wanted with built-in storage, ceramic tiles on the floor and bench tops, a gas stove, a sink and a fridge. Very basic, but functional. Bedouin women still cooked outside on gas framed rings on the ground, so the idea of having a specialised kitchen was quite a foreign concept. There were two bedrooms to which I added built-in wardrobes, one bedroom with an access door to the outside. This was because in a Bedouin household, men would enter via this door and the women would not be seen at all. The men would entertain each other in that room ensuring only family members could see the women at home.

Outside I built an *arisha*; a shade made from palm leaves with open sides to make the most of any breezes over the summer. I decorated it with rugs and low seating.

My Backyard Arisha in my New Home

The house was almost finished, but the 'garden' with its sixty date palms was an impenetrable jungle. I employed Yusuf and other men to come and trim the palms in my garden. Yussuf is a Saidi man born close to the Nile south of Cairo but who had been living in Dahab for years and was famous for trimming palms around the area. The garden was also full of rubbish, old Jeep motors, plastic bottles, plastic bags, rusting metal, and thousands of desiccated dates from previous seasons. I don't know why the goats had never been allowed to come in and eat them because sheep and goats love dates. By then there were many year's worth of them all over the ground attracting thousands of ants. You could not sit out anywhere for long without ants starting to crawl all over you. I soon discovered that the very tiny black ones bite fiercely and after feeling the initial nip, the bites swell painfully.

The ants had to go, so the dates had to go. The next crop of dates was already beginning to ripen in the upper fronds, although that crop would not be great as I doubt these palms had ever been pruned. While Yusuf cut the palm leaves, I worked inside on preparing my house.

"Oh my God! Oh my God! Yussuf, Yussuf! *Yallah!*," I yelled out with fright.

Yusuf was working not far from the door and came running immediately. He followed my wide eyed stare to the corner of the room to see a hand sized black spider crouching in the corner. Regardless of the fact he didn't understand a lot of English, he understood my fear. "Is it poisonous?" I asked.

"*Mafeesh. Mafeesh mushkila.* No problem," he assured me, grabbing the broom out of my hand and squashing the monster. "*Mafeesh mushkila*," he kept repeating.

"OK. OK. I'm Ok now. Are there likely to be many more of these things?"

"Camel spider," he said. "No problem." He swept the squashed and definitely dead arachnid on to the hand shovel and threw it into palms some way from the house. No doubt the ants made easy work of that body. Ugh! I'm not easily frightened but it was the shock of seeing the black legs scurrying away when I moved the rug from the corner. These spiders were huge and hairy and while I am not adverse to smaller, more normal spiders catching flies, these hand sized creatures were too much to consider as reasonable house pets.

I looked at him dubiously as I took the broom from him again. From that moment, I was seeing legs poking out from every corner. I was super careful about how I moved anything, expecting another one to spring out at me at any moment. My caution was not misplaced as during the course of cleaning over the next few days, I must have killed five or six of those spiders. It took me a long time to trust that I had removed them all. Maybe they sensed their impending doom if I'd have found more, because after that I never found any in the house. Hallelujah!

Midsummer was approaching and the heat was intense coupled with my early pregnancy. I didn't look pregnant at all so nobody questioned how much work I was doing. I never knew until later that the first trimester is often the most physically exhausting, as my body adjusted to the massive hormonal changes going on inside me. I was working six to eight hours every day at my house, returning to Kurt's house to sleep. He was still behaving very strangely towards me, not talking at all except for when he really had to. I just ignored him back, concentrating on preparing my house so I could move as soon as possible.

My rented house slowly turned into a home, as I unpacked the special small things I had transported over the previous months; lamps from Morocco and Thailand, saris from India, favourite objects I had found on my global travels. I bought mattresses, cushions and rugs for seating and chose places to hang mosquito nets and the hammock chairs I had brought from Germany. I had sold everything else back home, expecting that Dahab would be my home for many years to come.

I tried not to think about Kurt and his rejection. If it was just going to be me and my baby, then so be it. But I couldn't help feeling depressed at times and I had no one I could confide in. My friends in Germany and those I had left in the fashion world had all told me not to do it. They said that I was crazy to throw it all away and move to some relatively remote place in third world Egypt. They couldn't (or wouldn't) try to understand at all.

My parents were bitterly disappointed in my decision and while they hadn't exactly disowned me, they certainly hadn't made the move any easier. They made it clear that they didn't support my move. I had even had a discussion with my father over the apartment house where I had lived for more than ten years. I had been told it would become my inheritance and I loved it having made some alterations to it; my brother would inherit the actual family home.

When I said I was leaving Germany, my father had told me a local Doctor was interested in buying the property. I was shocked and sad. I called him asking, "Why are you doing this? You know you promised this as my inheritance." Not that I was so worried about the money but the fact he was going back on his promise. He was noncommittal about the reason and never sold the property in the end. Maybe he was trying to punish me for going so far from the families wishes. My mother vowed never to visit me in Egypt.

I was so lonely but the one thing I know how to do is work, so I just got up every day and worked. I worked hard with Ali to get that place ready for me and my baby. After the first week of putting up with Kurt's frosty silence and cold shoulder, I said, "We have to talk. It's ridiculous us continuing like this."

"Yes, OK. We can talk." He didn't offer more.

"The fact is I am pregnant. I'm happy I'm pregnant as I've always wanted to have children and a family. I have never imagined my life without them. I've been trying to get pregnant for years and now it has happened. Everything has changed at once for me and I cannot go back. I don't want to go back."

"Everything has changed for me too since you came." Kurt added.

"Really? You still live in the same house and do the same things. It was your decision to leave your job. I didn't even know you were unhappy with it. What has changed because of me? We have a Jeep for getting around, I pay for everything I need for myself. I don't ask for anything special from you and I'm willing to share everything I have with you."

"Well maybe not so much right now, but when the baby is born who knows..."

"Look! I want this baby, I want it so much. I'm happy I'm pregnant. If you don't want it, nobody here even needs to know you are the father. I won't tell anybody who the father is if you don't want anyone to know. You can just carry on with your life as before and I will bring up this child on my own. I am prepared to do that." Kurt remained silent. "You think about this. This is your chance to be a real father for this child. I'm not out to trap you. I want this child and you can decide if you want to be its father or not." There. I had said my piece and sat quietly.

"Ok. You getting pregnant has been a huge surprise. You said you didn't think you were even physically capable. "

"I didn't lie to you. You knew I had difficulty getting pregnant and also that I wasn't using contraception. You boasted that the 'problem' wasn't with you. You had managed to father two children, you said. If you were so concerned about having more, why didn't you use contraception?"

Kurt looked away. I was surprised when he suggested, "Let's take a short holiday to spend some time together. You have been working so hard on your house and I may start a new job soon. So let's see if we can go to the Nabq mangroves with Said for a couple of days. What do you think?"

"Yes. Ok. I would like to do that." At least he couldn't just keep walking out the door to "see his friends" whenever he felt uncomfortable.

"Nabq is south towards Sharm el Sheikh, isn't it?"

"Yes. Said goes fishing down there regularly and he has a hut there. We can sleep in that while he goes fishing for a few days."

And so it was, that we drove in the Jeep to the Nabq mangrove area for a few days. Foreigners are not meant to stay in the area overnight but because we were using Said's palm leaf hut to sleep in no one even knew we were there. It was a very basic, small hut made of palm fronds about two by three meters with a doorway opening to the East at the water's edge. There was nothing but thin kapok mattresses and cushions for furniture. There was nowhere to go, nothing much to do except spend time together.

Kurt relaxed over the three days and while not showing total commitment to me and the baby, he let me know that he wanted to be the father. We were to be a family on some level. I was still wary of him but I am always willing to see the best in people and decided I would accept whatever he could handle. I vowed never to encroach on his freedom (whatever he perceived that to be) and resolved that I would essentially be a solo parent except when Kurt was willing to play his role as father. It was better that my child would have even half a father, than no father at all. I was beginning to see that Kurt was a weak and somewhat selfish person, but he was kind and calm too.

Said spent most of the time out fishing or resting quietly. He cooked for us, including some of the fresh fish that he had caught. I knew I wasn't going to survive on a vegan diet in Dahab with its very limited supply of fresh vegetables so I ate the fish to stay strong for my baby. Kurt and I slept in the hut together under a mosquito net. Said slept outside rolled up in a large acrylic blanket (even though it was still hot during the night), covered head to toe so the mosquitoes couldn't bite him. After three days at Nabq we had no vegetables left so our last meal was essentially rice and fish. It was time to return to Dahab.

Over the next few days in Dahab I was astounded to hear Kurt proudly announce that I was pregnant with our child and that he was looking forward to being a father. I couldn't help wonder if he was just doing it to impress his Egyptian male friends, some of whose sole purpose in life seemed to be getting married and producing children. They were at least proud we were having a baby, a major life goal for every young Egyptian.

The next few weeks were busy, with me continuing to get my house ready to live in. I was also going backwards and forwards to Nuweiba, a hundred kilometres to the north, to change the registration papers for the Jeep. Bureaucracy in Egypt is a labyrinth of papers, signatures, stamps, different desks in offices and different offices, all making any process time consuming and expensive. But eventually the Jeep was completely mine.

I continued to stay overnight with Kurt and at least now our relationship was back on some happy level, we started to enjoy each other's company again. As long as he didn't think I was encroaching on his freedom we were fine. And I had no need and no intention of doing that. Egyptians didn't seem to find it odd that we had separate houses, most of the men were living in Dahab for work alone and travelled home every six weeks to see their families in Cairo or other cities for a couple of weeks at a time. Hardly any had bought their families to Dahab and the women probably didn't want to leave their extended families. Some men even had more than one wife and would spend equal time moving from house to house, family to family.

By the time I finally moved in to my home, with pruned palm trees and my own furniture and decoration, it was August, high summer and very hot. I walked in the door and let out a sigh. At last I was home. At last I had a space for myself and at last I was pregnant. For a brief moment I was in bliss. But as I lay down in my bedroom I realised I was never going to be able to sleep. Air conditioning was unheard of in Dahab at the time and the fans just seemed to move warm air from one place to another, never actually cooling anything down. I tossed and turned that first night in uncomfortable stickiness.

The next night I decided I would have to move my bed outside and sleep under the palm trees: spiders, ants and all. My pregnant body was exhausted and I was never going to get any sleep otherwise. I was petrified that first night wondering what might happen to me so the following night I asked if Kurt would come and stay with me until I got used to it. Looking back it seems odd that I actually had to ask him to help me. However he did come, and after a few nights I became accustomed to the open air sounds. The sea was only meters away through the palms and its rhythm lulled me to sleep and the swishing leaves of the palms soothed my fear. They became my night-time lullabies. I also often spent nights at Kurt's house but he rarely volunteered to sleep at my place.

A Bed Under Palms and Stars

Not long after I moved in, I was astonished to see Bedouin men coming to congregate under the palm trees. They were polite and non intrusive but I complained to my landlord that I didn't want strange men wandering around what I thought was my private area. His reply was, "You rented the house, not the garden." My eyes popped. "What do you mean?" although I understood his meaning well enough. I had taken it for granted that since the wall was around the house and the palm trees that I was paying for the entire area. And he had mentioned nothing when he saw how I had spent money to have all the junk taken away and have all the uncared for palm trees pruned!

"You saw me paying for all this work and you said nothing! This is despicable. I am not happy that strange men come into my garden now when you never said anything before!"

He just shrugged, "Well that is how it is. You are paying for the house rental but not the garden."

I was furious but realised there was little I could do. I resolved that I wouldn't stay in that house any longer than I needed to and started to look for another solution. However, I did love the area and I wasn't desperate to move. Other matters were more pressing, like getting through my pregnancy safely and looking forward to having our baby. I needed to find a doctor and most people in town recommended Dr Rumi in Mashraba. I went to visit him and found him to be a gentle and courteous man.

"I have delivered over four thousand babies," he kindly boasted as if he sensed my worries at the thought of delivering my baby in Egypt. I figured he probably really did have more experience at childbirth than most general doctors in Germany.

"I want to deliver my baby at home."

He looked surprised, "Well, yes ... that is possible. But most foreign women want to deliver in hospital."

"Well not this one. I want to deliver at home. Can you help?"

"Yes, of course. So long as everything goes according to plan and you remain healthy and strong, I cannot see any problem. So let's do an overall check, shall we?"

He determined that the baby was due late January and that everything was proceeding as normal for my stage of pregnancy. "What are you eating? What is your diet?"

"Well I was following a vegan diet with no animal products but I have decided to extend that to vegetarian here to include eggs, cheese and a little fish."

He raised his eyebrows. "Well that isn't enough to stay healthy. You should be eating meat."

"No. No meat. I haven't eaten meat for years and I won't start now. I am fine. I am fit and healthy with enough energy. I go swimming every morning and I ride my bicycle everywhere."

He looked astounded. "Ride your bicycle? You rode your bicycle here from Assala You have to stop riding your bicycle."

This time it was my turn to look astounded. "But I feel fine. It is only a few kilometres. What is wrong with swimming and riding bicycles?" I was also noting how portly he was and thinking he might benefit himself from exercising more often.

"Well I recommend you at least stop riding your bicycle. You don't want to lose this baby do you?"

"No, of course not. I'll think about it." I had decided I would live my life as normally as possible throughout my pregnancy. Having a baby is not an illness and women all over the world often continue as normally as possible. I felt absolutely fine and I was listening to my body. If I felt anything was amiss I would stop immediately. I got on my bike and rode home, confident that Dr Rumi knew what he was doing and he would look after me and the baby. I didn't tell him I was also going to regular yoga classes.

The yoga classes I attended were held in the Coral Coast Hotel on the beach front and I was attending classes twice a week. I loved them. Before it had always seemed so difficult for me to fit classes into my manic fashion schedule, so here in Dahab I could make them a priority. The yoga teachers were great too. Dahab was becoming known as a yoga holiday destination with groups travelling from Europe for a week's yoga holiday combined with living by the sea and spending meditation evenings at the water's edge or in the desert mountains.

I had also looked for new creative outlets now I didn't have to think about fashion constantly and started baking bread and muffins for fun. I found that my yoga instructors and others were requesting payment in barter - my baked goods for their services. That made me smile, as I remembered my grandmother's bakery back in Kaiserslautern. I was returning to creativities I hadn't enjoyed since childhood.

After my initial feelings of loneliness and depression faded, I started to make friends in Dahab too. My friends from Europe were also curious to visit and see this place in Egypt that had stolen my heart and prompted me to make such massive changes in my life. They came to stay and Kurt and I developed some income from scuba diving and safari. I would drive the Jeep and we would explore the South Sinai desert. We would also do mini diving tours to isolated places like Ras Abu Galum, a tiny Bedouin settlement to the north that has no electricity or running water but where the diving is superb.

Kurt was more and more comfortable when he saw I wasn't making any demands on his freedom and we both started to enjoy the thought of becoming parents in the near future. The rose tinted glasses of initial attraction were well and truly off but my pregnancy kept us close.

Aside from purchasing the Jeep in the months previous to my arrival, I had thought about investing some money into my life in Dahab. I discovered that the house Kurt was living in was for sale for very cheap price. I was interested in buying it, thinking that at the least I would have somewhere to live if need be. However the owner changed his mind, so that wasn't an option.

Kurt had then introduced me to an Egyptian friend of his called Sherif, who wanted to start a new business based in the Lighthouse area. Not all diving centres had their own compressor, so Sherif's idea was to open a specialised tank filling station called *Hard Rock*. Sherif needed tanks to rent out, so we made a deal where I would purchase the tanks and be paid a reasonable commission every time a tank was filled and hired out. Tanks do have a finite life but as long as they are cared for and not bled dry of air, they last for many refills. Over the years, the arrangement proved profitable for both of us.

Becoming Sherif's business partner helped me realize how I could establish myself in Dahab with small businesses. Sherif seemed to be a sympathetic person. He himself had been through some difficult times when his father (who had owned a number of properties in Dahab) died when he was just nineteen. As the sole surviving male in his family he stood to inherit all his father's properties but his uncles contrived otherwise. They had sent him to relatives in South Africa for a year. When he returned, they had essentially taken over all the properties yet Sherif was still directly responsible for his mother and sisters' welfare. I discovered this sort of behaviour among Egyptian families is not uncommon and he accepted it as best he could.

Sherif also had foreign girlfriends and had spent some time Germany, so he understood (more than many Egyptians) how Europeans thought and lived. Over the next months Sherif and I would become friends and spend a lot of time working on projects together.

One long time friend from Germany who came to visit in the early months was Dieter. He has been like a big brother to me for much of my life. He is a successful entrepreneur with a good business mind, so we sat together and talked about what other opportunities there might be for business in Dahab. I told him I was already a silent partner renting the dive tanks with Sherif but that I wanted something more creative for myself.

"I can bake bread and sell it!" I joked about my barter system for yoga and massages.

"Well, why not? There seem to be quite a lot of foreigners travelling here. And I haven't tasted any decent bread."

"I do it for fun really, not to make money."

"Well sometimes the best things start that way. Let's make a small business plan to see how many loaves you would need to sell to make money." So over the next few days we played around with numbers and figures, brainstorming what it would take to start a successful bakery in Dahab. The more I talked about it with Dieter, the more I liked the idea.

I mentioned it to Sherif. Would he be interested in being my

Egyptian business partner again? It is necessary to have local partners in businesses in Egypt. "Yes!", Sherif was interested so we started to look for possible locations for a bakery. I was adamant I wanted an area with vehicle access, not on the promenade with its exorbitant rents and hassling shop keepers.

One day Sherif called me, "I have found a place we should look at for the bakery. It isn't in the bay area and it looks terrible right now but I think it has potential. I want you to see it."

"Sure. Where is it? Where shall I meet you?"

"The corner of Peace Road and Sharm El Fanar. Meet you there in one hour?"

"Yep, OK. I'll be there."

When I got there, Sherif was already waiting on the street outside the rundown place with the illustrious name of El Prince Camp. 'Camp' in Dahab actually means 'cheap, tiny one room accommodation with shared facilities', not an area for tents as foreigners often think. Hardly anybody travels with a tent in Egypt. Bedouin tents are actually *beit shar* or 'house of hair', made from woven camel and goat hair and they are semi permanent placements, only moving as seasons or grazing requires. There were none of these in Dahab. As for El Prince, there was only one tumble down storey building with stairs up to the unfinished second floor. Building in Egypt is often done in staggered steps and it seemed El Prince's owners had run out of money, enthusiasm, or both. There was also a rundown restaurant to one end.

The camp had been built in a U shape with doors opening to the centre and as I walked through, a Moroccan *riyadh* sprang to mind. Pictures started to build in my head as I imagined a tiled courtyard and reflection pool in the centre, low seating areas, turrets and domes. I think Sherif was expecting me to say it was revolting but instead I said "Yes, I can see potential here. It makes me think of a Moroccan *riyadh*."

"Oh, so you like the place?" he replied, somewhat surprised.

"Yes, we can alter the restaurant area into a bakery café and rent out these rooms to dive masters and other foreigners on a long term base." Just as in my designer days, my mind was flooded with ideas and vision.

"It is for sale. If everything stacks up, I think we should buy it rather than rent. We'll have more control and worry less that way."

Considering what was happening with my rental home, I agreed with him. So we started the process of doing a proper business plan and decided to purchase El Prince Camp. The name would be changed to *Alf Leila - A Thousand Nights* in keeping with the stories of Sheherezade. The Bakery was to be *Leila's Bakery*.

Sherif of course knew I was pregnant, so we decided that the actual building and renovations would take place after I had the baby and we would then travel to Cairo to purchase all the building materials. Neither of us had any desperate need to hurry.

I was spending far more time discussing business with Sherif than time with Kurt. Sherif couldn't understand Kurt's attitude toward me. Why was he letting me do all this on my own? Why wasn't he supporting me? Kurt didn't really answer and by now he had found another job working at a diving centre at the Lighthouse.

I drew up concept plans for Alf Leila and Leila's Bakery and Sherif put me in contact with a German wife of one his friends. I discovered over time, that many of these talented foreign women married to Egyptian husbands were happy to literally stay at home, hardly ever venturing out. She was an architect so she converted my concept designs into construction plans and the slow grinding process of getting building approval started. There were so many constant visits to the Dahab civic offices, to the Nuweiba court house and to lawyers, that by the time I was awaiting the birth of our baby, most of the paper work had been processed. We were just waiting for final approval.

The Bedouin men wandering through my space continued to cause me more and more concern and I was fed up so decided to look for more options. Sherif found a cheap plot of land not far from Alf Leila and I decided to buy it. Here I would build my own house to live in, neighbours be damned. If we were renovating Alf Leila and the Bakery, we may as well build a house with the already contracted workers.

The baby's ultrasound in Egypt hadn't been very revealing, so it wasn't until I travelled back to Germany in September and had another ultrasound that we discovered we were having a baby girl. When I announced my pregnancy to my parents their whole attitude changed completely. This baby girl would be their first grandchild. My mother's vows of never visiting me in Egypt were happily forgotten and they decided to visit me in December before the baby was born. When they arrived I was able to proudly show off my rounded tummy, even though it was still not really obvious that I was eight months pregnant. We all had a great time together and everybody was looking forward to our new family addition the following month.

On the morning of their departure it started to rain, much

heavier than the time when Papa and I first went to Dahab. There was a torrential downpour from six in the morning and the electricity went out as electrical sockets are exposed in many places. I was still spending many nights at Kurt's house and his living room was the first to flood because it had no roof, just a mosquito net covering. We lay huddled in bed as water started to seep over the floor.

I splashed along muddy streets in the Jeep to my house to rescue the garden pillows. My plan was to ferry them inside to a dry area but when I opened the door, I found the rain running down the wall precisely behind my bookcase! The whole house was leaking like a sieve. So much for my beautiful tongue and groove wooden ceiling! The roof cover above was obviously useless. The kitchen was the only dry area in the house so I frantically moved as many precious items as I could in there, stacking them on the dry benches.

When I returned to Kurt's house I found his neighbours building a wall in the street to try to save their house from the raging torrents. It looked like a losing battle. I continued on to Mashraba, carefully fording the river that was again flowing under the bridge into the Lighthouse Bay. My parents were staying in the Nesima Hotel close to the beach. I found them huddled in their room as water leaked down the walls of their four star hotel. The waterfall was particularly spectacular in the bathroom where there was a relentless shower, despite all the taps being turned off.

The rain ceased as quickly as it had started and by late morning, the sun was shining again as if nothing had happened but the devastation remained. We waited on tenterhooks to see when the road to Sharm el Sheikh would reopen, as my parent's flight was due to leave at 5pm that afternoon. Lady luck was on our side when the road reopened at 1pm, leaving just enough time for us to travel to the airport for their check-in, providing there were no delays.

It was a tense trip, dodging piles of rock and rubble that had been deposited by the raging mountain torrents and swerving around large areas where the tar seal had been gouged out. We made it to the airport just as the Jeep's electrical circuits rebelled against the damp atmosphere and its engine began to stutter and lurch in protest. We literally coasted into a parking area as the engine died.

After saying good-bye to my parents we returned to the Jeep with our fingers crossed that it would start again. The engine coughed reluctantly back to life but not very convincingly, so we drove the Jeep directly to an auto repair shop. I was beginning to hate that unreliable vehicle as it wasn't the first nor the second time it had let us down.

We ran to the nearby bus station to catch the next bus back to sodden Dahab. We arrived to find there was only one dry mattress out of five between our two soaked houses. It was a miserable night but by the next day we could put everything out to dry in the sun to dry quickly. Getting everything clean was another matter; that took days of brushing and scrubbing.

Dr Rumi had predicted that our girl was due the end of January. The time came and nothing happened. Really, nothing happened. Not even a twinge. I had enjoyed a relatively easy pregnancy with no complications and no pain, not even the infamous Braxton Hicks practice contractions. I had no real idea of how the actual birth would proceed as I wasn't one to spend hours poring over books about pregnancy and birthing. I just knew I was healthy and women have babies all the time all over the world. I would be just one more.

It was over a week later in February when my waters finally broke at 3am but I was calm and felt no physical discomfort. When there were no sign of contractions by 6am, Dr Rumi told me I should go to the Dahab hospital for observation. He would meet me there. I was disappointed as I planned to have our baby at home but ultimately I just wanted a healthy baby. By 10am there were still no contractions. I felt nothing. The baby was monitored with no sign of heart rate stress but Dr Rumi looked serious.

"I don't want to worry you but there may be a possibility that we will need to do a Caesarean delivery. I don't have the facilities to do that safely here, so I want to transfer you to Sharm el Sheikh."

"Oh. Of course, if I must." I felt so disappointed but by now was also concerned that nothing was working out well. I didn't like the idea of a surgical delivery but as needs must.

I was bundled into the back of an orange Egyptian ambulance, (which was essentially an empty minivan) to be driven the hour and half to Sharm el Sheikh. Kurt followed driving the Jeep. It was bizarre to be alone in the back of that van with nothing but a bed to lie on, no attendant beside me and a driver alone in the front. I was facing backwards and couldn't see exactly where we were on the journey so I played a game with myself to guess how far it was to Sharm. When the mountains receded away from the road and the spaces became wider and sandier, I knew we were nearly there. We finally arrived at the Pyramid Hospital with its ostentatious pyramid of constructed triangle glass panes out front, a smaller less impressive version of the one outside the Louvre in Paris.

The doctor at Sharm examined me and said he didn't think I needed to prepare for a Caesarean yet. He said he would do all he could to help me have a natural birth. I was so relieved! But I was hooked up to tubes and baby monitors so I couldn't move from lying on my back in the bed. I hadn't eaten anything that day except for cookies and juice that Kurt had managed to find before I left. Egyptian hospitals are essentially self catering, you even have to purchase drinking water. I felt sick and weak from no food and wanted the birth to be over and done with.

Kurt was beside me in the delivery suite and I was grateful to him for that. They administered medication to induce the birth but the contractions never really came. I was doing all the work by force of will, pushing and breathing to keep a rhythm to deliver our baby. She still did not have a name. I was becoming more and more exhausted and slowly felt like I was going to die. I really felt I had nothing left. Just when I was really about to say 'I can't do this anymore!', Kurt said, "I can see the head. Come on Ella! You make this last effort. Our baby is nearly born! Just one more push."

I have no idea where I found the energy but his words were enough. He told me later there had been no sign of her head, he was just trying to encourage me. When her head did finally appear, the delivery team attached a suction cup and helped deliver our baby girl. She was finally born and I was so relieved to hear her cry of life. She didn't cry for long and they placed her close across my breasts. My baby, our baby, at last.

I slowly realised there was still a lot of activity going on around me but they were speaking in Arabic and I couldn't understand what was happening. The baby was lifted from my chest as they said they needed to clean her up. I sensed there was more from their concerned faces. After ten, twenty, thirty minutes I was still bleeding badly and the placenta was not detaching from the uterus. By the evening I was hooked up to drips in Intensive Care, suffering major pain from drug induced contractions that had never come during birth, with episiotomy stitches that felt like needles and my baby screaming in a cot beside me. I felt like I was losing my mind as well as my blood. I called for Kurt to come and take the baby. It was too distressing to hear her crying and I was too weak and in too much pain to deal with anything else. I was terrified, wondering if I would make it through the night, and I swear I saw a guardian angel at the end of my bed.

After blood transfusions, delivery of the placenta and surgery to repair the area of haemorrhage, I finally started to recover and got some strength back. When I eventually managed to climb out of bed and caught a glance of myself in the mirror I nearly didn't recognize myself. I was so thin and pale, my belly had completely disappeared and my eyes were white with anaemia. But I was so grateful to be on my feet and even more thankful for my lovely daughter. She was the motivation that pulled me through it all.

I was discharged the following morning with our gorgeous new baby, thirty-six hours after entering the hospital. The first thing I wanted to do was eat. I was starving! My body was well into survival mode and I knew I needed all the energy I could get to breast feed our little girl. Our beautiful, healthy baby girl! We drove to a hotel in Naama Bay, the Marriot Hotel I think, and I ate as much as I possibly could off the buffet. Kurt was astounded I could stuff so much in!

We had decided on three possible names for our baby girl - Lacy, Luisa and Luna. We found Egyptians had great difficulty trying to pronounce Luisa so that was out. Then we decided Lacy sounded too American so finally we decided on Luna. We had a baby girl and her name was Luna Sara.

I was very weak from loss of blood and the difficult birth but I was so happy to be home with our baby. Kurt had started a new job in Lagoona Diving Centre and couldn't be home with me during the day, so he arranged for his neighbour's wife to come and take care of Luna and me at my house. Aida was a typical, traditional Egyptian woman, a big mama with many children of her own. We figured as she already had many children, she would be able to guide me if I was having difficulties adapting to being a mother. We didn't bargain on so many cultural differences.

The first thing she insisted on was (like Dr Rumi) that I should eat meat. I hadn't eaten meat for maybe twenty years and I wasn't about to start then. We had quite a heated discussion that even if she cooked it, I would absolutely refuse to eat it. The idea of eating animals is impossible for me. She said "Well, then you have to eat chicken soup."

"I will *never* eat chicken soup!"

"But how do you expect to get strong if you won't eat proper food?" She talked to me like I was about five years old. I didn't find it funny.

And then she would take Luna from my arms and start to play with her, my baby who was only a few days old. She threw her in the air! I nearly died as my heart stopped in my throat. The scream couldn't even come out!

"No! No! Please don't do that!" as I took Luna back in my arms. 'Is this woman crazy?', I asked myself. Throwing my precious new born baby in the air!!!

The next day she decided that if I wouldn't eat chicken soup, I should at least eat fish. "Fish makes you strong, "she assured me. I had been eating some fish but it wasn't something I looked forward to. Aida had bought the freshly caught fish with her, which she proceeded to prepare in the sink and cook in a pan on the gas rings. I managed to eat a little as my thin body was ravenous for food. I certainly felt by then that I was eating for two as I had no body fat in reserve and what I consumed was all used up immediately. But after eating I stood up to do the dishes and realised all the fish guts and scales were blocking the sink. I nearly lost my lunch! The mess was disgusting and I couldn't get the water to run at all as some scales had fallen through the grate. I eventually called a plumber to unblock the sink and avoided going anywhere near the kitchen until it was cleaned.

I wasn't feeling better with Aida's 'help'. I was more upset and nervous about what she would do next. I told myself I would be fine looking after Luna by myself. So what if it takes me longer to tidy up in the morning? I am not working for anyone else and nothing has to be done on tight schedule. I can still go everywhere with Luna and get things done. Egyptians love children, so nobody is going to frown if I go everywhere with a child.

Kurt was staying the nights with Luna and I in my house for those first weeks, so we got used to each other as a family. When Kurt came home that evening I told him what had happened with Aida. "She has to go! I don't want her around. I will be fine. She is just stressing me out, not helping." Kurt found some polite excuse to tell her that I would be fine alone.

My milk started coming in after a few days and the pain that involved surprised me. I went to Dr Rumi for reassurance. His nurse explained to me that everything I was experiencing was normal (including the pain) and that I would be fine once Luna established her feeding routine for feeding (which it was). I did feel rather alone with no female European friends around to help me but I was managing.

Luna was such a relaxed baby, feeding easily and sleeping anywhere through any noises and sounds. She fitted into our lives like she had always been there. After four days at home, Kurt and I decided to go out for dinner with Luna. Everything was perfect and she slept happily through the whole meal. People fussed over her as a new baby and I felt happy that I had decided to have my child in a place that had clean, open air where children can grow up healthy outside.

Baby Luna at Eco Lodge

Camels in Assala　　　　　*Luna and Bedouin lady*

Broken down Jeep in the dessert

The next step was to register Luna's birth. The world is full of bureaucracy and Egypt is far from an exception. I suspect their modern methods are more unwieldy than those of their illustrious ancients thousands of years ago. I was dealing with it on a number of levels; the vehicle registration, the building permissions and now Luna. If a baby is born to unwed parents in Egypt they essentially do not exist as far as official identification is concerned. And no one in Egypt can function without official identification papers. Kurt and I weren't married. However, I found someone who managed to get fake marriage papers so we could register Luna's birth. When we went to register her name as 'Luna Sara Hartmann ' they insisted that the father's name be included too. In Egypt, one is given a first name followed by your father's first three names. However, they made a slight exception, so her birth certificate said 'Luna Sara Kurt Hartmann'.

Despite Luna being a perfect baby, the stitches from the episiotomy weren't healing well and I was struggling to get my energy back with the breast feeding. Some weeks after Luna's birth, Martina came to visit from Germany with two girlfriends. She was so looking forward to meeting her new sister and was instantly right at home in Dahab. She and her friends helped a lot and I was finally able to relax and get my health back. I am so grateful for her help at that time.

In May 2004, we decided to kill two birds with one stone by travelling to Cairo with Sherif to get a passport for Luna and buy the building materials for Alf Leila. Contractors won't invest funds to purchase on behalf of the owner, so no project will start unless all materials are bought and paid for by the person leading it. Also, the owner can't just hand over the funds to get builders to go buy materials as they may abscond with the funds and never be seen again. One woman I heard about, found her building material funds had been spent to buy a vehicle instead of materials.

Back then in Dahab, there were very limited construction supplies available, so we needed to cover everything from plumbing, walls to floors. We fully expected the building permit to be a formality since we were finishing an existing building, not starting something from scratch.

Kurt, Sherif, Luna and I boarded a bus to make the eight hour plus bus ride to Cairo. Kurt wasn't interested in our building plans but he needed to come to prove he was Luna's father at the German Embassy for her passport. That part was no problem but they said, "You can't have a male's name for a girl," as had been stipulated on her Egyptian birth certificate. Her name changed back again to become 'Luna Sara Hartmann'. I was learning. Just go with the flow, only make waves when necessary.

Sherif, Luna and I stayed on in Cairo to gather our building supplies. Sherif, who was born in Suez, was not much better than me at finding his way around the congested streets or markets, so he enlisted the help of a guide with a vehicle. He drove us everywhere down obscure back streets and into dark markets seeking the goods we needed.

Sherif thought it best to avoid too much attention visiting markets and construction areas, that had probably never seen a foreign visitor before, let alone a blond, foreign woman with a baby on her arm. I was in no physical danger but an uncovered foreign woman, would have meant they expected higher prices. I dressed in Egyptian women's clothes; a long *jalabiya* dress, a long black *abaya* coat over the top and a *hijab* head scarf. The heat was already oppressive in May but the most difficult thing was trying to breastfeed Luna with all that prohibitive clothing on. No special maternity clothes with secretive strategic splits! But I managed, as every Egyptian woman must.

We developed colour schemes for each room, chose flooring

and wall tiles for the interior and exterior, as well as window glass, cabinets, mirrors, electrical fittings - everything we could imagine. We even found copper bowls that are used to cook *ta'miya* (Egyptian patties like falafel but made with fava beans instead of chick peas) and decided these would be perfect for wash basins in the bathrooms. They looked like modern versions of the authentic ewer jugs and basins, traditionally used for washing hands.

Ten manic days in Cairo, brought back memories of the crazy fashion world I had left far behind me. Luckily, we were successful and found most of what we needed to build Alf Leila and Leila's Bakery. I was ready to return to relaxed Dahab. Then we only had to wait for the final building permit so that we could start the renovation. But no permit materialised and the authorities weren't forthcoming about what was causing the delay. Eventually Sherif suggested, "Why don't you start on your house? It can be a test run. There is no use applying for proper planning permission yet anyway as the lane in front is too narrow. All the other buildings there are built without permission so it's highly unlikely there will be any problems." I had paid so little for the land and the building materials were inexpensive, so I decided to take Sherif's advice and went ahead with building what would be my own house.

I was happy in my creative bubble that gave me so much joy. I drew everything first to be clear of what I wanted in my head but none of the workers could read plans or understand drawings. The only way was to spend every day on the construction site and explain to each man in my basic Arabic exactly what he should do. Luna slept peacefully or played on a rug in the middle of the building site.

The oddest experience was with the plumber. In my plans, I

wanted a dark blue bathtub placed under a window and duly conveyed my wish to him. When I checked how they had placed it, I noticed that the rim was not level and the workers tried to tell me the slope was necessary to allow the water to drain. I frowned and explained to the plumber, "The top of the tub should be level. The slope is already built into the actual bottom of the bath." He shrugged and they set about adjusting the level, filling it with sand to hold it in place. I got that removed but the surface was damaged.

When the worker who was placing the ceramic wall tiles took no care at all, letting rough cement fall into the bath, that was the final straw. The totally scratched bathtub could never be repaired and had to be removed. Each workman blamed the other! I later realised they had probably never installed a bath before, as Egyptian bathrooms just have open showers on wet floors.

It literally paid to be on site every day to ensure materials were not sold off nor construction shortcuts taken. The latter might prove the work useless at best or, at worst, fatal. One owner in the process of building apartments found their precious matching marble being used on another building site "because that one had run out and they needed it fast".

Project completion in Egypt is directly related to who can cause the workers the most hassle if they don't get it done. So by me working with them every day, ensuring they were on the job, my project was completed in extra fast time. By the end of July I had a new house, completed in less than three months and over summer too.

El Prince Camp was physically only about a hundred metres away but still languishing as a building site, waiting on its permit.

I had thought it would be perfect to be living in my house so close to our new project when we got the go ahead. I had given my landlord Said notice of my intention to move into my new house. However, over the course of the construction, after spending day after day in the area, I began to have doubts as to whether I would ever enjoy living there. The area is close to the tourist area of town, close to a busy road with the taxi drivers constantly tooting on the horns for any reason (or none at all!), and there were neighbours less than a yard away.

I loved my rented house with the spacious grounds, the palm trees whispering me to sleep. I was by then used to Bedouin men sitting quietly under the palms. I realised they were always polite and actually making efforts to avert their eyes if I was about. My new house had no value compared to those beautiful palm trees and that garden. "Said, can I stay in 'my' house?" I begged my landlord.

"Yes, of course. I haven't rented it out again yet."

I advertised to rent out my new house. The first tenants were a German woman and her Egyptian husband. I doubt they were officially married but as it's illegal for unmarried couples to cohabit in Egypt, many people obtain crassly called "Fuck papers". Couples get these *Urfi* marriage papers drawn up and signed by witnesses in front of a lawyer to say they agree to be married. When they no longer wish to be together, they just tear up the paper. Egyptian authorities don't seem to worry about foreigners like Kurt and I living together but it's much more difficult for Egyptians. All hotels must sign marriage papers before they can let rooms to Egyptian couples.

Despite knowing the floor was still being finished when they rented, it the couple refused to pay full rent. They were constantly complaining about everything and made my life miserable. I terminated their contract and was relieved when they left. I wondered if I was cut out to be a landlord. The house was still empty when Martina wanted to return to Dahab for a holiday with four friends. I offered the house to her and friends and they loved it. I then got the idea to keep the house for short term holiday rentals rather than long term leases. And so, my rental property Villa La Bohème was born.

I listed Villa La Bohème on the local website Dahab.net where, at that time, there was only one other house mentioned. It was a fortuitous decision as bookings started to flow, into what proved to be my most successful business in Dahab. And I was happy continuing to live among the treasured palm tree garden in Assala.

In October 2004, almost a year after we had applied for permission, Sherif received a letter from the *Magnes Medina* denying us building permission for Alf Leila and Leila's Bakery. We were both devastated. Apparently the existing building was less than the required five meters from the street cornerstone and had been built illegally. There was no point questioning how the previous owners had got as far as they did but we had to decide what to do with our now useless building.

Whatever we did, we would have to move the front of the building back the required five metres, either by reducing the current building or destroying it completely. The authorities were prepared to give us some concession by allowing us to use 80% of the site for building which was the old standard; the new one would have required a much smaller building. So there we were, with thousands of Egyptian pounds sitting in building materials and a useless camp that was an illegal building. Sherif and I had some serious decisions to make. Fast.

Luna with Abdu

Chapter 4

Building Leila's

I was totally frustrated by what was going on and couldn't even comprehend how it had happened. How could we have purchased a completely useless building with official papers? Everyone just shrugged when I asked as if to say, "Welcome to Egypt. This is how it works here."

I was so angry but I didn't really know who to be angry at, as it seemed as though everybody had tried their best to make sure everything was legal. I knew that I had built Villa La Bohème without officially registered papers and I took that risk because of the relatively small cost. Every other building on that single lane access was in the same position, as were many buildings in Dahab. The Bedouin after all, had been living there happily, long before any civic council told them they had to put in survey pegs to differentiate lots.

But with Alf Leila, we had spent money to ensure everything was done correctly. In the midst of this angry and frustrated frame of mind, I decided I would not be beaten. I would find a way to build Alf Leila and Leila's Bakery just as I had imagined. It would mean using most of my savings and borrowing money but damn it, I would do it!

I didn't take any time to research the idea further nor make a new business plan. I just said to Sherif, "Yes, let's do it!" After all, where had all the research and care got us? Sherif wasn't in a financial position to invest an equal share, so we adjusted how projected income would repay the difference and I asked for help from my parents and German friends. We decided to completely demolish the existing building and start from scratch.

Sherif continued to hold his daily court on the beach at the Lighthouse close to where Hard Rock was; the beach was his office and I would usually meet him there every day, sometime between six and ten in the evening. Most business days in Egypt do not start until the afternoon and end a little before midnight. To the outsider everything might look very informal but many expensive business deals are made looking out over the bay.

Sherif wasn't very interested in the actual construction of Alf Leila, but he was prepared to do all the negotiating that would be needed with authorities. I knew that I didn't possess the language skills or local knowledge required to be able to do that. This time we literally employed the 'who you know, not what you know' rule and decided that this time we would engage the services of an Egyptian architect with good connections to the *Magnus Medina*. Sherif knew just the best person.

At first Sherif's architect said he had two problems with our proposal. One, he would never work with a woman. Two, he wanted to create his own design, he could not build 'Ella's dream castle'. Sherif informed him, "If you want the job, you will work every day with Ella, and will do exactly what she tells you. She is the creator of the design." Maybe if I hadn't spent years as a designer in the fashion industry I would have felt more phased by his arrogant manner. However, I was used to dealing with men like him and just ignored his attitude.

Another Christmas came and went. Celebrating Christmas in an essentially Muslim country was a simple and low key affair. A Swiss friend invited Luna to their family house for St Nicolaus's visit on the 6th of December and at home that year I didn't decorate a great deal except for a Christmas tree and candles. Kurt and I made a fancy dinner at home together on Christmas Eve, opting out of restaurants and hotels serving traditional dinners - usually English in style. I felt a little nostalgic but also liberated from the usual European stress.

In the cool of January, Kurt and I took Luna on a family tour of Egypt. I wanted to research traditional Egyptian styles for Alf Leila and the trip also served for Kurt and I to enjoy time with our nearly one year old daughter. Luna was the apple of my eye, a happy, relaxed baby who seemed to love living in the clear open air of Dahab. I didn't regret for a moment my decision to move to such a warm, sunny, simple place where she was growing up in an easy manner, spending her days with me, Kurt or in this case, both of us. If I had stayed in the fashion industry I would have had to employ nannies and baby sitters for childcare and missed half her childhood.

I also never imagined that I would have just one child and broached the subject with Kurt. He was non committal, saying, "Oh, I just don't know. Maybe we should wait."

"Well if you feel like that you better think about using something!", I replied sarcastically. I was prepared to let nature take its course and wanted another baby. Maybe I could get pregnant again on a relaxing holiday. Financially, I was continuing to support Luna and myself on my own (sometimes Kurt as well) so another child would make little difference. I gradually realised that Kurt found it difficult to commit to anything. He drifted from job to job, not much interested in what I was doing but always with big business ideas of his own.

I rented a car, knowing full well a trip in my antiquated Jeep would be doomed to constant breakdowns and stress. For six weeks of mild Egyptian winter we drove south. First along the Red Sea coast through Hurghada towards the Sudanese border. In El Quseir, I fell in love with the Movenpick Hotel which seemed to be constructed entirely of natural stone and clay. We crossed the Eastern desert to Luxor and continued south along the Nile, through Upper Egypt to Aswan and then as far south as the temple of Abu Simbel, rescued from the waters of Lake Nasser. I was in awe of the inspiring ancient buildings and temples that Egyptians (while proud of them) seem to take for granted in their daily lives.

Then we travelled further inland to the Western Deserts close to the Libyan border, to visit the remote oases of Kharga, Dakhla, Farafra and Bahareya. Our little family covered over three thousand miles journeying through remote dusty deserts and negotiating crazy, city traffic. By the time I returned to start work with our chauvinistic architect, my mind was brimming with ideas for the *riyadh* and the bakery.

True to form, the architect completely rejected my idea for a natural building based around stone and clay. Apparently these were prohibited in Dahab. I wasn't in a position to argue but who really knows what is allowed or not, considering some of the buildings that get constructed? I gave up the fight on that and after three weeks of working with a grumpy, resistant Egyptian male we finally had plans for a modern *riyadh* that could be presented to the City Council for consideration. Everything went according to plan as this time approval came quickly, (aided no doubt) by our constant daily presence at the offices in the Medina. We sat there every night until at least after ten o'clock (Egyptian work hours) until we got the building permit.

In February, we demolished the old El Prince building and started from scratch with new foundations for Alf Leila and Leila's Bakery. At last something was happening! To make sure the construction went according to plan, I was once again back in the cement and mess with Luna playing in the dirt. Building Villa La Bohème had taught me a lot and I was determined to see this building was constructed to my specifications.

I was so stubborn and demanding that only one tradesman lasted the distance. He ended up doing all the masonry alone as he was the only one who understood my requirements for arches and domes and the only one who worked to keep everything consistently straight.

Building Alf Leila

Constructing the Arches

I was constantly covered in dust and sweat. When the architect saw how involved I was and how prepared to get more than my hands dirty, he finally accepted my ideas and skills. We were in agreement about most things by this stage and he was even becoming friendly, in a professional way.

I would confer with Sherif regularly in his 'office' but he didn't take much interest in the day to day construction. Kurt showed even less interest but I was too busy to worry about our threadbare relationship. He had started another new job but never seemed to have any money that he was willing to share with Luna and I. He did however love Luna very much and spent a lot of his time playing with just her. He also still had his beloved freedom and it was always up to me to make the effort to spend time with him, not the other way around. Despite me having the much more comfortable home in a quiet area, Luna and I would spend the majority of evenings in Kurt's tiny home.

Sherif had formed a relationship with a young Russian woman,

Natasha, and they seemed very happy together. She was a trained interior designer from Moscow and they had met while she was on holiday in Dahab in 2004. Like me, she had decided to change her stressful business life for a simpler one in Dahab and gradually moved her life to Egypt. We clicked right away and Sherif encouraged her to become involved in our building project in the summer of 2005. One of our difficult challenges was to utilise the existing ceramics and concrete tiles that had been purchased in specific quantities for the now demolished building. A lot had also been ruined in storage, so we spent hours measuring and calculating how many square feet we had left of each different pattern. With her interior design skills, Natasha produced graphics and drawings to help with the new specifications. We certainly broke a few rules in Dahab by being three females on a building site, Natasha, Luna and I, we were happy to get down and dirty in the dust and grime. Luna was such a great child to have anywhere; happy and interested in whatever was going on. The Egyptian workmen all doted on her.

Luna Playing in the Foundations of Alf Leila

Natasha and I became close friends, sharing many things about our lives, both in terms of design and the difficulties of being foreign women in Dahab. Like myself with Kurt, she wanted to be a mother and have a child with Sherif. She differed in one way though. Her expectations of men and relationships were that husbands should provide the best, build a home and look after the family. That was something most Egyptian men would understand as many Egyptian marriages are arranged between families according to those provisions. It seemed that more than love, she wanted status and security.

Perhaps with Natasha involved, Sherif decided he did not need to be at all and I saw less and less of him. Even for things related to accounts, I dealt directly with his manager. But he did continue to negotiate if we needed something from local government. He still gave me the feeling that he was there for me when I needed help with our business or even some things in my personal life, even if I just needed someone to travel with me to Sharm el Sheikh.

During that summer Kurt and I relaxed into a closer relationship with Luna at the centre and he decided he could live with me and Luna in one place. Not exactly the same space, mind you. His plan was to develop the roof area of my house and to create a space for himself. Despite him not having any personal finances to contribute I readily agreed to pay for the addition to my rented house. Driving back and forth on a daily basis with Luna was already becoming very tiring and time consuming. Kurt still had his 'man space' above us, but as there was no kitchen upstairs he spent most meal times with us. And as he never cooked or even washed dishes, I realised he had truly become part of the male chauvinistic culture of Egypt. How convenient for him!

Because of the prominent position of our site on the corner of the busy Dahab thoroughfares, building Alf Leila and Leila's Bakery created a lot of interest. The distinctive domes and arches intrigued people to the point where they were constantly inquiring about what we were building. Anticipation was developing, my plan was working. Construction was progressing well and by August I decided we should start to complete the bakery first and produce some goods as soon as possible. I myself did not have enough knowledge of how to set up a commercial German style bakery so I searched online for a German baker who could help me complete everything.

I found Reiner, a typical baker from North Germany. Reiner assured me he'd be in Dahab within two months and true to his word, he arrived on the first of October. I was so excited to meet this pivotal person, the one who could make or break the next stage of our project, that I drove myself to Sharm el Sheikh Airport to collect him. As I watched the passengers pass through the automatic doors, blinking involuntarily at the blinding sun, it was not difficult to recognise a typical German baker with his pale skin, blonde hair and intense manner.

"Welcome to Egypt!" I smiled at him.

"Thank you. Great to be here. Wow! The sun sure is bright. I've only ever been as far as Greece before and I don't think the sun was this bright." I discovered that flying to Egypt was the furthest he had travelled in his life, his Greek holiday being the only other time he had ventured into a culture different from mainstream Europe. 'This is going to be interesting', I thought to myself. He is in for some culture shock in Dahab with its makeshift buildings and goats on the street.

When he entered our bakery I saw Reiner's eyebrows rise. "This is your bakery?" obviously incredulous at the state of the building site.

"Ah, yes," I assured him. "I know it doesn't look much yet but things are coming together quickly." He looked at me as if I were mad - there were no windows, no doors and no floor tiles. I continued, "This will be the serving area and out back here the bakery."

Reiner stepped carefully over some building rubble. "Ah, I see," which he clearly didn't. "So the bakery will be through this doorway..." he trailed off as he inspected the dusty floor debris.

Reiner was astounded by my optimism. He couldn't imagine how we would turn that rough concrete and brick area into a productive bakery. However to his everlasting credit, from the outset he showed total faith in my enthusiasm and added only good will and encouragement. I appreciated his positive attitude immensely.

Reiner had a true baker's heart and soul. Baking was his passion. We immediately started planning what we needed to buy and he researched online for suppliers. The chef from the Dahab Swiss Inn was also very helpful as a source for certain special ingredients we sought.

Within one week Reiner and I were on the overnight bus to Cairo for our big shopping spree. Accompanying us was one of the most helpful and friendly men in Dahab known as 'Abdullah the Tailor'. He was a fountain of knowledge when it came to finding anything in sprawling, stressful Cairo. We arrived early in the morning and started shopping immediately. Ramadan was in

October that year, so Abdullah knew that it would take us longer to achieve anything. Just before sunset every day everything would close for *iftar*, the daily meal that literally breaks fast for all followers of Islam. It is a religious and social meal and everybody partakes in it, meaning that the whole city stands still. Not to mention the hours leading up to it when the streets are even more manic and congested as everybody 'rushes' home or to family and friends for the meal. It's a little like having Christmas Eve every day for a month.

Of course my personal life never stopped for business and I decided this trip would be a good time to wean Luna from breast feeding. I had tried before but she was such a demanding child I didn't have the willpower to say "No" long enough to keep the process going. I decided a clean break with me out of sight would be best. Little did I realize just how much milk I had been producing; I found myself with rock hard breasts leaking milk into my clothes. The things women have to deal with! I doubt the men understood why I was so insistent in my immediate requests to find a toilet to keep cleaning myself up, not always an easy task in Cairo.

A highlight was shopping at the infamous and massive *souq* of Khan el Khalili. This is where both tourists and locals jostle shoulder to shoulder, to purchase almost anything available in Cairo. You can find anything from tourist tat, gold and silver jewellery, furnishing fabrics and women's underwear, to food and spices, homeware, house appliances, and more! Khan el Khalili has everything, including the kitchen sink.

After four days of frantic searching, we sat exhausted on the bus returning to Dahab, exhausted but pleased with our efforts.

We had met with ingredient suppliers and set up accounts. We had ordered the oven, all the kitchen equipment and hand-painted tableware before heading home with all the other things we needed, including lamps and decorations. It had been a successful expedition.

From there it was full speed ahead to finish the construction, as we hoped to complete everything for the Leila's Bakery before the Christmas holidays. Essentially only the doors and windows were missing. The next task was an important one: Reiner and I needed to decide which recipes and products we would sell.

When the oven arrived as promised within a few weeks, we decided to bake for a stall at the yearly community market held in Habiba Kindergarten just off Assala *souq*. I set up a stall with our various breads, cakes, and sweets. From the moment I set the goods down on the table, they were sold. I repeatedly phoned Reiner asking him to bake more of this, more of that so the goods could be delivered, covered on the deck of a pick-up truck still warm from the oven. Everybody queued for our bread and pastries, and when I said the bakery was still closed because we had no doors or windows, they said, "You have a baker and an oven...Bake and sell!" The sales were successful way beyond our hopes and predictions. I couldn't believe it!

Within six weeks we were selling from Leila's bakery and were so busy we had to look for assistants. We hired two apprentices, Hesham and Mohamed, the latter quickly proving himself to be a special person. Mohamed had grown up in the Nile Delta region and had left home at the age of sixteen to earn money in Dahab, doing all sorts of jobs to keep the cash flowing back to his family. When he started at Leila's he was twenty years old and had been working at Hard Rock for Sherif filling dive tanks. The other guys laughed at him for wanting to work in a bakery but he ignored their taunts and made his own choice. With Mohamed's desire and motivation to learn all he could, it was not long before Reiner had an excellent and motivated assistant baker on his hands.

Even though I must have seemed a strange woman in his traditional Egyptian eyes, Mohamed also showed me a lot of respect. He seemed to accept all women as equals in general, which is somewhat unusual for Egyptian men. At one stage we saw he was struggling with health issues because his legs swelled and were painful from working in a small space on unforgiving concrete floors. His attitude was open enough to allow us to arrange a female physiotherapist to treat him with massage regularly. All his other friends were too shy to overcome the sexual connotations of what they perceived 'massage' to be but he was mature about it.

I knew that unfortunately Reiner's time would too soon be up and he would have to return to Germany. I again searched online for another German baker and found Dirk. He had just returned to Germany from the Spanish island of Lanzarote, so I was guessing he was more travel savvy. There was to be a one week work overlap so that Reiner could hand over to Dirk.

The changeover between Reiner and Dirk was difficult, their characters clashing on almost every level. The two bakers could not have been more different in looks and attitude. Reiner was pale, blond and very precise, with a positive attitude to life and baking. Dirk was swarthy, aggressive, with a critical attitude towards everything in Egypt from the very start, which was ironic as he could easily have passed as an Egyptian.

I had gained trust in Reiner and knew what I wanted to achieve with Leila's Bakery. Dirk showed enthusiasm for work but he resented following my direction or the recipes Reiner and I had created and successfully sold. He was always saying, "No" right off the bat, before he even understood what was being asked of him. I felt he trusted no one and believed he knew better than everyone else. He was happy if everybody did things the way he wanted, but often didn't communicate what he wanted. He treated the Egyptian workers badly too, so it created a difficult working environment.

Dirk also wanted a great deal more appliances and equipment but I told him we would have to wait until we had a reliable cash flow. I felt stuck between 'a rock and hard place' as I needed his skills and experience but he was proving to be a complicated employee. I told myself that it would all work out and that Dirk would settle down into life in Dahab. On a personal level at least, Dirk seemed to enjoy Dahab from the first moment with all the diving and partying on offer.

By December we had accomplished a great deal. Leila's Bakery and Café was finished! The counter was in place and the garden had been planted. We had also erected a colourful, canvas-backed fence, which showcased traditional textile patterns that were often hand appliquéd to adorn the insides of desert tents. Everything looked bright, festive and ready for action.

It was the perfect time for a party to showcase Leila's Bakery before the Christmas holidays and high season arrived. I broached the subject with Sherif, "The bakery is going really well. I think we should have a little party to celebrate." I wanted a quiet affair with our current and potential customers and friends. Sherif lit up,

"Great idea! We can make a huge party for Dahab. I know some people in Cairo who can come and do the music. And bring special lighting!"

"Well, that wasn't quite what I had in mind. How about a small party for our customers? Not everyone in Dahab needs to be there."

"I want everyone there! It will be a huge occasion and everyone will come. Everyone will know about Leila's Bakery and the hotel."

"But the hotel isn't nearly finished. And we haven't made any money yet to be throwing a huge expensive party..." I trailed off. I could see I was overruled and that there would be no stopping him. That was the first time we really clashed in our plans but I brushed it off and decided I should do the best I could to make it a success.

On one of my initial trips to Dahab, I had brought over a lightweight tent that I had once sewn for a party in Germany. It was the perfect backdrop for putting on a fun play to enact some stories from A Thousand Nights – *Alf Leila*. I hired costumes from Cairo's Operatic Society and gathered friends to be actors and help stage the drama. Sherif contracted the team from Cairo with a DJ and lighting at a cost almost equal to Dirk 's monthly salary; they arrived by private bus.

On the day of the party Sherif promoted the already anticipated event even more. Two camels were led around town with signs on their saddles inviting everybody to the opening and some of our costumed performers ran along the beach attracting further attention. After dark, a laser beamed all over the town and everyone knew that night was our opening. A promotional success, it seemed like *everyone* in Dahab came!

When it was time to perform our play, one costumed actor looked around bemused, "Where is the fan? It was here half an hour ago." It took a few moments to realise that Bedouin children had stolen many of the props. And it took some time to cajole the cheeky children into returning the items. Meanwhile, the crowd became so restless, that any willing audience members could hardly follow our stories through the noise and confusion. Despite the disappointment and disinterest we tried to have fun.

Luna Dressed Up for 1001 Nights

When we finally started to serve the complimentary food and drinks it was like the storming of the Bastille into the bakery! Bedouin children and teenagers were even trying to climb in through the open windows, so unruly as they grabbed handfuls of the hors d'oeuvres and sweets being served. I doubt they even chewed them enough to taste the smoked salmon! I was appalled; these children were not starving and would never have behaved like this at their own social events. Sherif finally realised that the chaos was rapidly turning into a riot. He quickly organised people to go buy extra food from an Egyptian bakery to feed the multitudes gathered outside and placed bouncers on the bakery doors to regulate the crowd. We could then accept genuine VIP guests inside to sample and enjoy Leila's Bakery food. But by then the atmosphere was so tense and uncomfortable that our friends and customers only stayed for a short while. I didn't blame them.

I myself was shattered, both physically and emotionally. We had been preparing for the party for weeks; putting finishing touches to the building and working all day long to make the food, only to see an hour and a half of chaos where those who really mattered were driven away by rude, obnoxious local behaviour. In the end I sat sobbing outside our new bakery, vowing never again to do a free party for the selfish public; it seemed to be such a waste of time and money. But I had to look on the bright side. Leila's Bakery was however, officially open and running successfully. Mission accomplished!

Once the party was over, it was back to daily life and my jeep was driving me to despair with its constant need for repairs. I wanted rid of it and as a joke one day I told Sherif, "I wish I could turn this pile of junk into land! At least that increases in value rather than an old car costing money." To my surprise, even though he knew well all the Jeep's problems, Sherif agreed to trade it for a piece of his land. Said he really wanted the Jeep. It seemed a fair deal if not a bit odd, bit I shrugged it off. Little did I know this simple transaction would later return to haunt me.

Leila's Bakery started slowly and sales kept improving. On the other hand, progress on the hotel, Alf Leila, was very frustrating. Although we'd been working on the building for almost a year, the workers were dragging their feet and work seemed to slow not increase. At this rate, the small hotel was going to take longer to finish than the pyramids!

I'd been talking with a friend in Germany, Martin, who was complaining about his life in the fashion industry, feeling like I had in previous years. I knew he had done a lot of 'Do It Yourself' projects and his skills were as good as most tradespeople in Egypt, if not better. I suggested he take a break and come to help us finish Alf Leila. I offered for him to stay in one of the completed rooms, work on Alf Leila as payment and go scuba diving when he chose. He arrived early in February 2006 and it didn't take him long to realise just how much work was needed, if we were to open before Easter as planned. He put off going diving to concentrate on finishing the building and I was so grateful to him for his help.

One of Martin's most important tasks was to complete the paving tiles in the courtyard. Originally I had specified that all the ground floor hotel rooms should be slightly raised on a small step, to ensure that there was drainage (especially in light of what I had seen from previous Dahab deluges). I was also aware of the Egyptian habit of sluicing everything down a drain instead of sweeping and mopping and I didn't want blocked drains backing up. But somehow a mistake had been made in the calculations and there was no step in the design, so Martin worked meticulously to ensure there were adequate slopes into central drainage holes.

Small finishing touches made the difference, as I aspired to soothe our guests' senses in artistic ways. Instead of room numbers I named them after spices – Cinnamon, Saffron, Curry,

Indigo, Ginger, Mint and Vanilla. I used some of my large Sari collection by hanging them over bed frames and we colour coordinated the bed linen and towels to each room's decoration. The en-suite bathrooms had uniquely tiled shower cubicles and polished copper basins made from the copper *tameya* bowls. Every room had interesting nooks and crannies and coloured glass in the windows to infuse the light. Incense perfumed the air.

The Arabesque Room   *The Saffron Room*

After about five or six weeks, Martin had completed Alf Leila and we had a functioning, small boutique hotel and German bakery. Our boutique hotel stood out with its elegant Moroccan *riyadh* design, pointed domes and balconies that were then, totally novel to Dahab. We could hardly believe that we were finally finished. We were also very proud because many people came to the bakery and asked to see our new hotel.

The Alf Leila Courtyard

We had done little marketing but when we officially opened word spread quickly, so we began taking bookings right away. My parents and some of my Italian friends were to be our first 'guinea pigs', staying over Easter to test out systems and functions. That period is high season for holidays in Egypt with Jewish Passover, Christian Easter and Coptic Christians who are about 10% of Egypt's population, the latter celebrating their Easter a week later in combination with an ancient Egyptian spring festival called *Sham El-Nessim*. Dahab was packed with visitors of all nationalities.

We decided a small celebration was in order and arranged to have a meal together in one of my favourite Dahab restaurants, Tarbouche House. This restaurant, (named for the red bucket style hats with a tassel on the top that one often sees in old photographs of Egypt and Turkey) was a small private restaurant away from the beach promenade. The chef owner didn't advertise, his reputation and success coming only from word of mouth, cooking only for prearranged groups.

Most of our group was assembled by seven in the evening; my parents, Kurt and our Italian friends. We were sampling the starters of small dishes of Egyptian *mezze* – hummus, tahina, *mahalel* - spicy pickled vegetables, served with fresh pita bread so were not in a hurry while waiting for Martin and Dirk to join us. Suddenly there was a deafening explosion that sounded as though it was very close. We all jumped and sat for a moment in stunned silence. "What the hell was that?" someone asked.

"Might have been a dive tank," suggested Kurt. "They have exploded before."

"Hope it wasn't Hard Rock," I added. Dive tanks are tested regularly for wear and defects that might cause weakness under pressure and while it is very rare for one to explode, hundreds of tanks are filled every day in Dahab.

"We can hope no one was injured. They do pack a punch," said Kurt. "We'll find out soon enough." In less than minute, there were two more explosions and we realised that perhaps there was something more sinister going on. Adrenalin and nerves kicked in as we sat quietly, our hearts thumping, not quite knowing what we should or could do next.

"Bombs in Dahab?" I said, incredulous. We were all thinking it. It was not unheard of in Sinai, with bombings occurring over the previous two years, first in Taba then Sharm el Sheikh. But small, peaceful Dahab? Within five minutes I received a text message from a friend in Germany, "Are you OK? We hear there are bombings in Dahab." Bad news travels super fast! People in Germany knew before we did for sure, that bombs had been detonated in Dahab. Shock went through our group, on many levels.

"Oh my god! Where is Martin? Where is Dirk?", "I wonder if people got hurt", "What should we do?", "What can we do?" Questions with no answers.

Within minutes of the text message Martin arrived. "I'm OK guys! There were bombs by the bridge!"

"Thank God you are OK. Where were you? Do you know anything?"

"Yes, I was there! I was shopping at *Big Ghazala* in the mall. There was this huge explosion outside, glass smashing. I'm glad I wasn't standing close to any windows. I stayed inside for a few minutes then decided I'd better get out of there. There had already been three bombs. Outside I could already see police and a crowd around the Santa Klaus jewellery shop. Glass and blood everywhere. I didn't try to get any closer. I just got on my bike and came here."

The evening of the 24th of April 2006 is etched in my memory. Despite the phone lines jamming some messages got through. Dirk was OK. The rumour mill was churning out crazier and crazier stories as to what had happened and we spent hours on erratic phone lines trying to reassure our friends and family that we were all fine. It was bizarre receiving messages saying things like "The Bridge has collapsed," yet Martin who had cycled by moments after the bombings was saying confirming quite the opposite.

It was no surprise that we had lost our appetites. We returned to Alf Leila where we sat on the west facing balcony of our brightly named Saffron room in disbelief and shock, staring out into the inky darkness of the mountains where stars still shined. Whisky or vodka was poured for everyone in an effort to calm our shattered nerves. Our questions went around and around in circles with no real answers. Who would want to do this to our quiet, beautiful oasis of Dahab? Why would anyone want to bomb Dahab? How come the world knew about it so fast? What will happen now? Will there be more?

About ten o'clock that evening I received a call from one of a popular German magazine, inquiring whether I would rent rooms with internet to their journalists who were covering the events in Dahab. They were offering ten thousand Euros for the stay. I replied, "I would never rent a room to any bloodsucking reporter ever! Especially not to cover such events at any price! I hate the media and the warped views you spread around the world! You only feed on the bad and we never hear from you when times are good. Don't call again." The whisky probably gave my thoughts greater wings but it was no lie how much I dislike the media as ghouls after the blood of disaster. Ten thousand Euros was a lot of money and the others thought I should consider it. I said, "Guys! I do have principles and I am not dropping my standards to support those vampires!" It wasn't until the early hours of the morning that anyone felt like sleeping. We all spent a restless night at Alf Leila so we could be together.

Before eight in the morning Kurt and I walked two hundred yards to the Bridge area to see if we could find out any details. Dahab was already crawling with the military and security police, with media personnel seemingly outnumbering the tourists. It takes at least seven or eight hours to drive to Dahab from Cairo and the closest airport is Sharm el Sheikh over an hour and half away. How had all these people got there so quickly? Overnight the whole of the parking area between Peace Road and the still standing bridge was absolutely packed with teams from the international media circus. Entourages of journalists, sound technicians, cameramen with their vehicles, satellite dishes, cameras and microphones.

The military had cordoned off the area of the bombings and it looked like a war zone. Dahab, the quiet Bedouin fishing village with beautiful diving, had been a traveller's refuge off the beaten track. But overnight it was splashed all over the world as a bomb site with horrible images, close-ups of the bomb damage, destruction and dead bodies. Dahab, where no illustrious official had ever bothered to visit before, was graced with the presence of the Egyptian Prime Minister, Ahmed Nazif, who arrived on the scene to offer his condolences amid a scrum of media and local onlookers.

The injured had been rushed to Dahab hospital in Medina which was woefully ill equipped to deal with anything of that magnitude. The overflow of injured patients were then literally carted off in the back of pick-up trucks to Sharm el Sheikh for treatment. I suspect many deaths occurred in that "golden hour" after the injuries occurred. At least twenty-three people died, mostly Egyptians but also German, Lebanese, Russian, Swiss, and Hungarian nationals, may they rest in peace. Well over a hundred people were injured including tourists from Egypt, Australia, Denmark, France, Germany, Israel, Lebanon, Palestine, Israel, South Korea, England and the United States.

By the time we walked the promenade that evening we were also astounded at how quickly everything had been pulled together. A small area was still cordoned off on either side of the bridge but a lot of clearing up had already taken place.

Considering the number of deaths and injuries that people had sustained, actual building damage was minimal, except for broken windows. The shrapnel holes in the pathway had been repaired, the bridge balustrades replaced, the promenade washed thoroughly and we were allowed to walk over the bridge. This was all done in remote Egypt, where it normally takes days, if not weeks, to get anything done. Divers were still combing the bay for evidence and gruesome body parts but there was little evidence of in depth investigation. It seemed more important to show the world everything was back to as normal as quickly as possible.

Over the following days all my friends were sick and tired of the media intrusion, none of which helped the actual victims of the situation. Our phones rang constantly with reporters snooping after anything they could report to the supposedly interested world. The media reported suggestions of attacks on Israelis. But there were hardly any Israelis in Dahab at that time as Passover had been weeks before, so I suspect they were not the main targets at all. Gradually rumours and theories about the disaster surfaced but to this day, it is difficult to know the truth about what happened. Blame was laid on insurgents from North Sinai and the resulting rounding up of thousands of Bedouin was tragic for the tribes. Apparently a bomber had placed a backpack on one side of the bridge, walked to the other side where he detonated the backpack then blew himself up. The third was closer to the Tourist Police station and the *Big Ghazala* where Martin had been.

What the media didn't show, was how Dahab was united in their solidarity as a community that grieved together over this horrendous event with all the anger, sorrow, despair, kindness, healing and hope it could muster. Egyptian, Bedouin and foreigners alike, we demonstrated for peace marching along the promenade from the Lighthouse through the bomb sites towards Club Red diving centre. The whole town was in shock and everyone wanted to help where they could. Ironically, I was glad that my parents were with us and they experienced everything as it happened. It would have been much worse for them from a distance, seeing the way that the disaster was portrayed by the press. My parents and friends left on their flights as booked and we tried to calm our shattered nerves.

Immediately after the bombings, tourists continued to visit. No flights were cancelled, so those who knew and loved Dahab actually made the effort to come to show their support. To celebrate Alf Leila opening, we decided to have a small ceremony for friends and supporters. It was a beautiful party requiring much less work than the one for the Bakery, but appreciated by nice people.

As the middle of hot summer approached, low season bookings in our new hotel dwindled to almost nothing and even the bakery had few customers. It seemed like Dahab was then forgotten as our town returned to peaceful quiet again and the press was no longer interested. There were no tourists and the promenade was empty in the oppressive heat. The hotel and bakery weren't making enough to pay the staff and it was stupid to bake and constantly waste food. I had used all my funds and borrowed money to complete the project and my coffers were empty. I had no more energy left for ideas or answers. It seemed the hotel, the bakery and our family life were resting on my shoulders. I was even worried about how I would pay the rent on my house. Although I'm sure I wasn't the only one in Dahab with similar problems, I was totally depressed. I decided to close the hotel and bakery for two months. Sherif was furious and a heated argument ensued. He yelled at me, "If anything closes in Dahab, it never opens again!"

"Well, what do you think we should do? I have no money left. You say you have no money left. We have no money to pay staff. What other options are there?"

He didn't have an answer so I went ahead and essentially shut up shop. I was still smarting from the fact that he had just bought a new car. I had been astounded when Natasha had come to boast about their new vehicle. I couldn't understand how impressing Natasha was more important than standing by our business.

The staff all understood the situation even though they weren't happy about it. Dirk had accepted a low salary relative to German standards, even though for me it was one of my biggest business outgoings. He returned to Germany as he had no way of remaining in Dahab without work.

With our remaining funds Kurt, Luna and I flew to Germany to spend a few weeks there with my family. Apart from attending my brother's wedding I essentially stayed at home. For the first time in my life I didn't go out shopping or to amuse myself because I had no money to spare. Despite the sobering situation, I was happy to know I was supported by my friends and family.

I returned to Dahab with renewed energy and again focused on marketing both businesses. I asked Kurt to help but he refused to work in either business, even short term. He of course knew of our precarious situation (relying on the hotel and bakery as our sole source of income) but I was beyond trying to understand him.

Our Egyptian workers returned from spending time with their families and Leila's Bakery ran fine with their efforts with me as overseeing manager. I needed an extra manager for Alf Leila as Sherif wasn't interested in the day to day running of it and Natasha had done all she was interested in regarding design. I found a new 'pearl' in Magdalene, a German who was working in Sharm el Sheikh. She moved to Dahab and together we inched the businesses back into profit and I was elated by the positive outlook. Our reputation was growing.

Leila's Bakery was contracted to do the catering job for the opening of the Dahab Specialized Hospital and while preparing for the event I started to feel unwell. I hardly ever get ill and was surprised by the nausea that came in waves. I joked, "There must be something about hospitals that make me unwell." Over the next few days I recognised other familiar symptoms - swelling breasts, uncomfortable clothing - and realised that maybe I was pregnant again. I had missed a period but that had happened before when I was under stress so I hadn't immediately assumed I was pregnant.

A test at Dr Rumi's confirmed my suspicions. He told me that a natural birth, let alone a home birth, was out of the question. I would have to have a Caesarean section to avoid the bleeding I suffered with Luna. I was happy to be carrying another child but I still had to work hard and Kurt and I drifted further apart. I suspected our relationship had no future but I didn't want to leave the father of my children. I spent nights crying myself to sleep about the future but had no regrets.

Kurt's own new 'baby' was 'I.love.dahab.com', a new website to promote Dahab. He spent a lot of his time and energy on that website with some success for promoting Dahab for but I never saw any income or support for our family. I felt bitter that Kurt received local fame and credit while I actually financed everything, including him. I had invested everything I had in Alf Leila and Leila's bakery, including all my time and energy. Dahab was beginning to feel like a choking prison that I wanted to escape. Yet how could I leave?

Desperate for a change I suggested Kurt, Luna and I take a holiday in Sri Lanka in February 2007. I hoped that travelling together as our little family would bring us closer together. I was amazed how easily Luna adapted to a foreign country. She was only three years old but was confident and outgoing with everybody. She already spoke three languages and had no fear of talking to anyone. With locals she would start talking in Arabic until she realised they didn't understand, so then she would try in English.

One day she became ill and developed severe breathing difficulties requiring hospitalisation, with antibiotic injections and medical observation. l stayed with her and smiled as she took everything in her stride, in such a happy mood the whole time singing songs for the nurses. She quickly made a full recovery but my parents scolded me, saying that I was irresponsible to travel while pregnant with Luna in such a country without vaccinations. I on the other hand, was sure that living in Egypt strengthened our resistance to illness. Sure, there were infrequent illnesses but we recovered quickly and regardless of what or where we ate, we never got food poisoning.

My hopes of bringing Kurt and I closer through the trip were dashed by a total breakdown in communication. He just didn't seem interested in talking to me, only playing with Luna. I felt very lonely, rejected, depressed and pregnant for the entire miserable six weeks while we were on holiday. It was a disaster.

We returned to Dahab and I focused again on both businesses. Magdalene had held everything together and both bakery and hotel were ticking along nicely. She became like an elder sister to me, supporting me in my efforts. I created events for the hotel, such as a Spa area in the courtyard with Sudanese sauna and massage and we rented the shop to a second hand clothing store called *Pink Elephant*.

By this time Mohamed was my main baker and doing a great job but he was restless and had decided to leave Egypt to find work. I could only wish him the best and hope my loss was the world's gain because he was an extraordinary young man. Sherif's cousins took over the baking but unfortunately, they were not in the same league as Mohamed. I developed new recipes and we even delivered once a week to Sharm el Sheikh but week after week, the chaos in the kitchen increased as the quality of the baking dropped.

I was six months pregnant by then and I had decided my son would be born in Germany because of the required caesarean section. Babies don't wait for anyone so I knew that the latest I could fly was early May because of airline restrictions. It was clear that I would be gone for at least three months so with Magdalene still managing Alf Leila, I handed overall responsibility to Sherif as my business partner.

Struggling with heavy luggage, I flew alone and heavily pregnant to Munich in early May to prepare for the birth. I arrived just in time to help my old friend Dieter celebrate his fortieth birthday and spent a week with my sister-in-law. My brother was in Hong Kong on business so we lived like roommates and enjoyed a relaxing week. I was well rested when Kurt came to Kaiserslautern with Luna, a week before the birth.

The doctors had let me choose the day of the birth and I chose June the fourth for Tom to be born. Everything went as planned and although I lost a lot of blood once again, I was fine and we had a healthy baby boy. Tom was such a sweet baby and Luna was so in love with him, she couldn't wait to show him to everybody. I spent a week in the hospital recovering while Kurt stayed with Luna in a nearby apartment that my parents had set up for us. They arrived to collect Tom and I on the day we were to be discharged from hospital. Kurt was complaining of flu symptoms the entire time we walked back to the apartment. I was still weak but had to go out shopping immediately to buy medicine for him and to get groceries so we could eat. I was already once again providing, only now for four people!

After three weeks in Kaiserslautern we went to Munich to stay with Kurt's son, Franz, and his girlfriend. I was feeling uncomfortable and ill with increasing pain in my abdomen. By the weekend of Tom's baptism it was so bad that I could no longer walk so my parents decided to take Tom and I back to Kaiserslautern to see my doctor. He scolded me, "Ella! You have been doing too much. You just had a baby by caesarean and have excessive bleeding." He sent me straight back to hospital due to a massive uterine infection. After a week of enforced rest I made a full recovery so we were able to fly back to Dahab at the end of July... to chaos. I wasn't surprised.

I knew Magdalene hadn't liked working with Sherif and his troupe and she had quit her job at short notice. I had no faith that

Sherif knew anything about running a hospitality or retail business but knew I couldn't do anything from Germany. While in Munich I had been in contact with Dirk and learned he hadn't found another bakers job after returning from Dahab. He offered to work at Leila's again providing Sherif agreed. As it turned out, Sherif (not wanting any more to do with managing Alf Leila or Leila's Bakery) was only too eager for him to return. Both businesses were losing money, so I called Dirk and he arrived back in Dahab in August.

With Dirk managing the bakery I again took over management of the hotel but knew that with two young children, I wouldn't be able to cope without help. Kurt was just Kurt; he only took care of the children when it suited him so I knew not to expect much help from him. I had to find someone to help at home and look after the children and after several attempts, I found a kind Egyptian woman, Selima.

Selima told me that she could work only if she could include her two children, a daughter seven years old and a son, two. It was very unusual for an Egyptian wife to even be allowed to work by her husband. But they needed the money badly as her husband earned a very low salary as an assistant to the Government appointed veterinarian. He was not the type of man to look for extra work. We agreed that Selima would either clean for me at home or she would take care of Luna and Tom at her house. Her family lived in a very small house with just two rooms and without running water. Her husband had a big heart for kids and animals though and outside they had chickens, ducks, a dog and cats. Although it was a very basic home there was so much love and fun around that I left the Luna and Tom there a lot of time, even from when Tom was only three months old.

Selima seemed to be a positive woman, who tried her best to make sure her family survived, always smiling. She came from a very poor village of the Delta and as is the custom among poorer Egyptians, had married in her late teens. The marriage was arranged between families and her husband was fifteen years older than her. When I met her she was just twenty-six but to me she looked ten years older. We became good friends, talking about everything and coming to terms with our cultural differences. Through Selima, I began to understand the lot of Egyptian women and what happens in their lives. She was also the one who finally forced me to speak Arabic. I understood a lot but after four years I still had no confidence to speak it and as Selima could speak nothing else, I learned to converse as did my children.

Initially Dirk should have only stayed until November, but our income was so low that I couldn't consider closing again over the coming high season and wanted to run the bakery until at least January. Dirk made a proposal to lease Leila's Bakery for six months to see how it developed. As he had no money to invest, I agreed on a lease where I would do his accounting to ensure the funds were managed properly and invoices paid. He made a quick return trip to Munich in September with the plan to return to Dahab in October to start his lease.

I finally felt like I was getting some things back on an even keel although transport was becoming an issue. Kurt still had his precious motorbike and wouldn't dream of trading it in. But I couldn't carry two children on my bicycle and needed a small reliable car. In those days there were no car dealerships in Sinai so I travelled to Cairo to buy one. Abdullah knew just where to purchase one. And so I bought my super red Maruti, the smallest

Suzuki ever manufactured, tried and tested as the most popular family car in India. I loved that car from the first moment I saw it. So between that and Selima looking after the children, I had time to rebuild the businesses and attend to the hotel.

In the autumn we had a change of tenant in our hotel shop, as *Pink Elephant* second hand clothes outgrew our space and moved elsewhere. We opened a boutique with clothes from my fried Ida, ceramics from Silvia and hand-made silver jewellery. At Christmas, we organised a fun event with a fashion show from Ida Raven and an art exhibition. It was a wonderful evening as models sashayed down the steps into the Alf Leila courtyard to live, traditional Bedouin music, while guests sipped mulled wine and sampled fresh sushi and sandwiches

Fashion Show at Alf Leila

I decided the children should experience Christmas with some

German traditions. As in Germany, I decorated the whole bakery from the beginning of December and even had St Nicklaus visit the children on the 6th. Only this time, St Nicklaus arrived at our garden on the back of a camel, much to Luna's delight. We opened advent calendars daily and kept the wreath candles burning for the four weeks until Christmas day.

Kurt's family also came to visit that year, with his brother staying with us in Assala while the remainder stayed in Villa Bohème. Our Assala home was the focus for barbeques and meals where we could all be together as a family. However, one day, I returned home from work to discover they had already eaten their meal without leaving anything for me. I was furious and vented my anger at Kurt as soon as they left the house. I couldn't believe how they (especially Kurt) could be so thoughtless when they were essentially having a free holiday! The very next day I booked tickets for myself and the children to fly to Germany on Christmas Eve, as at least I felt my family supported and loved me. When we returned home two weeks later Kurt behaved as nothing had happened but I was still stung from such rude behaviour.

I had begun a wonderful friendship with Francesca, an Italian woman who lived close to my house and like me, had two children of similar ages. Her daughter was only three months older than Tom and her son one year older than Luna. I had become acquainted with Francesca, when she and her husband had purchased some land from me when I needed money to construct Alf Leila. I had seen her on the beach many times alone with her son but she hardly said hello and seemed very reserved.

That soon changed when she saw me working in the bakery

struggling to hold everything together, often with three month old Tom in my arms. She quickly saw I needed help and was there without question and we quickly became firm friends. I discovered she was a person of strong character and a big heart but did not suffer fools easily and preferred to keep her life private. She never minced words and would speak her mind to whomever she thought was out of line including Dirk, Sherif and Kurt.

We found we had so much in common, including our children and the fact that we were both in unhappy relationships with their fathers. It was wonderful for me to converse in Italian which I loved so dearly and we shared great times cooking and chatting together. She had lived in Italy for many years with her Egyptian husband, before coming to Dahab to spend the pregnancy of her second child. For me it was a relief to get to know a European woman with similar attitudes who would travel alone without her husband. She returned regularly to Dahab, six weeks in summer and three weeks in Winter, so over the years we spent a lot of time together.

Shortly after Christmas 2008, my friend Martin (who had never returned to his western way of life) was by then working as a diving instructor in Sharm el Sheikh but wanted to return to live in Dahab. He asked if we would lease Alf Leila to him and made us an offer. We agreed and gave him a low price for a one year contract, to see how things would develop for both parties.

The contract began in March so in April, for the first time in many years I felt free from day to day work responsibilities. Francesca and I spent a great deal of time with each other while the children played happily together. Both of us were tired of our relationships and wanted to spend time away from our men.

Tom, Leila, Francesca and me

One day I commented to her, "I wonder how Ida is getting on in Siwa?" My fashion designer friend whose clothes had been in Alf Leila's shop, had moved to an oasis called Siwa in the Western desert close to the Libyan border. It was the one oasis that Kurt and I didn't visit when we made our Egyptian tour a few years earlier. "I would like to visit her and see what Siwa is like."

"I've never been there either. How far away is it?

"I'm not sure exactly. Quite a long way. You have to drive to Alexandria, then along the Mediterranean coast before turning south in to the desert. Shall we do it? You, me and the children?"

"Oh wow! Yes! Let's go to Siwa for a holiday."

And that's how Francesca and I made our plans to leave for Siwa a few weeks later in May. At first we were going to travel by bus but after long debate we decided we should drive in my little Maruti. There would be less space with two adults and four children but what we sacrificed in leg room we would gain by being independent travellers, stopping whenever we felt we needed a break.

We loaded the tiny Suzuki with kids and luggage crammed in all corners. Despite careful packing, space was still a premium so we stuffed more gear into the rear seat leg room and laid a blanket over it so Luna and Francesca's son could sit with their legs across it. There was only room for one baby seat in the back so the other had to be held by the passenger in front. The adaptations were certainly not up to modern European safety standards but no one in Egypt made a fuss. It was nothing to see a whole Egyptian family of father, mother and two or more children balanced on one motorcycle, without helmets.

My Maruti

We were all excited as we drove out of Dahab, first to Suez then across the Nile delta to spend the night with friends in Alexandria. We made regular picnic stops to break the journey up and let the children play in the sunshine, so they enjoyed the journey immensely. At the end of two days travel crammed in my tiny car, we arrived in Siwa oasis. Everyone looked astounded and impressed when we told them we had driven the little red car all the way from Dahab, South Sinai. For them Dahab would have seemed a million miles away as few Egyptians ventured into Sinai, and then usually only to Sharm el Sheikh.

Siwa has been inhabited for thousands of years, proven by the temple ruins from ancient Egyptians. Even Alexander the Great journeyed to the oasis on his epic travels. We had imagined finding a pleasant picturesque Bedouin village so it was a shock to see crumbling shacks with raw sewerage pooling in the streets. Nonetheless, there was still undoubtable charm in the large date and olive tree plantations irrigated by running water and the relaxed lifestyle of the inhabitants. They are not actually Middle Eastern Bedouin but descendants of Berber tribes who had come from the East centuries ago. Geologically speaking, Siwa is a little like the Dead Sea being meters below sea level and there are large shallow salty lakes as well as fresh water springs with hot and cold water.

Ida lived with her family in a house considered to be of high standards for Siwa, mainly because it was tiled and had electricity. Our room had two large beds for the six of us, one per family. We could hardly sleep that first night suffering from sticky heat and mosquitoes. At two in the morning I moved our mattress on to the roof and brought my mosquito net out of the car. Half an hour later Francesca followed with her children and all six of us huddled on the one mattress until dawn.

The next morning we thanked Ida for her hospitality and moved into a camp with two large rooms and our holiday began in earnest. Every day we chose a different direction and explored the spectacular desert landscapes. The children had the most fun with tours by Siwa Taxi, cute covered donkey carts gaily painted as tourist chariots.

On Holiday in Siwa

Our donkey was called Ali Baba and every afternoon he and his young boy driver would take us exploring through the palm plantations. We discovered beautiful pools in which to bath and swim that were constantly topped up from hot and cold water springs. With so much fresh water flowing in the desert, Siwa truly was a beautiful oasis.

After nine beautiful days on holiday with all the fun memories we had created, we journeyed back to Dahab. It had been an amazing trip but it was time to return to everyday life. We both had to face the realities of our marriages, how unhappy they made us and decide what we wanted to do.

Chapter 5
Life Changes

With my feet firmly back in Dahab, I felt depressed at what little I could see my future with Kurt would bring. With both businesses running well I had extra time on my hands, which gave me more time to realise how bad things were between Kurt and I. The only one he seemed to love was Luna. She was his princess in every way and he doted on her. As for Tom and I, we were just extras; me being the financial provider, Tom just a baby boy. The holiday in Siwa had been an interlude but back in Dahab I realised that Kurt and I were estranged as far as love and respect were concerned. He was Luna and Tom's father. That was it. I still wanted to make our family work on some level, but I had no idea of how do that anymore.

With summer always so hot in Dahab (day temperatures were often above 40°C) I decided to take the children to Germany and stay in Kaiserslautern for a while. Luna and Tom could get to know their grandparents and I could explore options and whether I could return to live in Europe. Once again, I handed over the responsibility of the hotel and bakery to Sherif. With both leased to committed foreigners, I expected things to continue to run relatively smoothly in my absence.

Sherif and I were still close in many ways and he seemed to feel sad about my difficulties with Kurt. He was Kurt's friend but he couldn't understand how his lack of interest in the businesses, leaving the responsibility for making an income to me. He knew I was unhappy in Dahab too. "Don't worry," he said, "I will take care of everything." He even made an odd comment that maybe things might have been different if I hadn't been with Kurt and him with Natasha. I shrugged the comment off as something said in passing.

Back in Germany, we moved into a small apartment in my old home in Kaiserslautern that my parents furnished for us. I was back where I had started, but now directly responsible for two small children and I wanted to find a way to remain financially independent. I started to look for a job to investigate the opportunities open to me. I wondered whether serendipity would again step in and offer me a new direction.

I still wanted to be close to my children as they grew up so I quickly realised living back in Germany as a single mother wasn't going to be an easy option, even if I did find a good job. Positions at my level of expertise in the fashion world were few and far between, literally. The closest position I could find was based more than a hundred kilometres, away which would mean paying for full time childcare and hardly getting to spend time with the children. My parents realised how unhappy I was and offered to take us on a holiday to Pesaro in Italy. I had holidayed there with them many times as a child, so it was like time travel to visit the place again. Nothing much had changed, not even the colours and patterns of the 1970's decor still adorning the walls and floors. I journeyed back to my childhood, happy that I could be there with Luna and Tom. They loved it as just as much as I had and it was a special time for us all, with my parents enjoying their roles as doting grandparents. We spent relaxing days playing on the beach, just across the road from the hotel.

Ten days later the children and I went to Rome by train to visit more of my old friends. I was retracing my passion and successful life in fashion, to see if I could again find some opening for the future. But I found that with the two small children at my side I saw everything through different eyes. Large cities in Italy don't lend themselves to travelling with young children. The high curbs make negotiating the streets difficult, buses don't cater for carrying pushchairs and many houses are multi-storeyed without lifts. It was a constant struggle and I certainly built up extra arm muscles lugging the children around!

My successful fashion designer friend (who then made dresses for wealthy Arabs) offered me a job, but I couldn't conceive raising my sun loving, free children in crazy Rome. He and I had been carefree students together but that life was out of the question as a single mother. The realities of living in European cities and Dahab could not be more different and I realised I was not prepared to return to the life I had previously known.

Our next stop was beautiful Tuscany where another friend, Peter, worked at an old winery with rooms for rent. Peter and I relaxed on his terrace talking and drinking wine into the early hours while the children slept peacefully, but still no new ideas emerged. There had been a time when living in in small Italian village in Tuscany would have been a dream for me. Not any more. My dreams and my focus had changed. I quietly cancelled any ideas of living in Germany or Italy in the near future.

In the meantime, Kurt (not one for planning a great deal) had travelled to Munich on short notice so we decided to meet up there. I dreaded seeing him and being reminded of our situation but I was looking forward to seeing Kurt's children Martina and Franz. Both of them adored their half siblings, Luna and Tom.

I felt I had formed a special relationship with Franz, since he had come to stay with us in Dahab some years earlier when he was a depressed, obese teenager. Kurt and I had offered him a health program to follow where he would exercise daily with his father and I cooked healthy balanced meals for him. He lost twenty kilograms and changed his life. He was happy in Munich with his girlfriend so I was relieved that I and the children would stay with Franz while Kurt would stay with his brother.

Meeting Kurt was even worse than I imagined. He chain smoked the entire time, nervous and irritated, so I guess he was as stressed as I was but he wouldn't discuss anything of importance, even avoiding polite conversation. He chose to act like he was a million miles away so we could only be a million miles apart. When I did push him for some discussion he kept complaining that I always wanted him to change. I did want him to change. I wanted him to be responsible for helping with our children, for some input and income. I asked him, "What is your purpose in life? What do you want to achieve?" He just told me I was crazy. I wondered if I was and knew I had to ask myself those questions too.

I met with Dieter who still lived in Munich and poured out my problems to my wise friend. He suggested, "Go through the Quadrinity Process and you will find a solution." I was sceptical but Dieter had done the course. He was happy and successful in his life and had always given me good advice and so I started to seriously consider doing the course. Dieter even offered to help me finance it by cancelling a previous debt I had to him. I decided to do it. I asked Kurt if he would take care of the children for ten days while I did the course. That was the first time that Kurt had ever had to look after both children by himself.

The Quadrinity Process was a live-in series of seminars that required participants to have no contact with any outside influences, focusing only on your inner self. I was to focus on my inner child, to hopefully identify long term negative patterns in my life and change them for the better. For ten days we lived isolated in a hotel in the woods close to Frankfurt, with absolutely no contact with anybody from our normal lives.

As I analysed my relationships I made self discoveries and saw repetitive problems. From these revelations I made vows to change things in my life (although I wasn't sure how to, at that point). The course stipulated that I shouldn't make any great changes immediately and to keep things simple for at least three months to let ideas formulate.

I returned to Dahab in September 2008, with the focus that I would enjoy living in Egypt for at least the next two years. After that Luna would have to be in a suitable school. There were only a couple of options for schooling in Dahab and some parents chose to send their children more than sixty miles each day to Sharm el Sheikh, but I was not convinced those were good options.

I was still using Selima for cleaning and childcare but her life wasn't consistent. For the most part, her family house was full of fun and laughter but there were times when I saw much sadness. Her husband was a man with a big heart for children and animals and he particularly loved Tom. But over the years I had become aware of a darker side to his character and wondered if in fact, he was even mentally ill. When the mood struck him, he would beat Selima and the children, sometimes viciously. Once I saw their daughter just after a beating and her chest was so badly bruised that I took her to a doctor. When I explained that her own father had caused the injuries the doctor warned me to stay out of their family problems. On another occasion, Selima and both children were so injured that I took them all to hospital for treatment. It was the least I could do.

I even investigated further with a lawyer but he insisted there was little I could do to help her if she didn't want to take action herself. Women could divorce their husbands but she stood to lose everything, even her children. It was horrifying to see how everybody (including the legal system) protected the man in situations like that. Selina was a strong woman but still not strong enough to overcome the stigma of leaving her husband with no real support system, in a heavily patriarchal Egyptian society. It was like I had a sister I cared about who suffered misery and despair but I wasn't able to change anything. I would often take Selima and her children to the beach or pool with us and we would have a great time together. I loved her children and she mine, but we couldn't be one happy family. The reality was that sometimes everything worked really well but at other times, she demanded more and more support from me, without doing her job and taking care of my children. And though I felt for her, I needed consistency in our lives.

I began to send Luna and Tom to local childcare in the mornings, so they could socialise and play with other children. Habiba was a wonderful centre run by an Egyptian woman, Fatma, whom I had first met when I was heavily pregnant with Luna. I had been driving my luckless jeep around Assala when a wheel got firmly stuck in a drain hole just outside Fatma's building. She saw what happened, marched outside and helped me out of the Jeep saying, "You just come inside with me and rest. My husband and the other men will deal with your Jeep." That, they duly did, while I drank tea with Fatma.

I decided once more, to try to make things better between Kurt and I. He still had no regular income and I had long ago accepted that wouldn't change so I just wanted us to be together as a family. Even though I prefer to get my exercise outside, swimming or on my bicycle, Kurt was happy that I made the effort to go to the gym with him in the mornings but never suggested other outings. The prospect of us spending more time together didn't seem to enthral him. I mused over my old pattern of me changing to suit him and getting nothing in return. He continued to spend most of his time on the website and development of a real estate agency, based out of an office in Masbat. I decided to just let things slide for a while – see what would happen. I did a Reiki course, enjoyed my time on the beach and kept an eye on the businesses. Life was good, the children were happy but I was bored and needed a new project.

Little Tom with a Camel

One day a casual acquaintance, James, phoned to ask if I would meet up to discuss a project he was doing to remodel and redecorate his home on the beach, turning them into holiday apartments. Perfect, I thought! We arranged to meet at The Blue House, a wonderful Thai restaurant with views over the Lighthouse Bay. It was a favourite among the locals and I was pleasantly surprised that James had bought a bottle of wine to share (he had remembered that I preferred it to beer). Our conversation at the Blue House was professional and relaxed and I happily agreed to help James with his project. We struck a deal for payment; my design and sewing skills, for his handmade jewellery and massages, both of which I knew he was skilled in. After I had given birth to Tom I had gone regularly to have massages at the Hilton where James ran the spa and he already had a display of his jewellery at Leila's Bakery.

I had been to his home on the beach just before I left for Europe, when I went to buy a gift voucher for Kurt for a drumming workshop that James was organising. I remembered the home as being special, two side by side apartments with garden at the front and large gates that were within metres of the waters' edge and a beautiful coral reef. It would be a worthy project to work on. I also recall that day, he had opened the gate very confidently wearing only his shirt and had been very charming, even a little flirty. He asked if I could give him a ride to Rush, the nightclub he was a partner in. Rush was an open air club venue, shaded, with palm trees and a small swimming pool hosting regular DJs along with offerings of alcohol and drugs. It was popular with locals but not a place I frequented, except for special events or parties.

On that occasion, I had just finished a yoga class with my friend and was going out to eat dinner alone so James invited me to eat with him at Rush. That had been the first time I had a social, one to one conversation with him. Wrapped up as I was in my problems, I was surprised how easy he was to talk to. I had appreciated his sympathetic ear when I was considering moving back to Europe and might not even return if I found suitable work.

On my return to Dahab I was back on a construction site, the difference being, with my sewing machine instead of as project manager. I left my house eagerly every day to go to James's where I could let my creativity flow; design and sew anything from new curtains to cushion and furniture covers. James treated me as an intelligent partner, seeking my opinion and listening with focused attention to my ideas. "What do you think of this, Ella? Should this cabinet be built into here ... or over here?" "We need to change the floor tiles. What do you think would look good? This wasn't something I was used to from men in Dahab! We talked about anything and everything and I was enjoying my time immensely.

Building Palm Beach

James had lived in Dahab on and off for over twenty years. As we chatted, I was surprised to learn of his very creative, entrepreneurial spirit. I had presumed he was a night owl close to the dark side of life, who preferred loud music and parties with his numerous girlfriends. I on the other hand, was a lark, with the responsibilities of two small children and to all intents and purposes, married. I had no idea that he could be so responsible and organised and that he loved working so focused on different projects.

When I first arrived in Dahab, James had run a pizza restaurant that I frequented when pregnant with Luna. He had also worked briefly at the bakery when I had been away in Germany in 2007, but there was a disagreement between him and Dirk, so Sherif had fired him. At the time James did say that one day I would know the truth about that situation and that I should be careful, but I just shrugged it off as male egos battling it out.

We had easy conversations as we worked together and I felt I could talk openly to him about anything at all. He knew some of the difficulties I had in my relationship with Kurt and I knew James's behaviour towards his girlfriends was totally different. Once he had invited us to a dinner party at his home and I was envious when I saw how romantic and caring he was towards his girlfriend, Audrey. When I had organised the spa night at Alf Leila, James had paid for her to attend and on another evening we spent at the beach, we saw them having cocktails in the sand. I was envious that Kurt would never think of behaving like that.

I also knew however that James had had many affairs and relationships over the years and Audrey complained that he wouldn't consider starting a family or commit to a long term relationship with her. She had asked my advice and in light of my situation, I had advised her to find someone willing to commit to her.

The antithesis of conversation while working during the day and the silence at home couldn't have been greater. When the children were in bed Kurt and I didn't say a word to each other. He would disappear up to his 'man cave' and I would remain downstairs, alone. Even if I took the initiative to organise a babysitter so we could go out socially it made no difference. Kurt would spend the time socialising with others and ignore me. Whenever I broached the subject of our communication problems, Kurt's answer was always the same, "I'm not ready. Give us time." Ready for what, time for what?

Halloween was fast approaching and the sixth anniversary of the start of our relationship. I organised Magdalene to babysit and to stay over so that Kurt and I could go out for the whole evening. I was nostalgic, remembering the fantastic night I had spent in Dahab dancing at Tota when we had our first romantic connection. How excited I had been and up for the challenge of riding back to the hotel on his motorbike. I wanted to recapture some of that magic.

I asked Kurt to choose the restaurant, so we went to a small seafood restaurant in the local market square of Assala. It may have had some charm for tourists (where they could literally rub shoulders with local Egyptian life on the edge of the grimy, busy street) but it could in no way be considered romantic. Pick-up truck taxis passed by constantly tooting, large hunks of meat with hairy tails still attached hung uncovered outside butchers shops, street dogs and cats begged for food and people generally loitered and gossiped along the roadsides.

"Would you like a beer?" Kurt asked.

"Actually, I think I'd prefer wine tonight." Kurt went to the store close by that sold Egyptian alcohol brands; no imported drinks are available to purchase retail although beer is made under license. He returned with beer. No wine.

I blinked in amazement, too astounded to say anything. I could have gone for wine myself but felt deflated, suddenly not really in the mood for celebrating. I felt my idea of rekindling any romantic flame between us was truly in vain. I retreated back into myself. What more could I do? I spent the entire meal sat opposite Kurt, who interacted with everyone passing by, yet ignored me completely.

Thankfully it wasn't the kind of meal to linger over anyway, so within an hour we returned home to prepare for the fancy dress party that night at Rush. Luna was still awake at 9pm attended by Magdalene, so we sneaked up to the second floor. Kurt sat down and lit a cigarette saying nothing, the smoke drifting over me. Fed up, I decided to take a power nap on his bed before getting ready for the party. When I awoke at 11.30pm he had fallen asleep beside me so I just left him and went downstairs to dress up.

There weren't many opportunities to dress up in Dahab so I decided to make the most of it. I pulled on a bright scarlet wig decorated with flowers, a colourful dress and high heeled boots. The lyrics "These boots were made for walking ... they're gonna walk all over you," sprang to mind as I pulled them on. I decided I would be no shrinking violet that night. I was almost ready to go by myself when, just after midnight, Kurt stumbled downstairs. At the sight of me dressed up ready to go he said, "So you'll go out like this? Then I have to dress up as well."

It was annoying that he hadn't planned anything, but I was happy that at least he wanted to enter into the spirit of the evening. I helped him get ready and finally by 1.30am we were in the car and on our way to Rush. We kissed briefly in the car but by then I was not interested in romance, all I wanted was to dance and enjoy one of the few social events Dahab offered.

The party was thankfully, still going strong and Rush was packed. A few people had dressed up but mainly it was just a good mix of foreigners and locals enjoying the music in the open air, palms framing the swimming pool beside the bar. Sherif and Natasha were there along with many of our other friends. We all danced together for about twenty minutes then I went to the crowded bar to queue for drinks. By the time I came back fifteen minutes later, Kurt was nowhere to be seen. I asked Natasha and Sherif if they knew where he was but they shook their heads.

This completely confused me. Where and why would he go to all the trouble of dressing for the party and then just disappear? I was still hoping against hope that there was a vestige of that romance from our first dance to share. It was our anniversary, after all. I craned my neck to see if he was in the crowd. Rush wasn't a huge place, so I wandered around searching the smaller inside bar with nooks and crannies but he was nowhere to be found. I danced half heartedly, alternating between anger and worry, about where he might have disappeared to without a word.

By 4am the crowd was thinning so I started to consider going home. Kurt had kept the keys to my car but I didn't want to get a taxi with an opportunistic driver, so I told Sherif I would just walk home along the beach. Dahab was a place I felt comfortable at any time of day or night and it would take me about half an hour. Just as I was preparing to leave, Kurt reappeared. "Where have you been?" I snarled.

"Oh, just about. I didn't see you." I was astounded. How could he miss me wearing a bright scarlet wig in high heels when I had been looking for him? He was obviously lying.

At that moment, and it really was just a split second, I decided to make a huge change. Kurt's behaviour that night was the last straw and I wouldn't be ignored like that one more day of my life. My voice was very even and precise, "I've had enough. Go wherever and whenever you like, with whomever you like. I don't want to be with you anymore! We're finished! It's over!" I snatched the car keys out of his hand and without another word, turned and left. I had never said anything so finite before and I totally meant it. Just like that, as far as our relationship was concerned, it was finally over. I had tried to stick to the Quadrinity rule of continuing the status quo for three months but I only lasted two. I knew I wanted a relationship with someone who would treat me with respect and love, with whom I could communicate and feel secure. I finally admitted that Kurt would never be that person.

I decided I couldn't go straight home. Magdalene was staying the night anyway so I drove to the beach and got out to walk along the sand as the sun was rising over Saudi Arabia. Dawn is always a special time of day in Dahab, quiet and peaceful, totally calm before whatever stress the day might bring. I stripped off my red wig and high heels and let the breeze caress my face. My ears were ringing from the music in the club but the lapping waves on the shore soothed my rage. Kurt wasn't worth my energy or my anger.

I was drawn to James's door. As I stood there, before knocking, I took a breath and told myself, 'Sometimes you have to close one door before you can open another'. I knocked tentatively and waited with baited breath. There was no answer. I was disappointed. I knocked again, more firmly. Then I heard his footsteps over the sound of lapping waves as he approached the gate. He looked somewhat nonchalant considering that I was knocking at 4.30am. I blurted out, "Hi. Hope you don't mind ... me coming here like this."

"Of course not, Ella. Are you OK? Come in. Coffee?"

"I've done it. I've broken up with Kurt." Speaking it set the new fact in stone. "We are finished. I need someone to talk to."

"Well, I didn't think you were here to start work early," joked James.

That morning he welcomed me, remaining calm and comforting as I told him of the evening's events. I appreciated how he talked to me, listened and how easy it was between us. Up until that morning I had never allowed myself to acknowledge any attraction to James but we secretly both recognised there was a mutual attraction and respect between us. I went back home some hours later, lightheaded and light-hearted, almost giddy with feelings that I hadn't felt in years. I had closed one door and opened another in the space of an hour and I was eager to see where it might lead. All hallows eve truly holds a spell in Dahab!

The transition between being friends and workmates to lovers, felt so natural for us. I continued to work with him almost daily on his holiday apartments, so it was easy for us to meet without starting town gossip. Knowing the mistakes I had made in previous relationships and with two small children to consider, I was cautious about anything becoming public knowledge and gossip. James was my secret.

Meanwhile, I did make it clear to my friends that Kurt and I were no longer partners in any way even though we continued to share the same house. In that respect, our normal living arrangements were fortuitous as we lived in separate areas of the house. Kurt was unwilling to move out as he was still enjoying the benefits of living rent free but I refused to continue providing his meals for him. The children didn't seem to notice much difference, they were so accustomed to us not conversing and they got to see their father as usual. We quietly arranged that they would spend four days with me downstairs and three with him upstairs.

So that James and I could spend time together socially we would arrange to leave town regularly. My little red Maruti gave us much more privacy and freedom than if we had to hire a car or take a taxi to go anywhere. We went to visit my friend Cada at Rock Sea Camp outside Nuweiba. She was the first to congratulate me on being in love, "This is the one! You are in love! Right?" She was right, we were in love and it showed. I was in a state of bliss that someone finally cared for me, wanted to be with me and treated me with equal respect. Nuweiba and Sharm el Sheikh also became our hideaways from prying eyes in Dahab. Occasionally our friends did see us together but they could see how happy we were and respected my wishes to keep everything quiet.

One evening when I had prepared far too much food, I invited James over to have dinner with us, thinking Kurt would be out for the evening. As fate would have it, the gas bottle ran out just before I finished cooking so James offered to drive my car to get a replacement. Just as he was leaving, he met Kurt coming in the gate. Kurt looked stunned when he realised James had been invited to dinner. The ceiling creaked and groaned overhead as he paced about upstairs like a tiger in cage for the whole evening.

The following morning Kurt lectured me, "You can't just invite other men into my house. It's not good for the children to see other men at the table. I never want to see James around here again!"

I replied, "This house has never been your house! It has always been mine from the very beginning when you told me you didn't want to live with me. My signature is on the rental agreement as you stipulated, and I have always paid the rent even though you now live here. If you don't want to see any of my guests then you should think about leaving to find a place of your own." He had completely lost my respect now.

"And by the way, James will be dressing as St Nicolaus this year. If you don't want to see that, don't come!" Kurt was obviously fuming but said nothing. I continued, "I never ask you where you go or who you are with. Nor do I care!". That was a dig as there were rumours that he was dating a widow who had a business next door to his real estate office and owned a property close to my Bedouin home. I was happy for him and not concerned that the affair might have started some months earlier.

On the 6th of December, the day James was to dress as St Nicklaus, I wanted no one to guess what hidden feelings I had throughout the day. I wondered why I had asked James when it caused me so much stress. Nonetheless, everything went as planned and Luna didn't even recognise James, even though she sat with him on the camel. Kurt behaved himself although underneath he must have been seething.

We finished the first apartment of James' Palm Beach Villa before Christmas that year and he welcomed his first guests. When it came to actual Christmas preparations, James and I spent time doing simple things together like baking gingerbread and decorating the tree. He was reminded of his childhood in Germany where he had lived until the age of four and that his mother loved festivities and celebrations, going all out to decorate and prepare special food. The children accepted that he was often around at our house (although he never stayed overnight) and we had so much fun all together.

As for Christmas Eve itself I wanted to avoid any more bad memories on days of celebrations and to remove all romance from that day. The children and I celebrated Christmas Eve with a German friend, her son and her mother, as well as Martin and his son who was visiting him, with a quiet blessed meal. The children spent Christmas Day with their father.

Kurt finally moved out of the house in early January 2009 and I felt I could gradually let people know about my relationship with James. Some close friends were very sceptical as they didn't like him. He had a reputation for being very blunt, rude even, and didn't mince his words, always telling people what he thought. They found this difficult to accept but I respected his honesty. People often view relationships according to what is right for them, not for others and I knew that I had to follow my own heart.

We saw each other almost daily and I was still on cloud nine, in love and happy. One day walking along the promenade at the Lighthouse James stopped and turned to me, "Will you marry me?" I was taken completely by surprise. My heart skipped saying

'Yes!' But this time I wasn't about to let my passion rule. My rather rude reply was, "You must be crazy!"

I knew I loved him but panicked that maybe I had fallen for the 'wrong man' again. "How do you feel about having a ready made family? It's so important to me that the kids have a responsible male close to them. You know Kurt isn't a good role model."

"I understand that Ella. The kids will never be a problem."

"And you know I plan to leave Dahab when the time comes for Luna's schooling. There is nothing suitable on offer here. It is important to me she has a good chance in life."

"Yes. I know that too. We have talked about it before."

"But you've lived in Dahab for twenty years. This has been your home. Could you really just up and leave like that?" I wasn't going to be trapped in Dahab.

"Sure! I've left Dahab plenty of times," James assured me.

"Yes, but that was for travelling. You always returned here."

James was determined to overcome any problem I came up with and I was just as determined to keep finding them. "And I want to see your bank account. Not literally, but I want to be like an Egyptian woman. I want a furnished home provided. I do not want to be the sole provider anymore!" I felt callous and calculating knowing that I was in some ways punishing him for Kurt's failures. I wanted a man completely different to him.

James was surprised but not fazed in the least. His simple answer was, "I never had to provide before. Now I will."

That was that and when I flew to Germany to visit my parents at the end of January with the children, James promised to remodel the top floor of my house while I was away. He said,

"There will be a completely new beginning for us when you return. A fresh start ... You'll see."

True to his word, he built a summer bedroom for me upstairs with another for the children, as well as a new living area. Even though the work wasn't completed I could see he had worked hard and it looked fabulous. The changes also helped Luna and Tom to adjust to Kurt's absence because the space looked so different and wasn't his anymore.

After discussion with other friends and family, I also decided that too much movement wouldn't be good for such young children, so Luna and Tom should only spend every second weekend with Kurt. As far as I was concerned he had never been fully committed to their care before nor given them priority. Kurt also had a completely different parenting style. He treated Luna like a princess, spoiling her rotten so that anything she wanted, he got it for her. James on the other hand thought she was demanding and rude so wouldn't let her behave like that, neither to him nor to me. The first time he reprimanded her I was a little taken aback, wondering how she would react. She just accepted that James was different to Kurt and changed her behaviour; acting the princess around Kurt but showing more manners at home with us.

James spent a lot more time at my home, we worked together in the mornings and spent time with the children in the afternoons. He continued to be supportive, responsible, communicative, full of love and energy. I never would have guessed that a reputed Dahab party animal was actually that kind of man. I was still wary but he showed nothing but genuine and consistent feelings towards myself and the children. James especially paid attention to Tom, encouraging him to help when he was working on the building. I noticed Tom's confidence grow as he came out of the shadow of his pretty, princess sister. He followed James around like a duckling attached to his leg.

Tom and James

James and Tom working together

We were all at the house one day, rearranging some furniture and Luna was watching James and me figuring some things out together. As out of the mouths of babes, she blurted, "Are you two in love?" We looked at each other and smiled, "Yes."

I asked, "Are you OK with that? You too, Tom ?" They just shrugged and accepted it. They had never seen Kurt and I communicating or working together like that.

Not long after that revelation I had a dentists appointment and as James had toothache, I took him along with Luna and I. As the dentist removed one of James's wisdom teeth, Luna bounced on his lap in the dentist' chair wanting to see what was going on. On the way home James was still obviously suffering, so we stopped off at the pharmacy to get painkillers. Luna tapped me on the shoulder, "Mummy. James has to sleep with us today. He can't stay alone. He can sleep in my bed." That was James's first officially accepted night with us, sleeping in Luna's bed.

James started staying over regularly and decided we were no longer going to share our bed with a spoilt child. He placed Luna in her own bed before firmly closing our bedroom door. For what seemed hours, Luna sobbed and screamed outside the door. She seemed so distraught it took all my effort not to go and comfort her but finally she went off to sleep in her own bed. After three more days of a gradually lessening performance, she was fine about sleeping on her own. I thought she might hate James for his stance but I was wrong, she still respected and cared about him like nothing had happened. Shortly afterwards, James decided that he would remodel the second apartment at Palm Beach and if both rented he would live with us. He had been in our lives almost six months by then and the children were happy about the idea.

Palm Beach Villa

The lease with Martin for Alf Leila Hotel was up for renewal. He kept making excuses that he was too busy to sit down and renegotiate the contract. I didn't make a fuss as he had always indicated he wanted to continue with the lease. The lease was four weeks overdue when we finally sat down to discuss the terms and to my surprise, he was adamant he wouldn't accept the 10% increase that had been mooted when he initially signed. We had given him a very good deal for the first year on a trial basis and he had used Alf Leila as a base from which to operate other hotels and holiday rentals with success. That had made Sherif feel uncomfortable and he wouldn't budge on the increase despite my willingness to negotiate. We were left looking for a new tenant and I lost a good friend. Martin and I had known each other for many years. It was a shame.

As luck would have it, a prospective couple appeared almost immediately and they took over the hotel in May. I was a little surprised that they wanted to live at the hotel as well as run it; living where one works is always stressful, but I wished them the best.

Meanwhile, James and I had been invited to a wedding in Alexandria which was to be held in the elegant Four Seasons Hotel. "I have nothing to wear!" I laughed. It sounded like a typical female complaint but it was actually true. Living the casual life in Dahab for so many years, meant clothes for special occasions had disappeared from my wardrobe and requirements. Dusty bohemian style was never out of place in Dahab, even faded and repaired clothes were fine, but I would feel ridiculous wearing them in a sophisticated hotel setting.

I decided to go shopping in Cairo to buy new outfits. I exclaimed, "Finally I have a man I can go shopping with! He enjoys it! He's perfect! ... And he's not gay!"

Everything at the wedding was chic and organised. We enjoyed ourselves immensely, propping up the bar until the bride and groom made a late entrance and the party really got going. I was giddy with enjoyment, in a relationship where I could share life and have fun.

James and I in Alexandria

Together we made plans for my annual summer migration away from the Sinai heat. "We can all fly to Germany, spend time with my parents. And then you and I will go to the most romantic city in the world, Paris!"

James was as enthused as I was and I began to search the internet for home exchange websites and try my luck. Dahab was a beautiful holiday spot so maybe someone would appreciate the constant sunshine and cooling waters in exchange for an urban Paris apartment. As fortune would have it, I didn't need to seek further than my friends. I found a friend of a friend was looking for a house in Dahab and all suitable accommodation was full. This woman was from Paris so she in return, offered us her brother's apartment in Paris. Like many Parisians, he would be away on holiday in June and July. Perfect!

Prior to leaving James's landlord, Abdul, arrived to use one of the Palm Beach Villas for their annual holiday. As my house was rented, we decided to live in the other Palm Beach apartment until we left for Europe. It was like we were on holiday in our home town of Dahab, living directly on the beach with Luna and Tom playing with Abdul and Salma in the shared garden or in the sea. We woke up to the rising sun and the sound of waves lapping over the coral reef and I fell in love with Dahab and my life there all over again.

James and I were adjusting to living in the same house as a couple. Sometime earlier when James and I had been spending almost twenty-four hours a day together over some weeks, I had started to feel constrained and frustrated. I figured that we were spending too much time together and tried to send him away. "I need some alone time. Why don't you go to the beach house, so I can do some things on my own?" I loved him more than ever but I couldn't focus on my needs with him around all the time.

"Why don't you just do things on your own even though I am here?" he suggested. "I don't mind if you ignore me and do your thing. Why do you feel the need to send me away?" I had to pause to stop and think. It made me realise that I wasn't used to fully sharing my life. When Kurt and the children were around I had always focused on pleasing them instead of just letting us all be independent. I had compartmentalised my life into sharing times and solo times.

I began to appreciate just how my life with James was really so different than before. We had unlimited communication on all levels about anything and everything. He accepted me as I am, both as a friend and a lover. There was nothing he wasn't willing to discuss and he shared intimacy with me, in a way that I had never experienced before. If you can ever say that you have truly found your other half, that is what I experienced with James. What I could or would not do, he did, and vice versa.

In August, just as the sweltering heat really hit, we all flew to Munich. We stayed in a hotel for one night, before visiting Franz and his wife. They had just had a baby and Luna and Tom were excited to see her. Then we took the train north west to Kaiserslautern, to stay with my parents. They had met James when they had visited Dahab in the Spring, when they been reserved (even sceptical) about our relationship. Who could blame them? But with time they saw how happy I was and that James and I had a closer relationship than I had ever had before.

James and I left the children with their grandparents and journeyed the few hours to Paris by train. The apartment was close to the Bastille with a balcony overlooking Paris's wonderful rooftops. On the table was a gift pack that included wine, pate de foie gras, chocolates and a page of recommendations for places to visit and dine in the area - the perfect start. We spent sunny days sightseeing and shopping for interior design items and I loved revisiting familiar haunts from my fashion days, describing to James what my life had been like. We spent romantic evenings together, dining out and making love in the most romantic city in the world. It was a divine time. In those early days I sometimes reflected on my initial impression that I was having an affair with a beach hippie/party animal but found so many more facets to James. He was as comfortable in Italian suits as he was in cut off jeans. He could curse and swear but could also be refined with wonderful manners, even lecturing the children about table etiquette.

With James by my side, I felt I was invincible and we returned to Dahab full of energy and hope. Francesca had been managing the fully booked apartments while we were away, so we decided to lease another apartment which would require renovation and presentation before renting it. Both James and I were making good money from all the rentals and it was a relief for me to finally have a contributing partner.

The only glitch was, the couple who had leased the Alf Leila Hotel hadn't been successful managers and had left on short notice. It was again left to me manage it but due to experience, I knew what was required to pick up the business and with James by my side, I had the energy to do it. Sherif had neither the skills, nor the interest in it, so after some discussion we agreed we should sell the property but everything needed to be working well before we could put it on the market. I agreed to manage the hotel until the end of January when James, the children and I, planned to visit his family in California. By then we would have to have found a new manager or leaser.

Sherif was also busy as he had taken over a seafood restaurant in Assala. Over casual coffees Natasha told me she was pleased Sherif had a new challenge. She said he was getting bored with just managing the Hard Rock filing station. By then Natasha had given birth to a baby girl and both her and Sherif and doted on her. They were doing well financially too, building and renovating properties to sell, as well developing a large villa and garden for themselves.

Natasha however, was having trouble with her Egyptian mother-in-law. She told me she would just arrive unannounced and take over Natasha' s kitchen and house, complaining about everything and leaving a trail of grease and grime. She wouldn't give Natasha any rights or indeed accept her as a foreign wife to her only son. It was putting stress on Sherif and Natasha's relationship but I was didn't get involved, other than lending her a sympathetic ear. We never went out together socially as couples. Sherif often told me he was "happy to see me happy" but he didn't like James and remained a close friend to Kurt. Anyhow, James wasn't directly involved in how I ran my businesses with Sherif, so I felt no need to defend my personal relationships. I understood that personality clashes should not interfere with anything concerning our work.

So once again I again started managing Alf Leila in November. We decided to invest further by roofing the corner terrace area that overlooked the bakery. I figured funds could come from the previous lease so arranged a meeting with Ali, Sherif's appointed accountant whom I always worked directly with. I discovered Sherif had been withdrawing money from the lease on a regular basis. The roofing would require all remaining funds so I would be financing two thirds of the project, Sherif only one third. I knew Sherif was busy with his new restaurant so it was up to me to approach him regarding the money. It was always up to me to approach him. I either saw him casually if I was eating at his restaurant or I went to his open office in the Lighthouse area. He never came to me. I decided to not push for funds to be equated as it wasn't a great deal of money and we could even it out when the property sold.

It was coming up to four years since we had opened Leila's Bakery, so it seemed a good idea to have a small celebration. It would also be a good opportunity to promote Alf Leila Hotel prior to the Christmas high season. I discussed this with Dirk and he was all for it. As luck would have it, it was also Natasha's birthday so she decided it would be good if she joined in the party; it would be a party for everyone! We had one month to plan for December 15th.

I was working long hours at the hotel to reorganise everything, overseeing the construction of the terrace cover and a small hotel kitchen, as well as plan for the party. Our rentals were all full too, as there was a television crew from Croatia staying to shoot scenes for some odd sounding program called "Farmer Seeks Wife". We arranged all their transport and airport transfers as they travelled into the desert. We had employed an au pair, so I could concentrate on work for those few months until we left for California. I had everything to look forward to, excited at the prospect of meeting James's family and to see the beautiful area of California that they lived in.

At the very beginning of December, two weeks before the party,

Natasha came to me, "You should talk to Sherif about the party."

"Why should I talk to Sherif? What does he want to know?"

She was not forthcoming with any explanation, "He just wants you to talk to him about the party."

"Why can't you tell him about the party? It's your birthday as well. He doesn't need to do anything." Natasha just shrugged. I was also thinking the last time Sherif had got involved with our opening party with all the unnecessary expense and theatrical disaster. "If Sherif needs me, he can call me."

Five days before the party, on December 10th, Natasha phoned me in an agitated state. She said, "Sherif has just freaked out. We have had a massive argument."

"About what?" I asked.

"He forbids me to have anything to do with your party at Leila's. He said I shouldn't have agreed to anything without his consent."

Was I hearing right? "You're not allowed to have anything to do with my party at Leila's? First, it is not my party. It's just an event to celebrate Leila's Bakery four year anniversary." I was incredulous.

"Ella. He is really mad about this. I told you before he has a bad temper."

"Yes you did. But about a small party? And as for your birthday, it was your idea to join in."

"Well, I won't be doing that. He says you have to call him immediately. Now!"

"OK, OK. Don't worry, Natasha. Take a deep breath. I will call him."

What was it about these controlling men? I sighed as I picked up my phone. Before I could even say "Hello", Sherif began screaming "What the fuck do you think you are doing?" and not waiting for an answer, continued raging on like a bellowing bull. "I forbid Natasha to have her birthday at the bakery! She is to have nothing to do with it or with you. I am sick and tired of your behaviour. I want to end our business partnership as soon as possible. NOW, if possible! You hear me?" I could certainly hear him but it was taking me some time to comprehend what he was actually saying.

"Well, it was Natasha who wanted to have her birthday here. Of course there's no problem if she has changed her mind."

"She hasn't changed her mind! I have! I forbid her to have any more to do with you and that crazy boyfriend of yours."

"What has James got to do with this? He is not even working here at the hotel or the bakery." Then I was totally confused.

Sherif spluttered out more venom, "I don't care. I just want you out of my business. Now! Finished!"

"Well we are partners in these businesses. Sure we can separate but it will take some time to sort everything out. Why now?" I was astounded at his ranting. "Why are you behaving like this? What has happened?"

"I don't have to explain anything to you. I just want you out! You have to decide what you want. The bakery or the hotel. You have to tell me now!"

I stalled, "Well we have to go over the accounts. There are two businesses with varying amounts of investment and drawings. And profits and unequal amounts of profit to allocate ..." Surely he was not serious.

He continued bullying me, "I don't care about talking about

that. That is not important. I just want you to decide now - Bakery or hotel?"

By then I was shaking and just wanted to get off the phone, "OK, OK. No problem. But I can't decide just this minute. We can work something out. Let me think about this and we can talk tomorrow." I hung up.

I stood there dumfounded, like a broken balloon with the air deflating out of me. I was in shock trying to comprehend what had just happened. Despite Natasha 's warnings that Sherif had a vile temper, that was truly the first time I had experienced anything like that. Why on earth was he so angry all of a sudden?

I called James to tell him what had happened. James had good intuition about things. "Well, regardless of being a bully, sounds like Sherif is very confident about his demands. He can behave as badly as he likes but he can't make you decide on the hotel or the bakery just like that. Or get away with it. Unless..."

"Unless what?"

"Unless he knows something that you don't."

"What do you mean?"

"Well, how did you agree to do business? Do you have all the partnership agreements? You need to get them all together. Now. Bring them home so we can get someone to go over them."

With a sinking feeling, I gathered every piece of paper I could find concerning my and Sherif's business partnership. Most of the papers were of course in Arabic and I couldn't read them.

The revelations from that evening changed everything, including my faith in humanity. I could never have predicted what came to light that night. Our Egyptian friend told us, "The company contract between Sherif and you is not valid. It doesn't have the final required stamps from the court."

I was in denial. "But that can't be true! Sherif said he had processed the final papers through the court. It took over a year." My friend shook his head.

"I even had them translated by the German Embassy in Cairo. So that I could understand everything and it was legal," I trailed off knowing that my friend was telling the truth. The papers were all legitimate and signed but Sherif had never bothered to register them. He had lied about it to me, banking on the fact I wouldn't realise. All those years, he was happy for me to build up the businesses knowing he could just take them over any time if he wanted to.

I stalled in contacting Sherif over the next days, the full gamut of emotions of grief flooding my emotions: denial, anger, strength, weakness. Not to mention feeling foolish and exposed, for believing I had done everything to make sure the businesses were legal. Gradually, I had to accept the idea that Sherif had always planned for that situation when it suited him. Legally, I had nowhere to turn.

Desperate, I asked different people for advice and it felt strange that some just shrugged their shoulders as if Sherif had doing nothing wrong, advising me that I should be grateful that he was even offering to let me have part of the property. Grateful? It was sad to think Egyptians were so inured to being ripped off that they accepted it at every nasty turn. As for the emotions running through me, gratitude was not one of them! This man, whom I had trusted as a friend and a business partner, had planned to cheat me from the very beginning and his wife was one of my best friends. I tried to talk with Natasha , to see if there was some part I could understand, some sliver of respect still left between us but she was on Sherif's side. I felt devastated and defeated.

Despite the inner turmoil, I had to continue to put on a good face amidst the chaos, as I was still managing a full hotel and the four year celebration was going ahead as planned. That party was one of the worst evenings of my life. Some people even questioned why I wasn't attending Natasha's party, as if it were rude of me. What could I say? Blurt out, "I'm not welcome because her husband is trying to cheat me! Besides I have to be at the party I organised, that she wanted to be part of!"

I was so grateful that James was by my side and I had an au pair to take care of Luna and Tom. I might not have coped at all otherwise. I couldn't eat or sleep and I felt like my whole world was spinning around me, constantly wanting to fall into a crumpled heap. I kept thinking, 'Stop the world, I want to get off!'

Chapter 6

The Nightmare

"Ella! Ella! Wake up!" I felt James shaking me but my brain was still dealing with the pictures in my head. "Ella, wake up. You're screaming. You're having a nightmare."

I slowly opened my eyes and breathed a sigh of relief as I realised I was in bed with James beside me. No one was actually trying to murder me. Seconds later, I remembered my reality and sunk back into depression. Maybe the nightmare was a better place to be. It seemed everything was spinning: my world, the days, my head. Awake or asleep, those worlds merged into one.

I had called Sherif a few times over several days, to try to understand why he was intent on destroying the partnership so quickly. I could accept that he had decided, for whatever reason, that he no longer wished for us to be partners, but I couldn't understand why it had to happen so fast. It seemed like madness had taken hold of him.

He would start raving and bellowing at me down the phone, repeating some stories of disputes we had had over the years. I had considered them business discussions really, minor disagreements or negotiations at most, and all resolved at the time. And he brought up other things which he had never even said a word about before. It was like he had kept every tiny annoyance he felt and sealed them in a jar. He had then chosen to open that jar and turn every grievance into abuse to be hurled at me. He said, "I will not accept you deciding anything for yourself anymore! The party was the last straw! You should have asked me! I'm the owner!"

The Nightmare

I mulled over my business meetings with him and realised just how few there had been (especially of late) but that had been his choice. Sherif always preferred to sit at court as King of the Lighthouse area with his followers in attendance. I had little time for some of those men. I knew of their reputations for forming quick relationships with foreigners (women mostly), bleeding them dry for as much money as they could before unceremoniously dumping them and moving on to the next victim. Some men in Dahab made a career of it and I became more aware of how many of these were in Sherif's group of sycophants, even Kurt, but I never thought for one second it could happen to me.

He blamed me for everything, yet he was the one who had chosen not to participate in meetings with me or those leasing our businesses, such as Dirk or Martin. Sherif was the one who had problems communicating with them on a business level but he blamed them at the time. I kicked myself. Maybe I should have seen it coming.

James was my rock. We discussed everything and I was so grateful that I had such a devoted man by my side. Sherif and Kurt both hated him but James was prepared to risk trying to negotiate. James suggested, "We know that Kurt is a close friend of Sherif's. Kurt might be able to help. It's worth a try".

One evening when Kurt came to pick up the children James spoke to him. I was in another room so Kurt didn't realise that I was able to hear what was being said. James broached the subject, "Kurt, you have most likely heard Sherif is trying to break up his partnership with Ella." Kurt was silent. "You know it has been successful until now. Do you have any idea why he wants to do this? Why he wants to destroy everything? Has he said anything to you? He never said anything about this to Ella before." James waited.

Kurt almost spat, "Ella was stupid doing business with Sherif in Dahab." I frowned, hidden from view. It was Kurt who had first introduced us and suggested I do business with him. He continued, "Anyway, she deserves what she gets. If it was me, I'd be going for a lot more money." His response left me reeling, leaning hard against the kitchen top so I wouldn't stumble. I felt like I heard James talking to the devil that day. I began to wonder if Kurt had been part of this plan from the very beginning, all those years ago. I had long since stopped thinking I could rely on Kurt but I never, up until that point, had thought he was devious.

One man who did offer to help was Hamsa, who was a real estate lawyer in Dahab. I expressed surprise, "Why would you want to help me? You work in the same office as Kurt. How can I trust you?" He revealed that he was in the process of breaking up his partnership with Kurt and that he wanted to help me as he felt I was being cheated and he didn't approve. He had seen too many shady business deals in Dahab and wanted to make a change. I thanked him but didn't take up his offer immediately. Could I really trust him?

James also began to reveal more of his opinion and observations of Sherif during his extensive time living in Dahab. James told me, "You know Ella, I have seen Sherif fail at running businesses before. Including what had been one of the largest successful camps." He told me, "It was only when you invested in the filling station and he leased the Hard Rock diving centre, that Sherif started having some business success. I thought everything was cool between you two. I had no reason to say anything before."

"And I had no reason to think there was a problem."

"I didn't realise just how much you were doing without any help from that bastard until I saw you managing the hotel like you are. I told you he should be doing more as a partner."

"Yes, I know. But I was so used to doing everything myself, there didn't seem much point asking him. Besides he just aggravates everybody." I sighed.

I had been completely deceived in those seven years, while I had believed our business partnership had been essentially solid and successful. Sherif had prepared a time bomb of devastation behind my back which he chose, for some reason, to detonate at that time. I had experienced his bad behaviour on some level and watched him treat others badly but I never thought he would turn on me. Maybe I should have seen it coming but by then, the end of 2010, it was past being important.

I was completely shaken that my perceptions of the people around me could be so totally wrong. I constantly asked myself, 'Just who can I trust? What else in my world is false?' I even felt alienated from the few I still considered friends. When I tried to discuss what was happening their eyes would glaze over; either they disbelieved, couldn't comprehend or wouldn't even try to. They would say things like, "Aren't you just exaggerating?", "You must have done something? Why else would he behave like that?", "I'm sure everything will be fine. He's just upset about something". Natasha said she couldn't put herself between Sherif and myself, she would not show support for me.

Sherif repeatedly said, "I am a fair man and leave the choice to you. Bakery or hotel?" In my heart there really was no choice. From the very beginning I had wanted a bakery, not a hotel. My heart was still with the bakery as I remembered my grandmother's bakery in Germany. Leila's Bakery had taken a lot of work to make it run successfully and by then, Dirk was doing well. It was Sherif who had found the property that offered an accommodation option. It still had many ups and downs back then and at that moment, wouldn't run successfully without my daily input and effort as manager. I wasn't unhappy to walk away from that.

The main problem was however, financial. The way the total investments into both businesses were made, I owned 62% and Sherif 38% of both businesses (having invested more than him initially overall). However, I calculated that the money invested in the hotel and the bakery weren't equal, with the hotel taking 60% of the total investment and the bakery 40%. So if I agreed he could have the hotel, he would take a much larger share of the overall investment, for putting in far less money at the beginning. Despite not having put in equal money initially, he sure was betting on a winner.

We talked about some compensation for me as settlement and he offered me a piece of land. This turned out to be in a location on the boundary of his and Natasha's villa without access to a road, water or electricity. It would be absolutely useless to me as a foreigner in Egypt. Their land development laws are difficult enough to negotiate as a national, and it is almost impossible for a foreigner to get official papers. That land would have been a white elephant for me and Sherif was probably banking on the fact he could just claim it again at some future date.

The very few who did understand the situation, told me bluntly that Sherif had set me up. They advised me to get a lawyer who understood how the world played dirty. That lawyer was Islam

Attia, an Egyptian with a reputation for doing whatever needed to be done to win a case, by dubious means or not. I took all the paperwork to him and asked, "What is the best I can do to get what I should be entitled to?" He agreed to look over my case.

All this was happening while I was still working full time, managing the fully booked hotel and our rental properties, as well as preparing for Christmas. I was adamant that what was happening in my business life would not my affect how the children would enjoy their festivities. It was difficult enough in Dahab (being in a Muslim country) to recreate the experience of Christmas celebrations that I remembered so dearly from my childhood. I even invited Natasha and her daughter to my annual event on the 6th December and we all remained civil to each other.

On Christmas Day, when the hotel was quiet, I took a lunch break and went to see Sherif on his throne at the Lighthouse. With a Damocles Sword over my head and others stabbing at my heart, I just wanted it over with. My intention was to try to come to an acceptable solution and make a final agreement so we could all move on.

When I sat down, Sherif's sycophants quietly got up and left. I was so emotionally dead and hollow I didn't really know where to begin, "So Sherif, What shall we do?"

Sherif exploded, "I'll show you what I can do!" He jumped up and stormed off in the direction of the hotel. I sat with my mouth open before quickly following him.

"I'll kick you out right now!" he yelled at me when we got to Alf Leila.

"Are you insane? We have a hotel full of guests and customers in the bakery. Why are you doing this?" I thought he was clearly unhinged.

He demanded the keys for the hotel, the keys to my car and the contents of the safe. I just stood wide eyed and open mouthed as he continued to roar demands at me. "If you don't give me these things I will go to the police and say you are a thief and have stolen everything. Everything is in my name!" He continued, "You cannot come to the hotel anymore. I don't want you here! I am the only owner!"

He called his close friend to bring his German Shepherd, he called men who worked at the filling station to come and support him; all against one slim, blonde, foreign woman. I had known these men for years and they didn't threaten me physically. But they followed Sherif's orders to bring a mattress down from the terrace to the hotel courtyard.

He stood defiant, "I will sleep across the entrance way from now on," he said. I was shocked to see him so aggressive and out of control. Did he have serious mental health issues that he had kept hidden from me?

Sherif stomped into the bakery and told all the staff that they should go home immediately, "The bakery and the hotel are now closed!" I was at least relieved to know all the guests were out of the hotel enjoying the Dahab sunshine on Christmas Day and there were few customers in the bakery.

I could see he was willing to destroy everything we had built up. I use that term loosely, knowing full well he had put little of his personal energy into actually creating anything. If I hadn't been required to have an Egyptian partner to own a business I could have done it all by myself. The scene he was making was too public for my business sensibilities. He was like a spoilt child, who, if he couldn't have everything, nobody would. He would destroy the whole sand castle.

I called James to tell him what was happening. He was enraged and wanted to come to the hotel immediately, rounding up his Bedouin friends to come and fight Sherif. Bedouins can be still very tribal in their attitude and not afraid to stand up to others, even physically if necessary. I on the other hand wanted to avoid what I thought would just be a huge scandal. I was still hoping for a solution through negotiation. I told James, "Just stay where you are. I am fine. I just wanted to let you know what was happening. Stay with the kids and make sure our guests are happy. Especially now that I am about to ruin their dinner plans. I'm cancelling the dinner tonight." We had planned a Bedouin style dinner in the desert for all the hotel guests and those in our rental houses, along with my family. I lied, telling them Luna and Tom were ill, which was so ironic as they hardly ever had a sniffle let alone an illness in Dahab.

I kept thinking, 'What if a guest returns now? This will be so bad for our reputation.' Although if I had really thought about it, what did it matter? Sherif was setting out to ruin what he considered to be his business anyway. I was relieved to find that Sherif did at least calm down enough, so that if any guests came nothing would look too out of order. At any rate, I was determined not to be intimidated by that lunatic. I refused to give Sherif the keys to the safe or to my car and I phoned my lawyer Islam Attia to come immediately, as well as Dirk, so he could supervise what was happening to the bakery.

Alf Leila

I sat down in front of Alf Leila with Sherif and Islam Attia, attempting to coax them into some kind of agreement. Sherif wouldn't discuss anything, he just kept dictating that I take the useless piece of land as compensation. My lawyer kept telling me to agree. I frowned and was beginning to smell a rat! Previously Islam Attia had visited the land with me and had told me it was never going to be worth anything. Now he appeared to be agreeing with everything that Sherif was proposing. He even agreed with him that I should pay for erecting a wall around this land. I kept insisting, "No. that is not even an option. The land is useless to me. I cannot register it to sell it."

It became more and more obvious that Sherif had been working this out for quite some time and he now laid his cards on the table. He had decided that I should have the bakery, but that I would work in the hotel until the end of the month after which time it would belong to him. I would have to pay to build a new water tank for the bakery, install a new electricity meter and I would also pay for a new contract in advance detailing ownership.

Dirk was by now also sitting at the table. He told Sherif, "Calm down man! Stop being so aggressive." Sherif did tone it down some but when Dirk attempted to try to reason with him concerning the details of the business separation, it fell on deaf ears. No chance. It was all supposedly fait accompli.

Islam Attia announced, "I will draw up an agreement this evening. It will be ready to sign tomorrow." Supposedly on Boxing Day I would sign the new contract agreeing solely to ownership of the bakery and to the payments for the extra construction. Islam Attia's fee would be five thousand Egyptian Pounds payable when I signed. He considered it simple - just like that! Sherif and my lawyer were both attempting to bully and blackmail me. I was exhausted and just wanted to shut them up so agreed I would see them the next day. At least Sherif had calmed down and removed the mattress from across the doorway. By five in the afternoon everyone had left, so I could get myself together enough to hide my inner turmoil before guests started returning to the hotel.

I didn't sleep at all that night. James and I again took the papers to a couple of Egyptian friends to check if there was anything that had been missed. Was there any legal way I could make this separation fair? They only reiterated that Sherif must have been planning it all from the very start. Despite Sherif saying otherwise, the documents had never been stamped at the Shakari office to make them legal and binding. I was still in denial that I didn't have a legal leg to stand on, not even a shaky one.

I decided to carry on with our Boxing Day plan which was to take a camel trip north with guests and family to the Bedouin settlement of Ras Abu Galum. I had already cancelled the dinner but wanted everything else to carry on as normal. A group of about thirty piled into jeeps, laughing and joking as we bounced along the rough road to the Blue Hole, where we climbed on camels to amble along the beach track to the settlement. It was a brilliant winter day for swimming, snorkelling and exploring and the Bedouin served us all a delicious lunch.

Luna on a Camel

The guests had a great time, even if I didn't. No one needed to know of my personal business problems. In my private hell, Islam Attia called constantly telling me he had the contract ready and I should go to sign it immediately, "And bring the money," always to bring the money.

Later that day, when I was assured all the guests were happy back in Dahab, I rocked up to Islam Attia's office with James to see what he really had to offer. He presented me with a contract, written only in Arabic, that he wanted me to sign there and then. I looked at him in disbelief. Did he think that after the situation I now found myself in, that I would now sign something in Arabic without consulting anyone else? He also then demanded ten thousand pounds instead of the five he had stipulated a day earlier, because he had "drawn up the contract on short notice". I said, "I don't have that amount of cash today. I will pay three thousand for your services so far. And I need at least a day to find someone who can translate this contract for me."

He was furious! He was yelling and screaming, "We had a deal! You should sign this contract. And you have to pay me more money!" I was becoming used to Egyptian men yelling and screaming, intimidating and bullying. They call it 'dousha' - making fuss and noise without much to show for it. Like childish tantrums at a supermarket checkout. As I collected the papers I told him, "I cannot possibly sign something without translation." I left his office with the clarity that I needed to get a new lawyer.

When the contract was translated it became even clearer that I needed a new lawyer. Islam Attia (true to his reputation) had decided he had a better chance siding with Sherif. The way the contract was written Sherif would still be able to refute the legality of my ownership as a foreigner and take everything sometime in the future. Determined to not be completely trapped, I called Sherif to tell him I needed to find a new lawyer and he would have to give me more time to get everything together. I still hoped that he would be reasonable over this, heaven knows why.

The only friends who offered to help directly were Francesca and her husband. As mutual friends with Sherif, they couldn't quite believe he could be so unreasonable and wanted to make one last effort to reason with him. A few days later they accompanied me to Sherif and Natasha's home in Assala, in an attempt to mediate an acceptable agreement. It was only minutes before Sherif was screaming at them too, "Get that woman off my property!" By the time he finished telling them that they shouldn't interfere, they understood I wasn't exaggerating about Sherif's temper.

I had no more ideas as to how I could resolve this situation with some pride, let alone some return for my investment. Why did I have to lose my hard earned money to this cheating, liar of a man who was trying to blackmail me? Finally I realised I couldn't do anymore on my own. I called my father in Germany. He listened to my plight with a calm, open mind. He said he would employ a German speaking Egyptian lawyer and try to sort things out. He also decided to fly out to Dahab himself to support me and would arrive early in January. I hoped that Sherif would have some respect for him as an older man, whom he had known during the seven years I had been dealing with him.

Sherif agreed to give me a week to hand everything over so on the last day of the year, December 31st 2009, I delivered all accounts and paperwork to Sherif's manager and accountant Ali. Ali already knew how the finances were for our partnership because I had been dealing with him directly for years. Additionally, Ali also knew that I was the one doing all the creating and how much effort I had directly put into both the businesses, unlike Sherif who sat back and had reaped the profits. But like most of the people who could see what Sherif was doing, Ali did nothing to help me.

I may have been down but not completely out, so I celebrated the New Year as well as I could with two people I felt I could trust the most, James and Francesca. We went dancing at Rush and although I had a heavy heart I was grateful to both of them for standing by me. My other friends were also close to Natasha and disliked James, so I gave up trying to explain what was really happening.

On New Year's Day, I looked down at my ringing phone. I was astounded to see Natasha 's name on the screen. I answered tentatively, "Hi?"

"Hi! Happy New Year!" she chimed. She continued telling me about how she had celebrated the prior evening, boasting almost. There was of course, not a word about my situation, about how her husband was screwing with my life and future. When I started to share how terrible I was feeling at the beginning of 2010, she had no more time to chat. Over the years that Sherif had been with Natasha he had bought a car, built and sold two houses for a good profit and they were living in a large villa with a substantial garden. Yet he never had enough money to support his side of our partnership monetarily and I was continually investing extra, to cover the debt or investment in Alf Leila. How stupid I felt!

Papa flew to Sinai in the New Year and it was such a relief to have him there to support me. He looked at everything very analytically, calculating my losses if I had to accept things the way Sherif was presenting them. It did not look good.

We eventually took the local bus to Cairo to meet the lawyer he had hired. It was a hellish journey in thinly upholstered seats with even less leg room than economy airplanes. The small TV showed slapstick style Egyptian movies, with the volume on max and the air conditioning set so low, I was grateful for my warm winter coat and scarf. After nine, cramped hours, we hopped off the bus into the Cairo chaos, the largest city in Africa with its teaming mass of over twenty million humans and manic traffic.

We intended to drive directly to the hotel and rest before the next day's run around. One can't expect that taxi drivers know all areas in a major city. Nonetheless, the journey to Tahrir Square (the most famous square in Cairo) close to the Egyptian Museum and Ramses road intersections, seemed to take forever. Maybe he just didn't understand my accent and his pride wouldn't let him admit it, but he constantly stopped to ask directions then made numerous wrong turns, before we finally turned up at a very mediocre hotel. Too tired to look for somewhere more suitable, we accepted the lumpy beds in noisy rooms.

I did have one secret mission to accomplish without letting my father know, so I snuck out after wishing him goodnight. I wanted to buy some special clothes for Luna and Tom in the nearby downtown area where clothes weren't expensive. I found exactly what I wanted.

Like a scene from a B-Grade movie we were directed to meet the lawyer outside a picture frame shop the following morning. In Europe, people complain that lawyers make too much money and make grand impressions with swish offices and stylish fashion. In Egypt it is the complete opposite, where they have small dusty offices, casual clothes or ill fitting suits and give the impression that they're making things up rather than having a vast knowledge of the law. Our lawyer was no exception and although we hoped he knew more than we did, we didn't know for sure.

He informed us that I would have to sign some papers at the

Sha'akari office to allow him to represent me and so we started our Cairo odyssey. The crumbling, grimy, neglected building which held the warren of offices was unbelievable for a government department. We had to pay numerous bribes, to men at various desks in various offices, to advance in any way. My faith that these people could actually do anything to help me was rapidly fading and I found it difficult to keep the disgust from my face.

By noon we hoped we had everything and were ready to drive to Dahab. At the last minute the working partner of my newly employed lawyer, decided he wanted to accompany us, so the five of us squeezed into a medium sized saloon for the eight hour drive. Needless to say it was not a comfortable journey yet again and we still had to meet Sherif that evening.

We also had had a brief meeting with Hamza, who as a real estate specialist in Dahab, understood all the moves Sherif would make, as well as the counter moves I would have to play if I wanted to ensure the bakery be safe from Sherif's future attempts to take over the whole property. Hamza told my lawyer, that I should definitely not put the bakery directly into my name because at that time, as a foreigner, I would not be entitled to conduct my business.

I was exhausted while Sherif and his lawyer were well rested and relaxed. According to Sherif there was to be no discussion. His position was clear in that he was willing to sign the bakery over to me but that was all. I swallowed the bile rising in my throat when I heard that! Sign it over! Like he was giving me a gift? Considering it should have been in both of our names from the very beginning!

He would also magnanimously compensate me for the hotel of 120,000 Egyptian pounds, by paying me 2,000 every month.

Paying interest is against the rules of Islam so never mind that he would be paying this off over six years, interest free. To show his honesty and intention he gave me 2000 Egyptian pounds in front of all those witnesses. A written contract would not be required; his word was good enough. Sherif refused to sell to my lawyer as an intermediary owner. So despite Hamza's advice, the contract for transferring ownership of the bakery was drawn up in my name, mentioning nothing of Sherif's debt to me. I would also have to pay for half the new water tank and the new electricity meter.

The following evening, we all went together for me to sign in front of witnesses. I felt totally betrayed like Caesar at the Senate and even had to drink a beer to 'celebrate' with all the men including Sherif.

Islam Attia continued to hassle me daily for 10,000 Egyptian pounds, yelling on the phone, "You have to pay me now!" I refused to be bullied any more so I decided to go to the Egyptian police. Some advised that I was crazy to do that but I figured the best form of defence was attack. I was actually a familiar face at the police station and I felt I had a reasonable relationship with them. I had gone there previously on behalf of staff if they had problems with the authorities (which was not an unusual situation). My case was just one more. I reported Islam as threatening and bullying me for breaking a contract for work he did not do. It proved a good move, as Islam did indeed try to report me. Each report negated the other, although I ended up paying him 5,000 Egyptian pounds to "finish the story" as they say.

Papa returned to Germany and my new lawyer began the paper trail process. I had to pay all the costs and of course, those were

The Nightmare

considerably higher for a German speaking Egyptian lawyer from Cairo, than a useless one from Dahab. I could only hope I would get what I was paying for: that Leila's Bakery would be truly mine. I was told it could take up to one and a half years before the papers were officially stamped in my name. Sherif's shadow still loomed over me as I had to negotiate with him the building of a separate water tank for the bakery and closing all connecting doors and windows to the hotel. It was by then, mid January, 2010.

Despite a horrific and draining start to the New Year, fortunately not everything in my life was negative. Back in October, James and I had planned a journey to California for the end of January so the children and I could meet James's family for the first time. We had booked our flights for the cheapest route, via Frankfurt flying in to Las Vegas, Nevada.

When James saw the flight route he looked at me, smiled, got down on his knees and asked, "Will you marry me? In Las Vegas?"

I happily replied, "Yes! I will."

I didn't hesitate, as I could see how serious he was to be my partner and a good father to the children. We planned to spend three days in Las Vegas with the children and get married prior to meeting up with his parents. We hadn't told anyone what we were planning, not my family, nor his.

I ordered a simple beautiful dress from my Italian designer friend and Francesca delivered it when she came for Christmas. I nearly cried when I tried it on; it fitted like a baggy sack rather than haute couture as I had lost over a stone in weight. I was glad I had also bought smart clothes in Cairo for the children. I wanted them to feel they were an important part of our wedding day.

Morose and depressed, not in the least excited at the prospect of our marriage, I sat down at my sewing machine to alter my wedding dress to fit into it as best I could.

Three days prior to departure, we could see massive clouds building over the darkening mountains. As evening fell, we watched the brilliant lightning silhouette the whole Gulf of Aqaba, as the crashing thunder became louder. As the clouds rolled overhead, the loudest clap announced rain that pelted down like it had years of penance to make up to the desiccated desert. The storm raged for hours overnight and everything got soaked, even more so than in previous storms. It was all hands on deck, including our au pair. With exposed electrical sockets being common, all electricity had to be turned off. All electric equipment (computers, televisions, stereos, lamps) had to covered with large sheets of plastic and then bookcases, furniture and mattresses all to had to be stored as best as possible. We spent hours sluicing water off leaking roofs and ceramic floors by torchlight in the still pelting rain to avoid flooding. By dawn the rain had stopped, so then everything had to be hung out to steam in the winter sun as we wanted to dry all we could before our departure. Other regions of Sinai fared even worse, with people dying in flash floods and many injured, not to mention widespread property destruction.

Exhausted and demoralised, we sat outside on our drying furniture under shining palms, spring cleaned by the deluge. "Whew! It's all a bit too much," sighed James. Understatement of the year. "What say we call my parents? Tell them we are arriving in Las Vegas and ask if they wouldn't mind picking us up?"

"Yes," I agreed. "At least we won't have the hassle of hiring a car and driving with jet lag. But let's not mention our wedding plans at all. I am not sure if I have the energy to go through with it yet."

"You don't want to get married now?" James looked crest fallen.

"Yes, *habibi*. Of course I still want to get married but maybe now is not the right time. I want it to be a happy time. A happy memory. And right now I am not sure I can get myself together for it. Sorry."

"Ok. I understand. Let's just see how we feel over the next few days."

"I won't say anything to my parents either when we stopover in Germany."

Finally, we were at the airport ready for departure. That familiar feeling of boarding a plane, relaxing into the seats while excitedly looking forward to new adventures, soothed its way through my tired body. As the aircraft transitioned from noisy, grinding, tarmac to a smooth flight, I felt lighter and happier and with every mile, Dahab and Sinai faded into the shadows behind me.

James's parents, John and Katherine, met us at the Las Vegas airport and drove us to an apartment they had booked for all of us on The Las Vegas Strip. It was a perfect choice, with a kitchen and living area, as well as a connecting room with en-suite bathroom for us.

I still had Dahab flashbacks to the nasty events that had occurred, but I kept preaching to myself 'Be in the moment'. 'This should be one of the happiest times of your life', I told myself. 'I'm getting married to the man I love and I have two darling kids'.

"Let's tell Mum and Dad. I think it will be fine," James

reassured me.

"Well, you know your parents better than I do. How will they feel about not being invited to the wedding?" We still hadn't decided for sure if it was going ahead, but if so, we only wanted the children with us.

"We will explain our plans, but also how we are still undecided. They will understand."

Katherine and John were thrilled that we were considering it, despite me reiterating that it would be a private ceremony without family. They insisted James and I should just rest and consider what we wanted to do. They whisked the children away, doing lots of activities and keeping them entertained while James and I spent some much needed time together, without distractions.

"The wedding is on!" we declared. "We'll get married in three days!" So the search for a venue began. Some places were just too tacky or corny to contemplate and being married by "Elvis" was not our style. Eventually we chose a sweet chapel called the Little Church of the West, which looked and felt perfect. It was the first chapel on The Strip in 1942 and is now a listed historic building. Built out of Californian redwood in the style of Pioneer English Gothic, it is no wonder that it is the most popular venue where even celebrities have taken their vows. James and I finally started to feel some excitement about our intended wedding!

That feeling was not to last. I received a message from my mother that Papa had gastritis and that my Grandmother had suffered a stroke and was hospitalised. My mind was back in turmoil. Could I cope with getting married and then potentially getting news of the death of my grandmother? She was ninety-five years old after all but I was so close to her. Of course she I knew she wouldn't live forever but the possibility of entwining her death with my wedding, had me in a spin again.

"Right!" said James. "I have a solution. You will turn your phone off and I will answer all emails for the next days. If something else happens I will deal with it and you can clear your mind of any problems."

"Out of sight, out of mind you mean?"

"At least for a few days. Life goes on Ella and we deserve to have some happiness. We need some happiness now."

"You are so right. What I don't know won't hurt me, especially if you deal with everything." I loved him even more than before, a man who was on my side. We would be married in Las Vegas!

John and Katherine were so comforting and supportive without making any demands in return. I changed my mind and said I wanted them to be part of the wedding after all. It was like I had known them forever and they were so understanding of our situation. It seemed silly to exclude them.

James did not as yet, have any wedding clothes, so we went shopping. Never underestimate the power of some retail therapy! We found a beautiful Italian suit for him and I bought some ankle boots for me. John took us to an office to apply for the marriage license.

On the eve of our marriage I told the children. Luna seemed very excited and wanted to see our clothes immediately but her response was, "You can't get married just like this, Mama!"

"What do you mean?" My heart skipped a beat thinking maybe she did not approve and would make a fuss.

"You don't look like a bride at all! You have to go to a hairdresser. And you need a veil!" A hairdo and a veil? That was all? What a relief.

So at eight o'clock on the morning of our wedding, Katherine drove us through Las Vegas in search of a suitable hairdresser who would take a bride at the last minute. The fourth hairdresser took pity on me so at 10.30am and I sat in the chair to have my hair styled to Luna's satisfaction. It was gathered into a bunch of curls on top of my head with a sleek lock down the side of my face.

With the wedding having to take place before midday when the chapel closed, Katherine and Luna went off to find a veil for me and shoes for Luna, while I was being beautified. They returned smiling, with a dozen red roses and a matching button hole for James. I was getting excited and a little nervous.

We returned to the hotel and Luna (who by then saw herself as Mistress of Ceremonies) informed me that, "Mama! James is not allowed to see you!" She organised everything to make sure James was out of sight before I could go into the room to dress. Luna and Tom were jumping with excitement to be part of the wedding party dressed in their new clothes from Cairo, Luna pretty as a princess in pink satin and Tom dressed in his miniature suit to match James's.

James went with Tom and John to the chapel first while I followed with Katherine and Luna. As I entered the chapel to marry James I couldn't stop smiling and felt like I was walking on cloud nine. The chapel was perfect and the staff so charming. With an "I do" and an "I do", our vows were complete within ten simple minutes and the papers signed. James and I were married!

Our wedding banquet was at a seafood restaurant on the Strip. But with jet lag catching up on us and Tom quietly falling asleep under the table, we didn't linger before returning to the apartment for a siesta. The festive surprises continued though, as Katherine had organised a lovely cake and we celebrated with table fireworks.

Refreshed after our naps, James and I went out for dinner dressed in our wedding clothes (including my veil) to an Italian restaurant at the Las Vegas Venice. We rode a gondola through the canals inside, posing for cheesy happy wedding photos. It was so kitschy and corny but totally enjoyable and light-hearted fun.

When we arrived at the nightclub to dance everybody made way for us. The doorman greeted us, "Just married? Welcome! Come in for free". We ended the evening playing poker, one of James's favourite games, before returning to the hotel at 4am, tired but so happy. And even more surprises awaited! Katherine and Luna had decorated our bed with rose petals and there was champagne chilling in a bucket nearby. We were so grateful and truly touched. "A perfect end to a perfect day. I am so happy Mr James ... I love you." "Me too, Mrs Ella ... and I love you."

After a brief sleep, we dragged ourselves out of bed to pack and do the four hour drive to John and Katherine's home in the mountains. Driving south west in the direction of Los Angeles we arrived at the sparkling winter wonderland of Crestline, California. My new parents in law's house was at an altitude of 5,500 feet, surrounded by stately pine forest. The icing on the cake was a layer of fresh snow blanketing everything, so pristine and beautiful.

Their home was so inviting and comfortable we just relaxed into it as if it were our second home. A room on the lower level was reserved for the grandchildren, who then of course included Luna and Tom. It was decked out with six bunk style beds for sleeping and anything that a child might wish to play with. Katherine was the grandmother from heaven, with toys, books, movies and even snow clothing in all different sizes. We pulled on the snow suits to play outside, building snowmen and sledding down gentle slopes.

It was also Luna's turn to celebrate, as she turned six early in February. Katherine and John organised a trip to Disneyland followed by an overnight stay for us and the children, including their new cousins. It rained the whole time we were touring around Disneyland but that couldn't dampen our spirits. No leaking roofs or flooding drains to deal with there!

Las Vegas Family

With the children happily settled with their new grandparents, James and I left for a three day honeymoon. We cruised through Seal Beach to Malibu then wound our way up into the mountains to visit James's good friends who were living 'off the grid'. Their home at the top of the mountains was surrounded by fruit trees, framing stunning views over the Californian coastline. Some twenty years earlier, James had helped them build that house. I could feel the love and care that had gone into its construction, the same James showed me when adding rooms to our house in Dahab.

We explored as far north as Santa Barbara then turned around, returning to Malibu to find a hotel with a Jacuzzi on the terrace. We sat in bubbles drinking bubbles, sipping champagne as the sun set over the Pacific. Any troubles in Sinai faded into the shadows as we enjoyed the last evening of our honeymoon. We found a restaurant serving sushi, the best I have ever tasted! Maybe even my taste buds were influenced by the happiness I felt that night.

The following morning we returned to the snow at Crestline, to spend the last few days of our trip with John and Katherine, before flying out of Las Vegas on the long flight via Frankfurt back to Dahab. I hoped the positive feelings and goodwill shown by all our families would be enough to lift me over any obstacles we might find on our return to Egypt.

James and I made a major life decision during that trip. We decided to commit to four more years of business in Dahab, after which we would move to California to start a new life. By then the children would need access to good schools and Egypt was just too difficult and expensive for education. We didn't have any further plans though, as to what we would do for work or business. There was time.

Back in Dahab Luna started attending school and every morning Kurt would show up at the bus stop to see her and give her candy. Every day as I drove away there was drama from Tom, screaming with injustice. One day when Luna returned from school she informed me that she would be receiving a mobile phone from Kurt as a belated birthday present. I frowned, how ridiculous! She is only just six years old.

I called Kurt. "Really! What are trying to do? Buy Luna's love?"

"I'll buy whatever I like for her. She is my daughter too!"

I bit my tongue, "Well you shouldn't buy her such unreasonable gifts. She is only six years old!"

"You can't stop me."

"And stop coming to the bus stop every morning to give her candy. Nothing but useless sugar and doing it just upsets Tom. Do you think of him?" I was just as angry that Kurt thought he could just step in and out of their lives whenever he chose.

The next day I went to collect Luna from school, "Oh, Madam Ella, Mr Kurt came to collect her some minutes ago."

Trying to cover my shock and anger I said, "Oh yes. I forgot Kurt was picking her up today." Driving back as I stopped at an intersecting street, I saw Luna pass by with her arms clinging around Kurt on the back of his motorbike. I was furious! Firstly, because Kurt was putting Luna in the middle of our personal problems by intentionally defying me. And secondly, at the thought of a possible accident caused by Dahab's careless drivers. Motorbikes always end up second best, regardless of whose fault it is. Speechless and shaking, I drove home.

We discussed what I should do with James. He reasoned, "Look. I have some sympathy with Kurt. He shouldn't have to sneak to see his children, doing things like taking Luna after school."

"I can understand that. But he seems to want to deliberately cause problems for me and favours Luna. Tom is often left out."

"How about we make it even then? We took the children away for one month. So we should at least let Kurt have the children with him for one month. It's only fair."

I hesitated, wondering how the children would behave after a month with Kurt. "Well you might be right. Let Kurt take some real responsibility for a change. I am just a little worried about their behaviour when they spend time with him but they already understand there are different rules in our house. I'll tell him when he brings Luna back."

It took quite some effort not to lose my temper when Kurt finally turned up with Luna. "Why didn't you call me? It was never arranged that you would collect Luna from school!"

"Because you would have said 'No' and I have a right to see my daughter!"

"Yes. You do. I want to talk to you about that." Kurt looked surprised. "I know I took the children away for one month to the States. So it's only fair you should have them for one month too. I can pack their clothes for you now if you like."

Kurt hesitated, "Now? You want me to take the children now? This evening?"

"Sure. I can bring their clothes over in my car." Kurt was living in a house not too far from our house.

"Well I shall have to arrange everything. Nothing at the house is prepared."

It wasn't possible for the children to move that day, but it was agreed that Kurt would have them stay with him for one month in March. I wondered how they would like living with their father over a longer period but no doubt he would take care of their day to day needs. March was also the month of regular rehearsals for the Circ de Bonboni (a children's annual performance show) and Kurt was involved with training for that , so it was convenient for him as well.

In my absence from Dahab, Sherif had built a water tank right in front of the Leila's Bakery entrance and all the connecting doors to the hotel had been bricked over. The cost of this was borne by me (of course!) and the work cost more than the 2,000 Egyptian pounds which Sherif was due to pay, so I received no monthly repayment from him and I owed him money. True to form, there was also no receipt for the work.

By separating the buildings, the bakery had gained some floor area and Dirk wanted to utilise it. Also with the bakery ownership now in my name, Dirk and I had to renegotiate a contract that would begin in April, hopefully to secure a longer commitment from both of us. It was a tough negotiation but I didn't want to risk remodelling the kitchen space, purchasing more expensive equipment for Dirk and then ending up with a large kitchen and no tenant. We signed a contract for four years, as Dirk said he would move to Austria at the end of that period. Leila's Bakery would be up for sale after that.

Remodelling the kitchen at Leila's Bakery began in March. As James and his team tore down walls they moved the surplus materials (furniture, doors, windows and other structural items) to Villa Bohème, as we had decided to add a studio apartment to the top of the Villa.

Sherif generally cooperated as we remodelled Leila's, it was after all, what he wanted. However, sometimes he complained about the noise disturbing the hotel guests, so we had to restrict work to when both the bakery and the hotel were not busy. The bakery was completed within three weeks, including a new outside seating area that covered over the ugly top of the water tank. Work on what would eventually become Atelier Bohème, had to be competed in stages when the Villa had no guests.

I discovered that Sherif hadn't changed the name of the electricity accounts as agreed, which meant more work at my expense. When it came to the monthly repayments of the two thousand Egyptian pounds, Sherif always came up with some previous issue I should compensate him for but there were never any receipts to show for the supposed work. I couldn't argue. After all, there was nothing on paper that proved he owed me anything.

Not long after we completed the remodelling of Leila's Bakery, Dahab's mayor came to visit. I proudly showed him around. He nodded with seeming approval and happily accepted some complimentary baked goods. A few days later, I received a call that our fence construction didn't comply to council standards. What standards? The wall had been completed for more than two years, yet no one had said anything, let alone complained before. Upon reflection, I wondered why the mayor had even bothered to visit and who was really behind the complaint.

In the garden, close to the kitchen, there was also a large ugly shed covering about four by four square yards that housed a power distribution box. It was there when we purchased the land and any effort we made to have it moved was declined. Maintenance workers were always happy to be hosted in the shade of our garden with free cups of tea. Yet, suddenly (along with the non compliant fence) our metal posts were also a danger because of the electricity shed. They would have to be removed.

For more than a month, myself and our original architect tried to negotiate a solution, to no avail. The final word was, that if I didn't dismantle the fence then the police would come the following day and demolish it with a bulldozer. I was essentially blackmailed into destroying what we had built with love and care. I had seen the total destruction and mess they created at other properties. I was once again so angry at the injustice of it all and, adding insult to injury was the fact the mayor was leaving within four weeks and after that, the issue would probably have disappeared.

A new addition to the team of workers who came to help with the heavy labour was Omar, the younger brother of one of James's Egyptian friends. Omar was a wiry, attractive young Saidi from Upper Egypt who didn't speak a word of English when he arrived. But from the beginning, he showed that he was very intelligent and had a great work ethic. He learnt to speak, read and write English with amazing speed. Within one month, Omar also became our gardener and James's main assistant, helping to build our studio apartment above Villa Bohème It took six months under the burning summer sun to complete the studio, but in October we welcomed our first guests to Atelier Bohème.

James had decided he wanted to run the regular transfers to and from Sharm el Sheikh Airport and for that we needed a suitable reliable vehicle. When the remodelling of Leila's was completed and the children were regularly staying with Kurt, James and I decided to make a short trip to Cairo to make some purchases and also to look for a vehicle. James had decided our ideal vehicle would be a Toyota Avanza and the Egyptian Toyota dealership in Cairo made a good impression on us. James jumped through all the hoops, crossed all the bridges, struggled through minefields of paper and bought his new car.

My life with James was very happy and our businesses were flourishing. All the holiday rentals were well booked and the bakery was busy. Omar was by then working full time on the five properties. I still had an au pair looking after the children so there was plenty of time for relaxation for James and I. We could see that the Alf Leila Hotel was empty and felt relieved that I no longer played any part in trying to make it a success.

"Let's have a wedding party!" I suggested to James. "It would be fun to have a party for all our friends since we couldn't invite them to our wedding."

"Great idea. How about we have it at Palm Beach Villas? We can just open the gates out on to the beach. There will be plenty of room."

"OK. And it's about celebrating our marriage, not about presents. We'll ask everyone to wear black or white and bring one flower as a gift. Nothing more."

We chose a summer weekend and held all bookings for that weekend so we didn't have to worry about anything. The party was a very informal affair with guests relaxing and the children spilling out on to the beach front to play games. Everyone wore black or white clothes, except for Luna, who wore her pink bridesmaid outfit from Cairo. I wore my wedding dress (which now fit more like it should) and was happy with my precious veil flowing in the Dahab breeze. James looked so handsome in his stylish Italian suit. Our guests, however, did not comply with my request for one flower. The place was drowning in bouquets covering every surface and space. There was some irony in that Kurt's new partner Nour, was the local florist and she probably made more money from our wedding than any other day.

We all enjoyed that summer immensely. Our life was going well with bookings for our properties, so when Cada contacted us about needing someone to manage Rocksea (their camp in Nuweiba) while they went to Germany, we jumped at the opportunity.

Rocksea

Rocksea was our favourite place in Sinai; it was beautiful to live directly on the beach and life in Nuweiba was the epitome of the spirit of the Sinai, with its Bedouin simplicity and natural beauty.

The Beach at Rocksea

The only clouds over our happiness, were Dirk and his aspirations for the bakery. In September, without any discussion with us, he opened another bakery as a branch of Leila's Bakery in another part of town but called it Dirk's Bakery. This new bakery was breaking our contract in many ways, as it was in his name and he received all the proceeds from that branch yet was producing everything from Leila's. I had always accepted that our relationship was somewhat tenuous with his massive ego and a tendency for secrecy, but on a business level, it had been successful.

I was very diplomatic with him but pointed out that what he was doing was unacceptable, as his branch was actually in competition with the main bakery. It transpired that what Dirk *actually* wanted to buy Leila's Bakery, so we started negotiations. I would have preferred an outright sale but he wasn't in a position to pay me like that. So it took some time before we came to an agreement where he could pay off the purchase over time.

Not long after signing the purchase agreement Dirk called me in a complete panic. He revealed there was a court case against him over money and that if he didn't leave Egypt immediately there was a high possibility he would be sent to jail. He asked, "Can you step back in to oversee the bakery?" I agreed.

Mohamed had returned to Dahab and was back working as Leila's baker. Some time earlier, unhappy with opportunities in Egypt, he had left Dahab to try his fortunes elsewhere. He had fled in small boat from Egypt's shores but had been caught and imprisoned in Lebanon. After some months in prison his family had paid an extortionate amount of money to get him released and he returned to Egypt. He had made his way back to Dahab much older and wiser from his experiences. I had great respect for Mohamed's abilities so he became the main baker and daily manager at Leila's Bakery. If he required any help he could easily contact me and everything ran perfectly, even with Dirk out of the country.

Towards the end of 2010, everything was running relatively smoothly. Sherif didn't cause too many issues over our shared building, Mohamed managed the bakery well and bookings for our holiday rental properties were good. To top it all off, James and I were even more in love then ever and I was happy with our lovely, complete family. Little did I know this would be the incredible calm before yet another, unbelievable storm.

Chapter 7
The Accident

I was much happier now I didn't have to work directly with Sherif or Dirk and it was in their absence from my day to day routine, that I realised how difficult they had actually made life for me. I questioned why they had all caused so much trouble; Sherif, Dirk and even Kurt. It was also ironic that James, whom some of my friends found so difficult, was an absolute rock to me. Love works in strange ways.

Luna had started school at El Kabany earlier in the year but to be registered properly she needed a new passport as hers would expire in January. Unfortunately I hadn't organised a new one when I was in Germany during the summer, so we had to fit in another trip to Cairo. With the busy Christmas period looming, we decided to go in early November.

James, Luna and I, left in our Avanza mid afternoon while Tom remained behind with Carina, our au pair. Omar who had proved himself very capable over the summer while working with James, was left in charge of all our rental properties. After a brief discussion we decided to travel north via Nuweiba and Taba to cross central Sinai to Suez, as opposed to travelling south via Sharm el Sheikh then up the western side of Sinai. The latter is much busier because of traffic, nowhere near as scenic and often more problematic at check points. Driving north also took us past the beautiful beaches of Nuweiba, then up on to the sparse, desert plateau. After ascending the tortuous winding rocky road from

Taba through granite mountains, the landscape widens into a stunning but desolate desert.

Driving directly west into the blinding, setting sun, James drove slowly on the straight open road despite there being hardly any traffic, just the occasional car and a few trucks. Trucks aren't permitted to travel on that road at night even though it's the main thoroughfare to Nuweiba port and to Taba, where they crossed through Israel to Jordan.

The light and the shadows across the desert accentuated the dramatic, silent majesty of the landscape. I was reminded of why I had been attracted this beautifully biblical land that had seen pilgrims and explorers cross it for thousands of years. I smiled across at James and gave thanks for him being in my life. We chatted quietly about what we planned to do while in Cairo, knowing we should arrive within five or six hours.

Luna asked "Can I get out of my seat? I'm tired and I want to lie down."

I remembered our trip to Siwa in my Maruti when there hadn't been enough seat belts but I replied, "No. This car has good seat belts so I think we should use them. Use my coat for a pillow if you like." It wasn't long before she nodded off.

Suddenly the road noise changed and I realised we had driven off tarmac on to gravel. There had been no warning signs and no workmen in sight, but it was clear the road was being repaired, although work had obviously finished for the day. James immediately released his foot from the accelerator, unfortunately a little too late to avoid heaps of sand spilling across the edge of the road.

As the tires gripped the energy sucking sand, we lurched

forward against our seat belts, before the car's momentum twisted us sideways. Suddenly everything was spinning. In the slow motion of adrenalin, I heard the crashing and crunching of mangling metal, as I was spun like a rag doll in a washing machine. The Avanza tumbled over at least three times, before coming to rest on its roof at the side of the road.

We were all still strapped in the upside down car. I looked over to see James unconscious behind the air bag, bleeding from his mouth and head. Luna was strapped in behind me and immediately said, "Mama, I'm OK. Everything will be fine." Beautiful Luna. I was so grateful for that safety belt.

Propping myself up as best I could while trying to avoid falling in the upside down car, I tentatively undid my seat belt. I checked James over. His face was covered in blood from a head wound but I was relieved to hear that he began moaning loudly. In my dazed state, I noticed that the whole car was full of sand, glass, blood and money. Money? The guests had paid us 5,000 Egyptian pounds on their arrival, which I had placed in a bag at my feet in the car. There were fifty one hundred pound notes floating loose in the car.

I looked out to see lots of people approaching the car. The driver and the passengers in a passing bus had seen the accident and were coming to help. My brain fog quickly cleared as I tried to get myself together. Let alone how badly injured James was, I knew laws pertaining to accidents in Egypt were horrendous and I didn't want to dare think about how much trouble was potentially coming.

I quickly collected the money and searched for our passports. Fortunately they had been placed in an open pocket, easily accessible to show police at various check points en route. I found them spattered with blood. What else? Car papers! Everything in Egypt always needs papers and there were those for the car and James as driver. They were in the glove compartment.

The first arrivals first helped Luna and I out of the car, then James, who was groaning ever louder with pain. Just that moment, seemingly out of the blue, an ambulance arrived. James regained some level of consciousness as he was placed onto a stretcher.

The men managed to turn our car over and I continued gathering our luggage and personal items. Nothing left in the car would be secure. We were all then bundled into the modern ambulance, a brand new, orange and shiny, fully equipped minivan. Within minutes we arrived in the Nakl township, which is smack bang in the very centre of Sinai. It oddly occurred to me how it was the antithesis of Las Vegas in a desert landscape, bleak and unwelcoming with depressing dusty roads, two restaurants, unpainted concrete, and broken buildings. As we drove into the ambulance station, the only things missing from the Wild West scene, were tumbleweeds. I was astonished to see a familiar face standing in front of the infirmary doors! A hotel owner whom we knew from Dahab, was more than a welcome sight for sore eyes. He immediately began to help us with translation.

The ambulance might have been brand new but the facilities in the examination room were abysmal (and I use the term "facilities" very widely!) There wasn't even running water. The congealing blood was washed off with saline and sterile swabs. As our adrenalin subsided we became more aware of our injuries. James was in great pain in his shoulder and his leg. Luna had a bleeding cut above her eye and a darkening bruise. I didn't have a scratch, although I suspected I'd develop a few bruises.

The police began to question us in limited language, demanding that we fill out reports straight away, regardless of how badly injured James was. He was white with shock, screaming in pain and in no state to do any such thing. They perused our passports for visas then confiscated the car's registration and warranty papers, along with James's drivers license. The hotel owner was helping but James suggested we call Abdul, his friend and owner of the Palm Beach apartments. He lived in Ismalia on the West bank of the Suez Canal and was a man of means and contacts. James said desperately, "He'll be able to offer us good advice."

Abdul suggested that the ambulance drive us the hundred miles or so to Suez where he would meet us. The only manageable access to mainland Egypt, and Africa for that matter, is the Suez Tunnel that passes under the Suez Canal. We were bundled back into the ambulance for the journey. As painkillers took some affect, James had become a fraction calmer by the time we reached the hospital in Suez. While we waited for Abdul to arrive, they x-rayed James and found he had a "broken" knee and broken collar bone.

Luna was also x-rayed but thankfully nothing was broken, she just had a rapidly darkening eye. When Abdul arrived he made some enquiries and discovered there was a specialist orthopaedic surgeon based in Suez, but also another more renowned from Cairo, who travelled to Ismalia once a week. Considering that we knew no one in Suez and Abdul was based in Ismalia we decided it best for James to be transferred to Ismalia.

The hospital staff in Suez however, had other ideas. With the prospect of a high income foreign patient, they weren't keen to let us leave easily. They refused to order an ambulance to transport us to Ismalia so we waited hours for another vehicle. When it eventually arrived we were astonished! It was a bare van with a bed in the back and open windows all round. As midnight approached, the choice was a rock or a hard place, so James was shoved unceremoniously onto the bed in the back of the van. I climbed in too as his sole attendant, while exhausted Luna crawled into Abdul 's car where she promptly fell asleep.

The driver, seemingly blithely ignorant that he had an injured passenger lying on an unfixed bed in the back, found every hole and bump on that road to Ismalia. As the van juddered over the rough road, rocking and swaying with every turn, James writhed in agony. In what was still Egyptian winter, we huddled under thin blankets that did little to keep off the freezing wind through the open windows. The ghastly journey seemed to take forever.

Upon our arrival in Ismalia we were relieved to discover that as a VIP patient, James would be given the 'luxury room'. The only snag, was that the room was on the third floor and the hospital didn't have a working elevator. James was placed on a stretcher too short for him and carted roughly up narrow stairs on it, swaying and screaming when his leg or foot caught the narrow walls. "What the hell are you doing to me ?", "Fuck!", "Arrgh!" James's swearing and groans echoed up the stairwell.

The 'luxury' room had two beds in it, a fridge and a small bathroom with impossible access for a badly injured patient. I recalled my time in hospital in Hong Kong and reflected on how luxury is so relative. Luna knew Abdul and his family quite well so she went to stay with them, leaving me to focus on James. Nearly twelve hours after the accident, where people had attended us within minutes, James was finally in the Ismalia hospital room.

The Accident

We were both exhausted.

The following morning, on the 8th of November, the surgeon was available to examine James. This entailed negotiating the narrow staircase down to the doctor's examination room again, the same procedure on the too small stretcher, the same agony for James, the same red language.

The doctor determined that the top of James's fibula was broken so severely, that to ensure any chance of repair it would require a bone graft, to be taken from his hip. His collarbone was also broken but that would hopefully heal of its own accord. The doctor decided he wouldn't carry out the operation that day as James was still in too much shock and we needed to find blood to match his own type, in case he needed a transfusion. We had to call the American Embassy, who advised us where we could purchase the blood if required. We hoped it wouldn't be needed.

The hospital provided no food and no one washed or tended to the patients, so I became James's sole caregiver. The nurses only administered the prescribed medicine, made the beds and did general cleaning in the room. This meant I had to go in search of suitable food in the neighbourhood. I had recently dyed my hair bright red, so felt I stood out like a beacon. I also felt very self conscious in my fitted clothes, which were far too tight for Ismalia where most of the women wore shoulder covering hijab. Ismalia is no tourist town.

One saving grace was that we were able to access the internet via our mobile stick in our laptop so we had connection to the outside world. I managed to organise Tom's care between Carina and Kurt, and Carina could also take care of our holiday guests along with Omar and Magdalene's help.

I contacted the insurance company to inform them of the accident and to try and get the wrecked Avanza transported to Cairo. I discovered this would be impossible, as only the registered owner could collect it or someone with assigned power of attorney. The latter required an official translator from a government office in Cairo, again with the registered owner. Since that person was James those options were definitely out! The car would have to wait until James could travel again.

The surgery was to take place the following day but no specific time was given. It wasn't until six o'clock the following evening when they finally began to operate on James, over two days after the accident. We had to pay cash up front for the operation. I had to make sure I had 8,000 Egyptian pounds for the surgeon, 800 for medicine and 1,600 for the anaesthetist. Luckily we had the money from the holiday booking as it was quite a mission to accumulate enough cash, with ATM machines limiting withdrawals to one thousand per day. I managed to send some cash to myself via Western Union and started preparing to gather the amount we needed.

As I waited nervously for the operation to be over, Abdul and his friends kept me company in our hospital room. We could hear James roaring in agony, as he was bought back upstairs to the room. His previous explosions of flowery language weren't anything in comparison to this new display. Abdul and company left almost immediately.

James had a heavy plaster and bandages from the top of his thigh down to his foot and could hardly move. There were drains from his knee and hip which dripped into containers already rising with blood and body fluids. He was hardly able to speak, writhing and thrashing about. He was complaining of pain all over his body; from his shoulder, through his hip, to his foot. "I can't bear this! This is too much! I want to die!" he cried out. He lifted his torso up from the bed and tried to beat his head against the wall in the hope he would knock himself out. I was beside myself as to how to cope, with no medical staff around. "Oh my god! Please, James! What should I do?" He was beyond answering so in desperation, I flung myself on top of him to keep him on the bed.

He eventually calmed down enough to explain that the anaesthesia had not worked completely. The drugs that paralyse you had worked, so he couldn't move but he had felt everything as they had removed pieces of bone from his hip to graft into his knee. He had been locked in hell. Apparently the anaesthetist, sporting the long beard of a dedicated follower of Islam, had shrugged it off saying that James drank too much so nothing would have worked! We both knew it was more than three days since he had had any alcohol and he didn't have a drinking problem.

The intravenous sedatives and pain relievers also seemed to do very little to ease his pain and despite being in a hospital, no one would do anything else to help. I was his living monitor as there were no bells or electric buzzers to call for assistance. I pushed my bed close to James's so I could be the emergency bell, should he wake and need a nurse. I never knew where the nurses would be as there was no central work station and I often had to open many doors to many rooms, before I found any medical staff at all.

After days of hell, one of the nurses was trying to administer more useless painkillers when she discovered that the cannula wasn't actually placed properly in James's vein. The injections were just bursting under the skin and causing more painful swelling. Perhaps that explained why the anaesthesia and painkillers were ineffective! When she replaced it with a new one, he did start to feel some relief and relax enough to start healing.

Luna, our little ray of sunshine, would sometimes come to visit, playing in the room and watching movies on our laptop. She understood we were trying to cheer the patient up and we would take care of him as best we could.

Post Accident Faces

My lawyer from Cairo also drove to Ismalia to explain to me that it would only take a few more days until my contract would be completed and be legally validated. Leila's Bakery would finally, legally, be in my name after almost a year. Some good news at least!

Five days later, the surgeon made his scheduled visit to the hospital, which meant once again navigating the treacherous journey with James on too short a stretcher down the stairwell to the examination room. The expletives were slightly milder this time round though, an indication that at least James was feeling better. The surgeon had good news, "You are well enough to leave the hospital. But I want to examine you again before you return to Dahab."

We needed to find somewhere suitable to stay for another week so Abdul arranged everything so that we could move into an apartment owned by Salma, his wife, which was directly on the bank of the Suez Canal. We then went about paying the account at the hospital. This payment was far more complicated than handing cash to the Doctors and the hospital didn't accept credit cards. That would have made life too easy! In anticipation of that, I had been withdrawing cash on a daily basis from ATM machines to make sure I had enough. As foreigners without a permanent residence, we had to pay twice as much as an Egyptian would, handing over different amounts at many different desks. Everything was suitably vague to ensure confusion, but we were in no position to discuss neither the method, nor the amounts.

After some hours everything was completed and we manoeuvered James into the back of a saloon car supporting him with pillows, his leg stretched along the back seat. It wasn't ideal but infinitely better than the open minivan from Suez to Ismalia. The apartment was lovely and finally we had a decent kitchen where I could prepare meals. There was also a room for Luna, so could be together again. The apartment complex was well presented and built for affluent owners but I discovered there were no supermarkets of any description in the vicinity. It was a mystery as to how the tenants cooked their meals or what they ate.

I took Luna and went in search of food and also for a place to get passport photos. I still planned to go to Cairo to apply for

Luna's new passport. I found a place for the photos and they insisted on applying some makeup to six year old Luna before taking them. She loved it, but I wasn't sure it fitted German requirements. Knowing how manic Cairo is, I wanted to leave very early in the morning for the German Embassy as it's only open in the morning. I booked a taxi driver for 6.30am the following morning, at the same time wondering if the taxi driver would actually turn up outside our house on Egyptian time or indeed, at all. There wasn't a thing I could do but wait and see. I was also very worried about leaving James alone in the apartment but there was no alternative. "I'll be fine," James assured me. At least the painkillers were taking some effect now. Luna and I prepared food and left it placed near his bed within reach.

At 6.30am Luna and I were ready to go but as I feared, there was no sign of our prearranged taxi nor did he answer my persistent phone calls. I was frantic and furious but also determined, so I ran to the end of the street to flag down another taxi. When I said I wanted to go to Cairo immediately and that I would pay a good price the driver just shook his head in refusal. He explained that his car didn't have the right papers for him to drive his car outside Ismalia; if he drove to Cairo with us, his car would most likely be confiscated by the police. My shoulders slumped. What more could this crazy country throw at us?

The driver was kind though and suggested we take a mini bus to Cairo. What did we have to lose? The driver waited outside while I explained quickly to James what I was doing and collected Luna. The driver took us directly to the minibus station.

Along with local Egyptians, we piled into a scruffy minivan. With every seat quickly occupied, we were soon on our way. The locals might have been surprised to see a brightly red haired foreign woman and a young blonde girl riding with them but they were nothing but kind and polite. And as a bonus, the bus fare was 8 Egyptian pounds, as opposed to the 150 pounds that the taxi would have charged had it turned up!

The journey in the microbus (as locals call them) was swift and without incident. Actual routes are not promoted in any official way because locals just know where they are going, so we were delivered without fuss somewhere into Cairo's teeming suburbs. These often all look the same and any signs were written in Arabic which I could not read, so effectively, I had no clue where we were. I checked my watch and realised we had just over an hour before the embassy closed.

We clearly must have looked confused and lost, as within minutes a woman asked, "Can I help you?" One of the things I loved about Egypt was the openness, the willingness to genuinely help. She looked kind.

"Oh, maybe. We need to get to the German Embassy as soon as possible. Before eleven."

"You'll never make it in a taxi by that time. The streets are too busy. You should take the Metro." She took us under her wing and guided us to Cairo's short, but relatively efficient underground Metro.

The ride was just perfect so we arrived at the German Embassy at 10:30 am, half an hour before it closed (I wonder what they did for the rest of the day?). I handed the application across the counter and waited for the staff to check over the papers. "I am sorry Madam Hartmann but we can't issue a new passport without a declaration from her father."

I was dumbfounded, again. "What do you mean? I have sole custody of her. Why do I need his approval?"

"I'm sorry but we require his declaration before we can issue a new passport."

I sighed. The whole purpose of that disastrous trip had been to arrange for Luna's passport before the end of November so that the Egyptian system could officially register her for school. Of course I didn't have a declaration from Kurt so it seemed everything was against us. Kurt would have to have to go to Cairo to collect the passport himself at some future date.

It was still the morning, so I was determined to try to get something positive out of the whole debacle. I called the phone number of a Syrian man who had expressed interest in purchasing Leila's Bakery and Alf Leila. He invited Luna and I to his home in a Garden City suburb where, when we arrived, it was like stepping into a wonderland. Egypt is so full of surprises one way or another.

His dream home was set around a courtyard, like a Moroccan riyadh, with a central swimming pool. Everything was so perfectly charming and beautiful; Luna went for a swim and was treated with chocolate. The Syrian was looking for a place to invest but had never been to Dahab, so I was very dubious as to his interest while I described the bakery and the hotel. I could see Dahab was never going to be the type of place that man would be happy investing in and didn't make any effort to convince him. I simply enjoyed the experience as a pleasant interlude behind high walls in dirty, dusty Cairo.

Luna also needed shoes. In Dahab her choice was plastic sandals or plastic sandals. It's said you can have anything you want in Cairo if you know where to find it, so we made our way downtown where there are shops side by side selling nothing but shoes. Downtown was where I had bought the beautiful wedding clothes for Luna and Tom. It didn't take long to find a suitable pair and we made our way back to the Metro.

We retraced our steps back to the point where we could catch a minibus back to Ismalia. I wondered how James was faring as we squashed in for the return trip. One of the exasperations or exhilarations of Egypt, is that what should be the same experience, can turn out to be totally different. It's like a roller coaster, that changes route with each ride.

On that return trip to Ismalia I feared for our lives. The driver wove so fast in and out of vehicles, passing them left and right at random, braking and accelerating, knocking us around in our beltless seats. As I glimpsed the speedometer registering over 140 kilometres, per my heart raced with terror as memories of our crash flashed through my mind. Had we survived that just to die in just another hideous 'accident' on Egypt's infamous roads? Beside me Luna slept blissfully unaware. James was doing fine when we finally arrived back and I was just relieved to have made it!.

November 16th was Eid el-Adhar, the Muslim holiday called the 'Big Feast', commemorating the story of Ibrahim, his son Ismail and the sacrifice of a sheep (similar to the Biblical story of Abraham and Isaac). Those who can afford it, ritually slaughter animals on that day and the meat is distributed to those less fortunate. It's also a time for family meals together, wearing new clothes and children receiving toys. For the first time James left the apartment when we went to share a meal with Abdul and his family. He coped well, all things considered. On the following day Kurt came to bring us various items and to collect Luna to return to Dahab. James and I remained in Ismalia for another week before seeing the surgeon again.

That was the week of a 'thousand and one movies', viewed one after another to pass some of the time. We must have looked an odd couple, me with my knitting and James reclining with his leg raised, nursing a broken collar bone. My patient care had progressed to massaging his leg twice a day and changing bandages; everything was improving as James began to mobilise his foot.

My Cairo lawyer called. I was instantly excited, thinking that after all that time and hassle, Leila's Bakery would finally be in my name. "I have news," he said. "They have decided not to ratify your contract. You cannot set up your company. I'm sorry." I was past being shocked. To learn that after eleven months of waiting and being continually told everything would be finished in "a few days", the reality was that the whole effort was a complete waste of time and money. I was back to square one and looking for a new lawyer.

Several weeks after leaving home, James went for his examination. The x-rays clearly showed the multitude of screws and a plate holding the bones together and that everything was healing according to plan. James was given the all clear to return to Dahab. Before departing however, we had to find a special brace that the surgeon recommended but of course, wasn't provided. We drove through crowded traffic with James propped up on the back seat from one pharmacy to another in search of the brace. We found something suitable at the fifth one we visited.

Back in the taxi, we were winding through traffic when the car suddenly swerved and I was thrown forward against the seat belt. As the sound of metal clashing against metal reached my ears, adrenalin flooded through my veins and I felt my heart thumping against my rib cage, blood pounding in my ears. Another car accident? Thankfully, it was a minor scrape and James wasn't injured, despite not being able to wear a seat belt.

I just wanted us to be safely home in Dahab. Yet we still had to attend to the Avanza which remained in Nakl. Vehicles in Egypt are exorbitantly expensive and we needed the insurance money to be able to replace it. We were worried about what might have happened to the car while we were stuck in Ismalia. We arranged a taxi to Nakl as well as a tow truck to accompany us, planning for the damaged Avanza to be delivered back to Cairo where the insurance company could deal with it.

Both James and I just stared open mouthed at our Avanza. The wreck before us looked nothing like the car that had left Dahab. "Oh my lord, James. How did we even get out alive?"

Me and the Mangled Car

He let out a low breath and shook his head. "Unbelievable. I never thought a broken leg and collar bone could be considered lucky."

"Yes. We are SO lucky ..." At the time of the ccident we had obviously been too shocked to take it in. Every panel on the Avanza was smashed, the front and rear bumpers hanging off, the bonnet crumpled, the roof caved in, and every window broken. The wheels might have been in place but our Avanza was well and truly 'a total wreck'.

We went to the police station to ask for the papers they had taken from us; car registration, car ownership and James's driver's license. The policeman behind the counter had no desire to understand what we were asking for. Our taxi driver was another godsend as he helped with translation and eventually one officer disappeared into an office with our request. When he returned our taxi driver translated, "He says they are not here."

James frowned, "What does he mean? 'Not here'"

"He says the papers have all been sent to Al Arish. The central office for North Sinai."

James looked about to explode, "So what happens now? How do I get MY car?" (with sarcastic emphasis on the 'my').

"You will need to get papers from Nuweiba before you can tow the car anyway. That is where the car is registered."

"Let me get this right. I have to go first to Nuweiba to get papers from the court office there, to get permission to tow my wrecked car because that is where my car is registered. Then I have to return here to Nakl, to collect my car's registration papers, my car's current registration and my drivers' license because those papers were taken off me by Nakl police after the accident ... when I was semi conscious ... and were sent to EL Arish for some bloody useless reason. I am already in Nakl, in the centre of Sinai, with my car, but I cannot take it. Bloody Egyptian bureaucracy!"

And so another Egyptian paper chase started. We sent the tow truck back to Ismalia (another complete waste of money) and continued to Nuweiba where the office we needed was already closed.

I suggested, "Let's go to Rocksea. We need a break and we may as well stay overnight here and collect the papers in the morning."

"Great idea." James smiled, releasing some of the stress that showed in his face. "It's so nice to be back home in South Sinai."

The following morning we collected the required papers before continuing to Dahab and on home! Our wonderful, helpful driver then returned to Ismalia via Nakl to drop those papers back at the Nakl police station. There was nothing for it then but to wait for a message from the court in El Arish, to say we could collect the car.

With Christmas fast approaching and bookings bountiful for our rental properties, we slotted back into Dahab life as best as possible. Omar and Carina pulled together to help me with the apartments. Mohamed continued to manage and bake at Leila's as Dirk still could not return to Egypt.

James was a terrible and horrible patient. With his collarbone still unstable and in constant pain with his leg, he found everything difficult. He had to rely on everybody to help him, yet he was extremely grumpy and completely intolerant. We arranged for a German physiotherapist to treat him every few days with massage and exercises to give him some relief. When Katherine learned of the situation, she immediately offered to come and stay with us over Christmas to help with the children or however else she could.

Almost daily, we telephoned the Nakl police. We desperately wanted to get what was left of the Avanza to Cairo, to claim on our insurance and purchase a new vehicle. We knew everything was a long winded process but no one would offer any information as to why it was taking so long to get the papers from El Arish. Finally we got word. James would have to go in person to claim the car. We arranged our Ismalian driver who already knew the situation and had proved so helpful, to come to Dahab to collect us. He was one of those Egyptians who keep calm and work their way through the minefield of processes often required and he could act as translator for us too.

I kept insisting that I go along as support and James was just as adamant that he would go alone. It was the first time we had a real argument. We both got very angry and were equally stubborn. I yelled at him, "You are totally insane thinking of doing this on your own in your condition! You can't stop me from going!" His reply was equally angry. I stormed off to sleep on the sofa, determined to leave with him at 5am the following morning.

He was still sulking so I didn't bother with any conversation, as I climbed into the front passenger seat. It was a silent drive, all the way to Nakl.

We arrived early but were told by the police there were no papers there, that we would have to go north to El Arish to collect the papers. We were also told that as foreigners we were not allowed to take the most direct route north without a written permission from the Governor. There were insurgents in the desert who committed crimes and kidnapping, even murder so it was a no go zone for foreigners. They wanted us to drive many extra hours east to Suez, then north to the coast to get to El Arish. We pleaded with them, "But we live in Sinai. We understand there are dangers but also know the real risk is small." They couldn't "issue the permission" in Nakl, they said. James was upset, swearing and cursing. I considered his temper and insurgent threats and decided we had better go the quickest route, if at all possible.

I asked politely, "Can you give us a police escort so we can go directly north? You can see my husband is injured and the extra hours in a car will make him even more ill. Please ..." We spent some time trying to negotiate with them but they wouldn't budge. Then we found a way forward. With a suitable amount of silver crossing palms, we were on our way directly north (again!) with an armed policeman in the car. I had to squash into the back seat with James, who was still refusing to talk with me.

The road was in a terrible condition, made worse by a sand storm that became denser as we drove into it. I was petrified by the near blind driving conditions, wondering if we really had taken on too much. By the time we got to El Arish we had passed two road accidents. It was a huge relief to just survive the drive.

We arrived with five minutes to spare as the office we needed apparently closed at 2pm. That office was also at the top of three flights of crumbling stairs and of course there was no elevator for James. By the time he reached the top landing in frustrated agony, he looked like a volcano about to blow but still, wasn't speaking to me.

Inside the office, there was a young man in a suit seated behind a desk. James didn't wait for introductions before launching into a tirade of wild insults and expletives, "Fucking bureaucracy in Egypt! What is this crap that I have to travel all this way just get my car?" It wasn't seconds before they were both yelling at each other, while I stood in wide eyed astonishment trying to calm James down. The man in the suit (to his credit) allowed James to vent his anger before revealing that there was a case against James for injuring a child in the accident. We stood horrified to learn that he might be arrested on the spot. So that was the true reason why we had not been able to get the Avanza papers earlier and why James had to go in person. Why waste police time looking for him when he would be forced to go to them? Could the story get any crazier?

I intervened, "That isn't true. Luna is my daughter. She's fine!"

"Well Madam. The report I have here says she was injured and the driver of the car, Mr. James here, is responsible."

"Well I am her mother and I was also in the accident and we are both fine. So what do we have to do to refute this claim?"

"Either the mother or the father has to sign a declaration that there will be no charges pressed and Mr. James will be free to go."

"Sure then. Let's do it now." I looked at James and smirked, "Good thing you bought the mother of the child with you then, isn't it?" By then, after his outburst and all of the effort it took out of him, he had calmed down. We smiled despite the debacle. The ice between us thawed.

It turned out the man in the suit was actually the Governor of North Sinai, a very important man who could have caused a lot of problems for us. He spoke English well and had actually studied in the Unites States, so James and he found common ground. They even ended up chatting and joking.

Aside from my declaration that I wouldn't be pressing charges for Luna's injuries, there were many forms to fill out concerning the car. Of course that meant by the time we were finished completing everything, the court that would stamp and sign the car's release papers was closed. There wasn't anything for it but to find somewhere to sleep in Al Arish, in order to return to the office the next day.

Even though the sand storm showed no signs of abating and the thought of driving on that road at night was terrifying, I wasn't happy about having to stay. Our helpful driver had a friend in Al Arish who gave us a tip to find a tourist chalet by the sea. We finally got James relaxing in a reclining position so the driver and I could go in search of food. We eventually found something good to eat at the local fish market.

Al Arish had at one time been a moderately successful town on the Mediterranean coast. But its proximity to Gaza with smuggling and growing insurgency, meant that by then few tourists ever ventured there. I could see the resulting depression in the unkempt streets in what had been an attractive seaside resort some years before.

The following morning (strengthened by a good night's sleep), we returned to the court to wait three hours for the papers for the car, as well as James driver's license and permission to remove it from Nakl. We discovered our personal police escort from the previous day had already driven back to Nakl. No policeman was keen to drive to Nakl-in-the-middle-of-nowhere either, so again silver crossed palms as we tried to convince the checkpoint police we would be fine going it alone. After all we had driven to Al Arish via the same route the previous day in the sand storm, which had thankfully, blown over. Success! That return journey was an uneventful drive through the bleak, featureless desert landscape of north Sinai.

En route we called the tow truck from Ismalia to meet us in Nakl. Finally, six weeks after the accident, we would be able to get the Avanza towed to Cairo to claim on the insurance. Considering all the hassles and unforeseen problems that always seem to emerge, we decided the best thing to do would be to accompany the Avanza to Cairo to make sure we would be there to deal with anything that occurred along the way.

The insurance company told us the car would have to be delivered back to the Toyota dealership, so I also telephoned dealership in Cairo to say we were coming - 'sha Allah!'. It was after 4pm by the time we left Nakl and I estimated we wouldn't reach Cairo before 9pm but the staff at Toyota assured me that would be fine and that staff would be there to meet the tow truck.

We needed somewhere to stay and I will always be grateful for the friendliness and hospitality of Egyptians, in this case, the our driver's brother. He and his wife even gave up their bed so James could have somewhere to rest his by then, very weary body. At 9.30pm we received a phone call from the tow truck driver. There was no one at the Toyota dealership and no one was answering any phone calls! He told us that, despite the temperature that night dropping drastically, he would spend the night sleeping in the open, smashed up car to make sure that nothing was stolen from it.

We arrived furious to the Toyota dealership the following morning. We had been told by the insurance company that we had to take the car to them and they hadn't done as they'd promised. "No was here to meet our tow truck driver ... as you assured me they would be!" Their disinterested reply was that they would have to charge us 150 pounds per day until the claim was finalised, selling the wrecked Avanza back to the insurance company.

By this time both James and I were totally fed up. "Look!" I said. "You sold us this car and you sold us the insurance policy which you said we HAD to have. The insurance told us to bring the smashed car here until the claim was settled. No one was here last night, despite your staff assuring us they would be, and our driver had to sleep in the car, despite freezing conditions. And now you want to force us to pay an exorbitant daily storage rate? You all can just fuck off! This is a total scam and we WON'T pay it. You are now responsible for this car until we get everything settled!"

And with that, we stormed out to go to the insurance office.

There we had another heated discussion about what would be required. I was totally out of patience with their attempts to avoid paying out on our claim. I expended more expletives and told them, "This is enough! There are no legal reasons for you not paying out. There were no other parties involved in the accident, the police have cleared James of any fault and you must pay us the money! The car is only six months old and you will pay us 85% of the purchase price as agreed! You tell us exactly what we need to do, right now!"

There is nothing like a crazy foreign woman ranting out loud to get some effect in Egypt. After my outburst they started to say, "All will be OK. All will be fine," and that James was no longer needed in Cairo so we could return to Dahab and anything else could be sorted out via email. They were clearly eager to get us out of their office.

Our driver returned us to Dahab. Home sweet home. After those three days James was a total wreck, physically and mentally exhausted. He was meant to be resting his leg for at least three months, not manoeuvring in and out of vehicles or up and down stairs. But we had Christmas to look forward to and his mother arriving to visit.

Home Sweet Home

Tom with a Goat

He had woken me from a deep sleep and I struggled to comprehend at first what he was saying. "He has just been here. Screaming at me. Telling me I can no longer bake at night because we are upsetting the guests. I can't even finish today's bread..." I realised straight away that Sherif was back up to his old tricks. He had gone into the bakery and forced Mohamed to stop there and then, that the guests in Alf Leila could not sleep because of "all the noise". Really? Too much noise? Now? After five years without problems? Weary of the whole scene, James's injury, the continuing car saga and then Sherif and his revolting behaviour, I told Mohamed not to worry, we would deal with it as soon as possible. Of course, there wouldn't be any bread products to sell to customers the next day.

I called Sherif to try to resolve the situation. According to him, if we continued to make noise and disturb his guests, Sherif would get Leila's Bakery closed down. I expressed surprise considering that we had never had a complaint in five years of running the bakery and nothing had changed, as far as I knew. At the same time, I was painfully aware that Leila's bakery still wasn't legally in my name.

After some negotiation, we agreed that if the hotel was full, (which meant the hotel would have to use the rooms close to the bakery) we would then not bake at all at night. Otherwise we agreed to start baking from 5am and that I would search for noise insulation material to line the walls. That would take some time as it would need to be sourced in Cairo.

I informed Dirk who still had to remain out of the country or face time in an Egyptian jail (not something you would even lightly wish on your worst enemy!) and assured him the bakery was still able to operate. I was also surprised to learn from bakery staff that Dirk had found a new kitchen in another building that he was planning on using anyway. I wondered what he was up to, but said nothing.

As usual on December 6th every year, I organised a children's Christmas party in our garden, so Santk Nikolaus could bring presents. It was always fun Dahab style, with Santk Nikolaus often arriving on a camel. That year was to be no exception so I busied myself with preparations and the children got excited.

On the evening before the party, I got yet another maniac call from Sherif concerning the bakery. Perhaps he had just heard that I had been unsuccessful in getting the bakery changed to my name. This time I just sighed, holding the phone receiver slightly away from my ear while he ranted and raved. The gist was, that he was "going to destroy me", "make sure the bakery would be closed down," because if I "had no guests then I would have no customers" and so on. The latter reason was probably the truth behind the whole issue. The bakery continued to have customers and constant success while the hotel, Alf Leila, was struggling along with a few guests. Sherif didn't really know how to run a successful business and he was jealous.

"You know what?" I told him. "I've had enough of your disgusting antics. I don't care anymore. Do what you like. Just be sure that I will make sure the whole of Dahab knows what sort of pathetic creep you are! A thief and a bully and no one will want to do any business with you ever again. Now just fuck off and leave me alone." I hung up and decided that man wouldn't spoil one more day of my life. I wouldn't let him.

Of course in reality it affected me. I knew that legally I was still in limbo with an unratified contract and I hadn't yet found a new lawyer to take over the issue. I knew I couldn't honestly sell the business to Dirk if the contract wasn't legally filed to begin with.

At the party the following day, Natasha arrived with her daughter, behaving as usual like nothing was amiss. I had to take my hat off to her, she had the cheek and the confidence of the devil. It took all my self control not to mention anything in front of the other parents, about her obnoxious husband still trying to steal my business from me.

A week later, Katherine arrived from California and she was like a breath of fresh air in the whole foul situation. Initially when we had told James's parents of the situation concerning the accident, they had immediately offered help but we had declined. Gradually however it dawned on us, just how debilitated James was and how busy the Christmas bookings were, so we had agreed that any help would be appreciated. Katherine had immediately reorganised her life and holiday season around a two month visit to Egypt to help us.

Her suitcase was full of Christmas crafts and we sat down to make Christmas decorations and treats, just like she had with James when he was a child in Germany. It was so much fun to have new enthusiasm around the house. Katherine was an angel in disguise. Business was good and at the local Christmas market that year we sold huge amounts of gingerbread and cookies. With five guest houses full, our own house full of fun and laughter and with Omar as gardener, Carina with the children and Katherine helping out, we had a great team supporting us. James finally got to rest and recuperate.

The Accident

On Boxing Day, James got a call from the insurance company concerning the car. Being a predominantly Muslim country nothing closes down for Christmas and Coptic Christians celebrate in the first week of January. Apparently, it wasn't true that everything could be completed via email. The sale agreement to sell the scrapped Avanza back to them had to be signed by James in person. This time he insisted on going alone. I didn't argue when he said he would take the overnight bus to Cairo. He returned the following day to tell me the story of his adventures.

He had met with a translator early in the morning and discovered that he would have to go to a special office in the bustling and congested used car market area. He had made his way through the extremely crowded streets to get the office and upon arriving, no one wanted to prepare a contract because James was a foreigner and that could mean risk for Egyptian authorities. He ended up paying inordinate amounts in bribes (which he hadn't banked on) to get the paperwork completed, meaning he ended up without enough funds to pay the translator.

With money not forthcoming from the ATM, the translator thought James was duping him and they had a physical fight on the street with James hopping around on crutches. Like most Egyptians, the translator had no bank account where money could be transferred, which is when James called me to transfer money via a very efficient system within the Post Office.

In agony from his leg and frustrated by the banking system, James finally arrived at the insurance company office. There he signed all the papers and was told everything would be processed and the money for the smashed Avanza was to be paid out. By noon that same day he had boarded the bus to return to Dahab.

Success! He arrived back physically shattered but very proud that he had his independence back and could still deal with things himself. That trip was a turning point in his recovery and a lot of his "difficult patient" attitude disappeared.

I decided it was my turn to have a break, so I took the bus to Rocksea to spend time with my girlfriend Cada for three days before New Year. She was managing the camp alone. Cada picked me up at the bus station and we had a wonderful day under clear blue skies beside the beach, with the type of weather that makes winter in the Sinai so special. She remarked, "Hard to believe they are predicting rain for the day after tomorrow."

True to the forecast, clouds loomed over the granite peaks the following day, building a stormy atmosphere just like all those years earlier, when I had been diving with Papa. When it finally started pelting down at 7pm that evening, I watched my short vacation drown in the gushing water. I hired a taxi to return me to Dahab in case roads became impossible to use and I knew what sort of chaos would ensue because of the leaking buildings. Our team spent all night pushing water off roofs to ensure the buildings survived and the guests stayed happy and dry.

At the end of December, an email arrived from the insurance company telling us that there were unfortunately some items missing from the car, including the spare tire. They said they couldn't proceed with the claim at that point. I rolled my eyes. Did they think we were born yesterday? I immediately picked up the phone and mustered my most determined, confident voice, "I am sorry to hear that some items were missing by the time you inspected it. However, I assure you that all the items were there when it was delivered to Toyota, which, you will remember, was at your request! I personally checked everything was there before we left the car. I tell you again. Even when no staff were present at Toyota to receive the vehicle, despite Toyota assuring us there would be, our tow driver slept in the car so nothing could possibly be stolen! So if anything is missing from the vehicle now it must have been taken while stored at Toyota. I suggest you take the matter up with the Toyota dealership where it was stored." James listened in, grinning. Of course we hadn't thought to even check for the spare tire after all the hassle at Nakl. The insurance office believed me and the claim was back in process.

James and I spent New Year's Eve at Rush and I was so happy to have him by my side as my husband. We were looking forward to a new year of challenges together. We toasted each other, "Let's see what 2011 can throw at us!"

On the 3rd of January, we received another email from the insurance company, "Please confirm receipt of the money." What money? "No, we are sorry but there is no money in our account. Do you have a record of the bank deposit?" Eventually after a few more scanned signatures sent via email, everything came together and the money was deposited into our account. Finally! Also James's uncle had generously offered to make up the short fall from the insurance to help buy another new car and that money arrived the same day. Time to celebrate!

Mid January we went to Sharm' for an appointment to check on James's leg; he was told he should avoid walking on his leg for another month. After the appointment, we decided to check out the few car dealers based there. It was late afternoon when we made telephone calls, explaining what sort of car we were looking for and headed off in search of the car dealers in the back streets. There were never any showrooms or official car lots, so each dealer had three or four cars parked on the side of the road for sale.

At one stage we were picked up from an agreed meeting point in a parking lot by a shady looking character (who quite frankly, could have stepped straight out of a gangster movie) complete with a suit, dark glasses and slicked back hair. James and I looked at each other, suppressing giggles. Is buying a car in Egypt illegal? Our eyes popped even more as were driven down dirt roads in the fading light, to the car park of an abandoned hotel. There were actually many cars displayed and we found a Kia and a Renault that might have been suitable but still weren't exactly what we wanted. It became clear that we really wanted another Avanza and none were available in Sharm el Sheikh.

Despondent, we returned to Dahab to decide what else we should do to find a suitable car, preferably another Avanza. James had an idea, "Abdul always has good contacts in Cairo. I'll phone him." We will never know if that was true but we really did want another Avanza and we trusted Abdul. We agreed to buy it and the instructions were to send the total purchase price for the car immediately to secure the sale.

That threw us into a quandary. We didn't know the dealer, nor had we even seen a picture of the Avanza but we trusted Abdul. All night James and I tossed and turned. We decided we would pay 10,000 Egyptian pounds as a deposit on the car and pay the rest when the final sale took place.

We went to our bank to organise a transfer to the dealer's bank account but the bank assistant informed us that, as the account was with another bank and it was late Thursday with banks closed Friday and Saturday, the money wouldn't be deposited for at least three days. There were no branches for that bank in Dahab, the closest being in Sharm el Sheikh over an hour away. We didn't have enough time to drive to there before the banks closed.

Egyptians are so resourceful in dealing with situations like this and our bank officer managed to send it directly to another branch with the dealer's ID number attached. The dealer was able to collect it within the hour. With the intention of paying cash for the Avanza on Sunday in Cairo, we withdrew the remaining 110,000 Egyptian pounds and stuffed it into a small, unobtrusive looking back pack. One has to wonder exactly how much cash is carried around Egypt like this.

James and Omar boarded the bus to Cairo with the money in the backpack, paid cash for our new Avanza, completed the sale deal easily within an hour and were on their way back to Dahab in the Avanza by six o'clock that evening. James was so excited when he called to say how smoothly everything had gone.

He spoke too soon. They were stopped at the check point before the Suez tunnel and told they could not proceed. There was no number plate on the car as we wanted it to be registered in Nuweiba to avoid future administration problems. I had driven my Maruti from Cairo with no plates with and had never even been questioned at the ten or so check points I had to cross to get to Dahab. When James called to tell me of the hiccup, I laughed, "So a blonde foreigner can drive a car without number plates no problem, but a Saidi will get caught every time." Omar was of course driving. It took hours of debate and bribes, before they were issued with transition number plates and able to get back on the road to Dahab. We were all relieved to greet them at six in the morning.

Katherine and I were up and about as it was to be a busy day for us. We were travelling to El Tur to extend our visas. At one point on our journey I was stopped for "speeding". I knew that was a ridiculous charge as we were in my tiny Maruti which I never drove fast and we had been overtaken by many vehicles. I asked to see the photographic evidence and was told I could see it the following day in Sharm el Sheikh. But that I would have pay the 200 pound fine there and then before I could proceed. I wasn't the only car stopped for what I was sure were trumped up charges, but everybody had to pay and no one could do anything to stop it in corrupt Egypt.

Everything went smoothly at the immigration office. Katherine and I filled in time waiting for our passports to be stamped, by visiting Moses Pool hot spring and shopping for the best, inexpensive vegetables at the local market. On our return route to Dahab we collected Katherine's friend Molly from Sharm El Sheikh, who had arrived at the airport earlier that day to join Katherine for a short holiday.

Omar also left that day to return the vehicle plates to Suez. He was exhausted from driving overnight but said he would catch up his sleep while travelling and return on the next available bus. Little did he know it would actually be some days later. Massive thunder clouds again built up over the desert mountains, dropping a deluge that blocked roads and destroyed homes. We were again busy saving the rental houses while Omar was stuck on a bus waiting for the floods to recede and the road to be cleared. We also had a brand new Avanza parked under the palms trying to make sure it didn't get damaged in the hail storms!

James had to go to Nuweiba to register the new Avanza, so he took one of his best Bedouin friends, Yasser, to ensure things went smoothly. Yasser was one of those people you feel you can trust 100%, as he demonstrated nothing but honesty and Bedouin hospitality. He loved to share his life with anyone, whether in the desert and by the sea. James discovered it would take some weeks before the registration papers would be completed but, as he still couldn't drive anyway, he was happy to wait.

There was just one more vehicle hurdle to jump, which was to register my Maruti in my name. It was still in Sherif's name and I sure didn't trust him anymore! That was why he had demanded the keys to my car when he threw his fit about separating the hotel and bakery. He knew full well it was my car (bought and paid for with my personal money), but that the registration was in his name to avoid having to re-register it every year as foreigners have to (Egyptians only have to go through the time and money wasting process every two years). We had made the same arrangement with the Jeep I had bought previously.

So I went with Yasser to Nuweiba to jump through the required hoops to keep my little red Maruti on the road. It was a bizarre and comical ritual of handing over money at various counters, queuing at one desk after another, sometimes the same desk a number of times, and of course "paying off" officials, to make sure it would be completed in one day. Finally the head of police checked everything was ok including the existence of a fire extinguisher, first aid kit and emergency display triangles, that the lights worked, wheels turned, etc. His check was followed by a mad rush back to all of the counters to have everything finally signed off and receive the precious little car license cards, before the office closed. My Maruti was officially and legally mine!

At the end of January my parents arrived for a holiday, arranged so they could meet Katherine for the first time. Luna was recovering from chicken pox so we rallied around her, hoping she would be well enough to travel back to Germany with my parents. I planned to fly over in February to collect her and Tom. It was also Carina 's birthday and her contract as au pair was finishing, so we organised a marvellous evening in the mountains with a Bedouin dinner to celebrate.

James and I lay down next to the fire watching the young party. Somehow we were feeling our age as we criticised their antics. We were however, looking forward to more partying ourselves in the coming days. Our friends Sophia and Tyler were getting married at Castle Zaman, north of Nuweiba, and we were looking forward to it. I had been encouraging James's recovery by giving him a goal for that day; to stand beside me without crutches for the first time since the accident. He promised he would, even though he knew it would be hard to reach that goal.

Chapter 8

Revolution

The 25th of January, 2011, arrived as most January days do in Dahab, with the warming sun silhouetting Saudi Arabia, to reveal clear skies over sparkling water and the resilient ragged mountains of Sinai. January 25th was National Police Day, a national holiday, but that didn't affect Dahab much. The banks were closed but there were plenty of ATM machines available for those needing cash. It was a perfect day for Tyler and Sophia's wedding. We had known them both a long time; Tyler being a successful photographer who had met Sophia when she was working in scuba diving.

Our friends were to be married at Café Zaman, north past Nuweiba, which was renowned as one of the best restaurants in Sinai. The venue itself was spectacular, with handcrafted stone walls and archways, built like an ancient fortress overlooking the gorgeous Gulf of Aqaba coastline. The whole venue had been reserved for the wedding. It was to be quite an event.

I loved the chance to dress in something fashionable and James looked wonderful in his beautiful Italian suit. He stood beside me without crutches for the first time in three months. Only briefly mind you, but proof he was well on the mend. True to casual life in Sinai, some Dahabians had dressed up, others not at all, but everyone was determined to enjoy the festive occasion. James loved catching up with people he hadn't seen for more than ten years and there were animated conversations of days gone by.

The ceremony was beautiful and we partook of a rare feast of sumptuous food and drinks, surrounded by wonderful friends. After the food at Castle Zaman, the party moved south to the Nekl Inn on the Nuweiba beach front, where it continued early into the morning. Many of us stayed overnight at the resort. After a leisurely breakfast close to the beach, we drove back to Dahab to attend to our rental apartments.

The following day my parents were returning to Germany, taking Luna and Tom with them, so we had goodbye lunch at a beach restaurant. My father quietly took me aside and asked if I was aware of what was happening in Cairo. I looked at him quizzically and said, "No. Why, what's happening?"

"There are a lot of demonstrations in Cairo with thousands of people demonstrating on the streets. I have only briefly seen what is happening on the news, but it seems like they are asking President Mubarak to step down from leadership. There are police blockades and military everywhere."

"Really? I had no idea. As you can see, everything in Dahab is as normal. I've been too busy with the wedding and work to even bother catching up on news. I'm sure it isn't really a problem."

"Well with us leaving through Sharm el Sheikh today with the children I want you to stay in close contact."

"Sure Papa. I'm sure everything will be fine. No one else in Dahab has said anything." I was booked to fly a week later to go to Germany for a short break and then bring the children home.

My parents took a taxi with the children and Carina, who was also leaving Egypt. Katherine went as well, to stay a final night with Molly in Sharm el Sheikh, who was also returning to the United States the following day. By that evening the internet was down and we started to wonder just what was really happening in mainland Egypt. Television news channels were blocked, effectively cutting off most media, so it was only through gossip with Arabic speaking friends we got any information and we couldn't really trust any information anyway.

When Katherine returned from Sharm el Sheikh she was anxious about Molly, whose flight had departed Egypt via Cairo. The chaos at the airport had meant confusion and high security, so she had had to say a brief goodbye before even entering the airport. She had no idea if Molly actually made her flight to the United States or was delayed in Cairo. When Molly did eventually manage to contact us from California, she was excited and enthusiastic about how well she was treated by the Egyptian airport staff. She said they were so kind and helpful, making sure "the American lady" got on her flight via Frankfurt to the States. She had no problems.

Nothing was really out of place in Dahab but rumours were flying. Friends panicked, talking about evacuating. I however, with the children away in Germany, had no fears at all. There was no sign of any dissent but there seemed to be even less police than around than usual. Perhaps they had been called to Cairo? The banks remained closed after the national holiday and the ATM machines hadn't been topped up with funds, so getting cash began to become a problem.

We tried to find out more of what was happening in Cairo. We were aware of the thousands, if not millions, pouring into downtown Cairo and Tahrir Square, where the demonstrations were focused. Despite tear gas and bullets flying, the Egyptian people were defiant about staying on the streets in Cairo, demanding that Mubarak step down as President. Military forces appeared to be standing to one side, not interfering nor supporting security personnel. Egypt had never seen anything like it.

There were mixed messages about personal security. The Italian and United States embSaassies among a few others, were warning their people that they should prepare to evacuate and that there would be flights arranged from Sharm el Sheikh. There was no such warning from the German embassy. I began to wonder if bringing the children back to Egypt was going to be a sensible thing to do but then I told myself that nothing was wrong in Dahab, and all the tourists were still having an easy, relaxed time.

With our first wedding anniversary at the end of the month, we had planned a cocktail party at Villa Bohème. In previous weeks, James had asked some of our guests to bring bottles of duty free imported alcohol for the party, as they were almost impossible to purchase in Egypt and super expensive. With the help of Omar he had decorated the garden and it looked charming and festive. Some of our friends declined to venture out, pleading fears over what was happening in Cairo but the only problems that actually occurred, were massive hangovers from the amount of cocktails consumed. I'll never look another strawberry daiquiri in the face again!

It was strange to wake up to normal days in Dahab with clear skies and sunshine, before remembering that a few hundred kilometres away, a mass revolution was taking place with millions of demonstrators involved. Surreal, was the word for it. People were talking of food supply shortages. We joked that the Bedouin wouldn't survive without sugar in their tea, or flour for the bread they bake daily.

Revolution

On the first day of February, the internet was restored and our email was full of cancellations. Up until that point the occupancy of our rental properties had averaged at almost 75%, which was great considering it was winter and low season. We had been doing fine financially. We had been so busy in fact, there had been little time to think about our future plans to move to the United States. That all changed with the revolution.

With the children away and with dwindling guests to care for, I had time for long chats with Katherine about what living in the States might mean. "Why don't you come to the States with me and see how it feels for you? Travel around a bit, get a feeling for the different places." She suggested.

"Yes, seems like now might be a good time. Especially as all the bookings for the near future have cancelled. But that also means we have no income we can rely on and I don't want to start eating into our savings. Who knows when we will need those?"

"Yes, I understand," agreed Katherine.

"And what about the children? I can't leave them in Germany with my parents and I wouldn't feel happy sending them back to Egypt without me. We don't have the funds for them to travel to the States as well." I felt frustrated.

"Don't worry about that. We can help you and pay for the children's tickets to the States. It will be good for you to see how they would adjust to life in the States. Ella, I don't know how you have managed all this all the time here. Dahab is a beautiful place for sure, but with the children and running businesses, it seems so difficult. Time to look for a new life," Katherine encouraged.

"Wow. That is very generous of you. Maybe you are right. Turn a negative into a positive. Up until now I have had no spare time to even contemplate going to the States again. Let's see what James thinks."

Later when I discussed Katherine's offer with James, he agreed it would be a good time for me to fly to California. He said with his increasing mobility and Omar as his right hand man, he would be able to handle any bookings, in the unlikely eventuality that any came in. Omar could move into the house with him. All our ducks were lining up in a row.

The only loose end was Leila's Bakery. Dirk had returned from Germany, so was continuing with his plans to purchase Leila's. However I still wasn't in a position to sell the business openly and honestly, as the ownership papers were not yet in my name. I had retrieved all the papers from the expensive but ineffective Egyptian-German lawyer and delivered them to Hamza in Dahab. Hamza had already given me good advice over the split with Sherif. I hoped I would have more success with him, as I handed over power of attorney to him.

I decided since I was going to be away and wouldn't be able to keep overseeing management of the bakery, I needed a loyal Egyptian working there. I decided to offer Mohamed a partnership in my share. I trusted him and he was quite capable of baking and managing the place alone. Under the circumstances, I couldn't be sure Dirk wouldn't just up and leave again. Mohamed was very happy with the arrangement, beaming when I paid him his first percentage of profits from the bakery.

Katherine contacted her travel agent, arranging for the children and I to fly with her from Frankfurt to California. On the 3rd of February, I left Dahab for Germany in a sombre mood, not really knowing when James and I would see each other again. Egypt was in turmoil with Mubarak still refusing to concede to the will of the Egyptian people. I felt terrible boarding that flight to Germany, with so many things uncertain.

I hadn't been away from Egypt for one day when the telephone rang. It was Dirk. He was complaining about the situation at Leila's asking, why did I "give everything to Mohamed", there were "no customers" and so on. I explained that I had made Mohamed a partner for valid reasons, to ensure the bakery could run without either Dirk or myself, especially considering the uncertainty in Egypt. I asked Dirk why he saw everything in such a bad light. After all, with Mohamed as manager, he too was then free to do what was best for his family and leave Egypt if he wanted to.

But Dirk wouldn't listen to my advice. He kept calling me daily to complain about the situation. I told him, "Calm down! It hasn't even been two weeks and the situation will resolve itself. Stop panicking!" I kept asking myself, 'Why should I let these men drive me crazy?' It was enough on its own to know that I could still lose everything I had invested into those businesses in Egypt. I had lost money on the Alf Leila Hotel and I could now lose the bakery and the rental properties, depending on the results of the revolution.

At the same time that all of this was going on, Luna turned seven and we had wonderful birthday party for her at my parents place. On February 10th, we watched the scenes of Tahrir Square in Cairo on television, as we listened with bated breath to President Mubarak's televised speech. It turned out to be an anti climax and we wondered what Katherine would have to report, when we collected her from the airport later that evening.

She said everything was super quiet in Dahab with no sign of any unrest, everyone just waiting to see what would happen in Cairo. There was the foreboding fear that the military would step in and fighting would begin in earnest, but up until that point the soldiers were being viewed as heroes for standing by the ordinary citizens.

Tom in the meantime had developed chicken pox, which wasn't surprising since Luna had it some weeks earlier in Egypt. He was feeling miserable, so I settled him down in front of the television. I was flicking through *Kinder Kanal* for children's programs or cartoons, when I caught scenes of Egyptian jubilation on the television. Mubarak had stepped down to the people's demands! The scenes from Tahrir Square showed a cheering populace, ecstatic with happiness and hopes for a true democracy.

I called James to see how things were in Dahab but he said there were just a few young men riding around the back of pick-ups, with Egyptian flags flying, horns tooting constantly and jubilant faces. I was so happy for them too but knew my journey was now taking me thousands of kilometres away from Sinai's Dahab.

I mulled over the fact that I was facing the loss of most of the value of my Egyptian investments, as no one could be sure how the revolution was going to affect the Egyptian economy and especially in the case of South Sinai. I also had no idea how we were going to get any start-up capital, to invest in any business in the United States.

My parents were not at all thrilled that we were considering going to live in the United States. As far as they were concerned,

Europe (particularly Germany) could offer us far better opportunities. Katherine, the pillar of strength that she was, assured them that James's side of the family would offer all the support they could, making sure we had somewhere to live and helping to give us a new start. I felt unsure of what we were doing more than any other time in my life, but I also felt I had strong family supporting me. Paramount to considerations, were the children's education and the possibilities for new businesses or employment.

On Valentine's Day 2011, we boarded our flight to San Francisco. The flight was uneventful but on arrival, our luggage was nowhere to be seen. The delay to find it meant we missed our connecting flight to Los Angeles, where Ken was waiting for us. It was a very tired group that finally climbed in the car, to drive to Katherine and John's mountain home in Crestline.

With a combination of stress and jet lag, I found myself awake most of the night worrying about the future. Kurt had also been in contact asking, "So what are your plans? What are you going to do? Where are you going to live?" I had no answers for him. For the first time in my adult life I felt completely adrift, relying on others for daily life and not having any clear idea of how to proceed. All I knew was, that we had the idea of moving to James's home country and finding a way of living.

Katherine and I discussed how we might register Luna for school and I asked her, "But how can Luna go to school here? She is only here on a tourist visa."

Katherine just smiled and said, "There are hundreds of Mexican children here without any visa at all and they manage to enrol so don't worry about that." Over the previous years Katherine had fostered many children and enrolled them in the local school, so she knew the principal and all the teachers very well. "It will be no problem for Luna to attend school in Crestline for a few months," they assured me.

Crestline was again a winter wonderland and so damn cold. It was a few days before we saw the shining sun and went out for walk to explore the village and forest. We didn't have a lot of winter clothes of our own, so again had to delve into Katherine's stock of ski suits for all sizes.

There are quaint log cabins and pole houses supported on long wooden foundations, to cope with steep sloping sections. Katherine showed me Molly's holiday home a few doors away from theirs, where we could live for free until we got established. It was a beautiful alpine village, where everything was built to cope with snow and rain (which isn't what most image of the California climate). That particular winter it snowed often, sometimes up to half a meter in one snow storm. When it wasn't snowing, it was often raining. I found the roads perilous and I thought that alpine climate would never suit me. I was now so used to the blue skies and glorious weather of Dahab, that I doubted I would be happy living without my daily dose of sunshine.

James called with more bad news. He had been back to the doctor for a check-up and been told his shoulder wasn't healing well. It would require surgery which was estimated to cost 4,000 US dollars. At that moment we didn't have that amount nor were we likely to earn it over the following months.

Luna was examined by a Doctor and been given extra

vaccinations as required. Within four days of landing in the States Luna was able to go to school. She was so excited but awoke before her first day with a headache and promptly vomited her breakfast. "I'm fine Mama. I still want to go to school." It was a pretty walk up through the forest to the storybook school, the Valley of Enchantment School. Everyone was so friendly and interested in the new blonde girl, who had come all the way from Egypt. By then Luna spoke German, English and Arabic fluently.

She was also able to attend a Boys and Girls Club, where the children have extended after-school activities. It was a relief that everything was for free in the US system, (including books) so Luna was taken care of. Tom on the other hand, felt very frustrated. He was used to going to Habiba to play with other children when Luna was at school but in Crestline, the preschool care was very expensive and out of the question. I spent a lot of time just playing with him to keep him happy and occupied.

Molly came to visit and she was still so enthusiastic and impressed by her holiday in Egypt. She couldn't speak highly enough of how friendly and helpful everyone had been to make sure she got home safely. Her enthusiasm was infectious but I wasn't ready to forgive all the difficulties I had encountered in my life there. I wondered if I ever would.

I looked into possibilities for suitable work and discovered that the Los Angeles Fashion Week would take place in March, mentally making plans to attend. Perhaps I would make contact with a potential employer or glean more ideas? I also found jobs available as personal shoppers and thought that maybe I could do that. Because of the beauty and novelty of Crestline's alpine beauty, Katherine and Ken often offered their home for holiday accommodation just like we did in Dahab. With guests arriving for the weekend, we had to clean and prepare the house. There I was on familiar ground.

With no home for the weekend we drove to Rancho Mirage in the desert, where Katherine had booked a room for us all at the Hilton. She went swimming and played with the children, while I lay snuggled in bed replenishing my energy. Katherine was my angel. By the evening it was raining cats and dogs as we splashed our way to the restaurant for dinner.

"Let's go to Denny's!" suggested Katherine next morning.

"What's Denny's?" asked Luna.

"A restaurant where we can eat breakfast." Katherine was enjoying showing the children a slice of American life.

"I'm going to have chocolate chip pancakes with bacon!" chose Luna.

"I'm hungry!" said Tom. "I want a pizza and a chocolate milkshake."

"Pizza for breakfast, Tom?"

"Yep. Pizza for breakfast!" Needless to say Luna and Tom loved it.

I felt constantly chilled to the bone. The desert in California was very different to that of Dahab, despite the well tended palms dotted everywhere and I hadn't spent so much time in a cold winter, for a very long time. With a perfect blue sky after the downpour from the previous night, I could see clearly across the desert landscape, to breath taking, snow covered mountains.

Katherine took us on a treasure hunt through second hand stores and garage sales in stylish homes, set in beautiful gardens.

She was searching for Toy Story characters for a cake she had made. I itched to buy some of the lovely inexpensive items but with no confirmed future shadowing my thoughts, curbed my buyer's impulse. Everywhere we went I was looking for inspiration. I kept asking myself questions, Could I see us living here? What could we do? Would I like it? Would James like it? Would the children like it? But nothing grabbed me and answered, "Yes!" I was looking for a clearer picture.

We met more of James's family members at a soccer game where his niece was playing and the children joined us back at the Hilton to splash in the heated pool. We also met up with Molly for lunch in the desert countryside, again so different from Sinai with rough rolling hills covered with rocks and stones. Luna and Tom played with children from Molly's extended family, as we all enjoyed a pleasant afternoon before driving back to Crestline.

I logged onto the internet and found more complaining emails from Dirk. Dahab and those problems seemed so far away but I still had to deal with them, not that I had any new ideas for Leila's Bakery. I got the feeling that Dirk was just moaning for the sake of it. I shut down the computer and pushed Dahab out of my mind.

Luna loved going to school, Tom found new games and things to play with and we settled into feeling as if we had a slightly normal life. Even just baking lasagne at home with the children, was a treasured moment. With my need to be creative I started to knit like crazy, creating one sweater after another, keeping my hands busy and my body warm. I missed talking and working with James but he was managing his injuries and our problems back in Dahab. I knew Omar would be taking good care of him. We were so lucky to have such loyal Egyptian staff in our lives.

The following weeks developed into some sort of routine. We would live in Crestline with Ken and Katherine during the week. Then if Ken's and Katherine's house was rented, spend weekends in the desert with other extended family or move into Molly's mountain cabin. Moving around was no problem, we lived out of suit cases anyway.

One weekend James's aunt invited us to Long Beach to see the sights there. She booked us into a wonderful place and even arranged gifts for Luna and Tom on our arrival. We spent the day with her at her beautiful beach home, where the children had fun flying kites on the constant sea breezes. The area was stunning with views over the Pacific Ocean but everywhere was so populated. The expensive homes clustered and crowded the beachfront, jammed against each other on exorbitantly priced land. Again I asked myself the questions and got a "No" in return.

Another weekend, we visited James' Uncle Jim who lived at Santa Ynez, behind Santa Barbara. The landscape reminded me of Tuscany, with its rolling hills covered by vineyards and wineries. Art owned a ranch there with a comfortable house overlooking the wide valley.

By then it was the end of March, so the spring weather was warm and inviting. I felt myself involuntarily take a deep breath of fresh air and suddenly I was at ease. I let myself dream and yes, I felt we could live there and be happy. As if Jim had read my thoughts, he offered us a small house he had on the ranch, to live in, for free! We could even work for him to make a start, a place we could rejuvenate. Thank you, Universe for delivering!

Not long after that, I got a call from James. He was tired and stressed and needed me back in Dahab to help with the bookings for the rental properties, to discuss the possibilities for his much needed surgery, and to deal with Dirk and his manoeuvres for Leila's Bakery. As for the latter, the negative emails were relentless. That man sure knew how to complain! Our time in California was drawing to an end.

Luna loved her days at the Valley of Enchantment School and the Boys and Girls club. "Why doesn't Luna stay here with us to finish her school year?" Katherine suggested. I must have looked startled, so Katherine continued, "Since you want to come and live here anyway it makes sense for her to complete the year, as then Luna will be eligible for the American Home School Program."

With thoughts of leaving my baby girl I could only manage a, "Oh really?"

"She could continue the program in Dahab until you move here and she won't have any catching up to do."

"That certainly makes sense." The reality of actually planning to leave Dahab was still a dream to me.

"She could stay with us until the end of June. You know having her here is no problem for me. I'm used to fostering children and Luna is a grandchild to me now. I would love to have her here."

It made sense in so many ways. I agreed that Luna would stay when Tom and I flew back home. To make sure Luna didn't miss us too much I gathered a stash of small gifts for her, wrapped up (like a personal Advent calendar) to be opened each day, containing little things like a bar of chocolate, a scented bubble bath or a small toy.

Before I left, I also started my application for a Green Card. The reality was slowly sinking in that California would be the goal for our future. It was with a heavy heart that I boarded the plane, firstly because I was leaving Luna there, and secondly because I could now see a light beaming out from the United States West Coast, like a harbour entrance in a stormy sea. I wanted to keep seeing that shining beam when I was back in Dahab, back in the turmoil of business troubles and occasional chaos.

James was there to greet us with wide open arms and a big smile, at Sharm el Sheikh. I had so missed our life together. It was a relief to see him walking again without crutches. Not perfectly but certainly well on the mend.

As I drove through those strange and wonderful mountains to Dahab, I was reminded of the first monthly visits I had made there. Back then everything had held such promise and enchantment. The mountains still had their beauty and their charm but life in Dahab was sullied by the lies, cheating and the exhausting difficulties of Egyptian life. I wondered then, with Mubarak deposed and in jail, if the Egyptian people would truly be able to choose their own leader. I hoped so.

While in the United States I had access to many news channels and watched the euphoria and excitement for the people in Cairo, as they realized they had toppled a leader who was essentially a dictator of a corrupt, bullying regime. However, whenever I spoke with James he said there had been little reaction in Dahab other than some buildings being rapidly and roughly constructed on empty sections. That included a section next to Leila's Bakery where there was an ugly concrete construction underway.

James and I discussed what was happening with Dirk at Leila's bakery and we scheduled a meeting with him. The sight of James was like presenting a red cloth to a bull for Dirk, so Hamza (who was now acting as my advisor) accompanied me. My friend Sophia was working for Dirk in managing and marketing, so she came too.

I knew that there had been a downturn in tourist numbers in the weeks immediately following the revolution but by May, life in Egypt was settling down and tourists were returning. We had steady bookings again for our rental properties. Dirk however, was continuing to run another small bakery under his name some 500 metres away from Leila's. To open the discussion I asked, "Dirk, what do you really want for Leila's Bakery? What problems do you really have? What makes you so unhappy?"

Dirk explained, "You know the business is still very bad. I'm still not making any money."

"Well I understand it was difficult in February and March but they are always quiet months anyway. Business is picking up again in Dahab."

He insisted, "Well, the bakery is losing money."

"In that case, is it wise to open extra bakery branches in your name with extra rents and staff? You are actually using Leila's to bake for your own bakery."

He ignored that logic, "I want a 40% reduction in rent immediately." I was at a loss for words. He continued, "And I want to replace the name of Leila's Bakery with Dirk's Bakery, so it is in my name. I'm doing all the work for it."

The gall of the man! He knew that I had just returned from California and that James and I were planning to move there in the future. He thought he could just nail me to the floor and walk all over me! It was daylight robbery of my bakery and not for the first time; I wondered how some people could sleep at night.

As I sat at that table I decided that no matter what I did, he would continue to look for any way he could to break his contract. I shook my head, "I can't accept those terms. I would be losing everything I have struggled to build and to keep."

"Well unless you do, I will leave anyway," he threatened.

"Fine then. If that is what you want." He looked a little shocked that I could let the contract fall through but neither was he prepared to budge from his unreasonable demands. "You can finish at the end of June. Two months from now."

Over the coming weeks, Dirk started to behave as if we were going through a marriage break up instead of ending a business arrangement ... at his request! From that meeting on, he refused to speak face to face with me. Any communication between us in that tiny town, had to be through Sophia or via email.

I then had two months to plan the redevelopment of Leila's. As is my nature, I wanted something new for the bakery, believing that "The only constant is change." As I no longer had to think about running a hotel and James and I shared running the rental apartments along with Omar, I had more time to devote to the project.

I had already considered what I might do with the spare room at the back of the bakery, renovated at Dirk's request. I decided to make chocolates and sell ice cream. An ice cream counter would need to be placed outside beside the bakery entrance, so a sheltering wall would have to be built too. Handily, that would also mean that I didn't have to see anyone entering Alf Leila Hotel, as Sherif was still a thorn in my side.

We removed the cactus garden (which was at that point, the

only barrier between the two entrances) and built a framed bamboo matting fence to serve our purposes. Of course, this wasn't to Sherif's specifications, so despite the wall being built entirely on my property, he immediately started to make a fuss. He dismantled it as soon as we left for the day.

When I returned with James to assess the damage, Dirk came bolting out of the bakery bellowing like a bull at James, "You can't come here! You're banned from the bakery!" I never really got to the bottom of Dirk's behaviour towards James. I suspect it related to some years earlier, when James had worked at the bakery and then, as the friend he was to me, James had warned he felt there was some cheating going on. Nothing was ever proven but Dirk had fired James.

Literally on the other side, I was arguing with Sherif's hotel manager, "I can build a fence on my property as I see fit. Sherif will just have to get used to it. It was built entirely on my section and hasn't anything to do with Alf Leila. Sherif had no right to remove it." I have no idea what that scene must have looked like to an impartial observer but now in my minds' eye, I just shake my head and agree with the "Dahab Mental Hospital" label that some have cheekily labelled the small town.

We rebuilt the fence and that evening I settled down at the neighbour's seating area, to wait for the fireworks that were sure to start when Sherif returned. When he appeared some hours later, he didn't see us sitting in the shadows. He ranted and raved to his manager, "This is my property!", "How can she just build this without permission?"

I stood up and asked Sherif, "What is your problem? The fence is built entirely on my property and I need it for wind shelter."

Sherif seemed a little mollified at his tirade in front of the neighbour, who was well aware of all the difficulties I had gone through with Sherif. He backtracked by saying that he thought the bamboo fence was ugly and I should have at least spoken with him about erecting "a more attractive wooden fence". I told Sherif he was welcome to do that but the bamboo fence was to stay until such a time that it could be replaced ... at his cost.

On the other hand, I decided to offer one last olive branch to Dirk. It seemed crazy to me to change the name of the business, with Leila's Bakery already so well established. Especially as he wanted to continue living in Dahab with the bakeries and I was planning to leave in a relatively short time. I sent him an email, in an effort to get through to him somehow:

Hi Dirk,
I feel very strange about our disagreement over the bakery so I'm writing this to you with an open mind. I feel that it's important that we can look each other in the eye and at the moment, this doesn't seem to be the case.
Please try to read this to the end without freaking out. I do not want, nor have ever wanted bad blood between us. Ask Sophia to continue reading if you can't. It seems to me that men destroy and make war... so take a breath... this is my white flag!
I ask you take some time to think, be honest to yourself and to pretend like nothing happened last month. Ask yourself, what do you really want? I get the feeling that since February you haven't wanted to continue running Leila's Bakery. Since then, you have wanted to get rid of me even though we had an existing contract and you have been searching for an excuse. The problem Sherif created in December wasn't the beginning of the issue and you had been searching for new premises even prior to that. You also said my husband was a reason but the argument at the meeting was six days before James came to help me with the fence. You had already decided you wanted to leave and never told me of any of your plans. It is all a shame really

because you're successful here at my bakery and you want to stay while I'm tired here and want to leave. It is very sad that we lose our way like this in the end.

However, I think sometimes it's better to stop and turn around than continue to run in the same direction. My goal is to move to California with my husband and my children and I wish to settle everything here, so that I can go. Since February, I have the feeling that this would no longer be possible with you leasing from me, which is strange after all these years. Are you going to open your bakery at the Lighthouse on July 1st? Do you regret your decision or are you satisfied?

I actually don't want to take back Leila's Bakery unless I'm forced to. I felt at our meeting that I had no choice, as your demands were too high. So how about if we can agree to meet somewhere in the middle and you can call everything Dirk's German Bakery? I would use the back room of the bakery to produce something different or simply use it as storage for some of my things.

However, if you really want to leave, you should do so, and we should stop arguing and clear the air to stop all this controversy. It appears to me now that you are not sure and that you are feeling forced out, whereas when we had our meeting at the beginning of the month, you were sure you wanted to leave. If you need more time to think, we should discuss that too.

Maybe we can think of a way to remain partners at Leila's Bakery. Perhaps you get selling space and I sell your products along side my chocolates and ice cream. Or you continue in the location if you wish and pay no rent but we make a suppliers contract. I won't bake bread, you will have a bakery somewhere else and Leila's Bakery can become a café, very different from your store.

I have no idea where to proceed from here but I think we should talk so we are doing the right thing for both of us. You love your bakery and I love mine. Whatever I do will be with joy or not at all. Decide what you wish now but unfortunately I can't agree to 40% less rent and change the name without receiving something in return. If I agreed to that I would feel that you have just taken the bakery away from me.

Again. I want to leave and I do not wish you any ill feeling, so let us find a solution. I have no interest in parting in anger and please do not put James in the middle. He and I have been together over two and a half years and we made a new contract during this time. If we find a solution, it should be possible that you can find one too. I feel there is something else behind you both bickering and it gets on my nerves.

So how what do you think? Now that I have shared my thoughts, I'm waiting to hear yours.

All the best,

Ella

I sent off the email as my white flag but I had no idea if or how Dirk would respond. At least I felt better.

At the end of May, James and I travelled to Cairo for him to have surgery on his collarbone. That hospital experience was so different to those in Suez and Ismalia. Everything went smoothly and according to plan, and with spectacular views over the ancient Pyramids, we could even pretend we were tourists on holiday. Egypt, the land of contrasts.

A couple of days after James's surgery I decided to renew my visa at the infamous Mogamma government offices. As soon as I entered the notorious building I knew I'd made a mistake. The place was crammed full of people, many looking confused and running in all directions, while others cooked food at stalls or served ubiquitous *shai-* sweet black tea. The whole place appeared to be in total chaos and I'm sure it is the same every day. It seemed a miracle I found the right window for a visa, or that I even got to the front of the queue.

"Where are your passport photos?" demanded the clerk abruptly.

"Oh. We haven't needed those lately when applying in El Tur…"

I trailed off.

"Well, you need them here. Passport photos for you and your son. Next!"

Tom was back in Dahab with Omar and his Saidi friends; no way to get a photo of him. Then I had a brain wave; I duly got our current passport photos photographed and printed out.

After waiting a further five hours and enquiring ten or more times as to what was happening, I decided I needed something to eat before I fainted. I returned to the chaos, to find my passport ready with a visa, if not only valid for six months as opposed to the year I normally got when applying in El Tur.

We spent the following week in an apartment set up for us by a friend, Noah, waiting for the all clear from the surgeon. With James feeling so well we managed to update the car insurance and had some social time for going to the cinema and doing some shopping.

Dirk had replied to my email while we were in Cairo; he would still be leaving Leila's Bakery on the 30th of June, so another era was about to end. Despite him being the one reneging on the contract, he informed me that the final two months rent would be deducted from the bond he had paid and also demanded that I pay him 14,000 Egyptian pounds for the renovation he had wanted to extend the bakery (the very one I had been dubious about and had wanted to make sure was covered in our contract). He threatened that the keys to the bakery wouldn't be returned unless I paid him the money he was asking for. Hamza, my adviser, told me the tenant always has the upper hand and unless I got the keys back, I could do nothing. Like many things in Egypt, the contract was hardly worth the paper it was printed on.

Dirk refused to let me talk to any of the staff on the bakery premises. One day Mohamed came to me in private, "Ella, I would like to stay at Leila's, baking and working for you. I don't want to work for Dirk." I was very happy to know this but Dirk was furious. He complained, "But I taught him everything he knows! If it wasn't for me he wouldn't be a baker!" It was true that Dirk had taught him, while both were being employed by me.

I had already made contact with a company in Sharm el Sheikh for the supply and display of Italian style ice cream. I asked for everything to be delivered on the 1st of July. I also wanted to make chocolates and continue with the baked goods I thought most popular. I realized that Dirk had been setting this up for many months so there wasn't anything left to negotiate. For me, life is just too short for such petty behaviour. I was soon to be reminded of just how true that is.

On the morning of June the 10th, we got a frantic call from Noah, our Egyptian American friend, who had organised the apartment for us in Cairo. He was at that moment standing in the apartment of another American friend, Samantha, whom he was working for on a part time basis in Real Estate. When he hadn't been able to contact her for three days by phone or visits to her Mubarak apartment, he became very concerned and contacted the police. They had decided to break and enter her apartment where they found Samantha had died in her bed.

Noah was distraught over her death, but also over the police who were rummaging through her belongings wanting to know where the key to her safe was. He was rightfully appalled and phoned anybody he could think of who might come to the apartment to protect Samantha's property. James, as a fellow American, was one of those people. So we went together and a few other friends turned up as well.

It was a dreadfully tragic scene. By the smell of decay Samantha had obviously been dead for some days. Eventually, with so many bystanders, the police reluctantly started to do their job properly and arranged for Samantha's body to be removed to the hospital morgue and the apartment was locked up.

The police interrogated Noah like he was a murderer and that Samantha's death was his fault. With an Egyptian father and American mother, Noah spoke both Arabic and English fluently so he would have been the perfect person for any mediation or translating that needed to be done. The police weren't interested. Noah was forced to go to the police station to give a statement and James decided to go with him. They harassed Noah all night before releasing him the following morning, minus his confiscated American passport. It was a shame he was treated so badly considering he lost both a friend and his job with Samantha's death.

Meanwhile, I phoned around to find contacts for Samantha's family in the United States. I also phoned the American embassy expressing my concern that the police might take Samantha's personal belongings and to ask them to contact Samantha's family. Samantha had an Egyptian ex husband who had continued to support her with alimony but he too was in the United States on business, so there was no one in Egypt at the time to arrange for a funeral or attend to her estate.

By late evening, when I had heard no news from the embassy I decided to call Samantha's sister to make sure she had been informed of her death. She already knew but appreciated our call and said she definitely wanted Samantha's body to be buried in the States. She said she would find someone who could fly to Dahab and handle everything.

As for Noah, three days later his passport still hadn't been returned to him and he was still under suspicion for murder. We decided to accompany him back to the police station to help him. As Egyptian police seem to operate mainly at night, there is no point trying to get much done before 10pm, when the police chief arrives at work. We were told the 'judge' from Nuweiba hadn't yet arrived so we would have to wait and drink tea. By 1am I gave up and went home, James arrived back about 2.30am. Noah finally called us in the morning saying he had his passport back.

I had time to reflect on Samantha's death and my problems paled into insignificance. I was lucky in so many ways with my wonderful children and husband, supportive family and felt sad about the manner of her death. Samantha had been larger than life, a statuesque almost brash woman, unafraid of speaking her mind with a loud, happy manner. She had seemed to lead a happy but relatively solitary life in a harsh land, where she had died alone, no one even aware of her death for some days. Always be grateful, I told myself.

Noah contacted a lawyer friend of Samantha's, Farid, who had handled her real estate deals, so he could manage the winding up of her estate. We learnt via email that Ashley, Samantha's niece, would be travelling to Egypt to attend personally to Samantha's estate. She would first visit the Egyptian family of Samantha's ex husband in Cairo then travel to Dahab but we didn't have an exact arrival time. We offered accommodation free of charge in Atelier Bohème, so she would have a comfortable private place to stay.

A few days later, we were expecting Ashley's call but heard nothing. We called Farid and were surprised to learn that he had picked her up from Sharm el Sheikh the previous evening and taken her his friend's camp. "This is very strange," James looked puzzled. "Why would she choose a cheap, public camp?"

"And why hasn't she called us? She seemed to be happy that we would meet her here."

"We had better go to the camp and find her."

We found Ashley sitting alone, distraught and confused. Farid had told her she must not leave the camp or talk to anyone. Flying to Egypt was Ashley's first time traveling far from America and she had no idea about exploring foreign lands. She had asked Farid many times to call us because we were waiting for her but he had ignored her requests.

"Come with us Ashley. Let's get you out of here. How do you feel about a drink?" asked James.

"Whew! I would love that. I've been sitting here like a scared rabbit, not even daring to venture out. Is it safe?"

I didn't know whether to laugh or cry. Dahab was a safe place by any standards, although I too remembered my first worries about walking around places strange to western eyes. Some men take advantage of naivety to bully and create fear. "It is absolutely safe. You will see for yourself why Samantha chose to live in Dahab."

We led her along the alleyway to the busy promenade, which she could see was full of tourists of all nationalities. We wandered past the shops and restaurants to a bar by the sea and Ashley visibly relaxed in front of our eyes. "A beer never tasted better." She let out a relieved sigh.

Farid tracked us down. "Ah Ashley. Nice that you have met up with your friends." I held back from sneering as he furtively joined our little group. Farid did well to hide any annoyance that we had rescued his victim, from whatever plans he had in mind.

"The funeral will be tomorrow," he quickly informed Ashley. "Tomorrow morning actually, in El Tur." We all looked shocked. We knew it was agreed by that time, that Samantha would be buried in Egypt as the cost of flying a corpse back to the United States was exorbitantly expensive but we all expected a few days notice for the funeral. El Tur was some hours travel away from Dahab on the Gulf of Suez and was apparently the only place a Christian could be officially buried.

"Oh! So little time," I said. "We'll have to call people, Samantha's friends. Now! To let them know as soon as possible as they may want to attend the funeral." After many phone calls it seemed that no one could attend at such short notice.

"Well, I'll definitely go," said James. "Ashley will need support and I have no intention of leaving her alone with that shark," referring to Farid.

And so it was that Farid, Ashley and James drove to El Tur the following morning in convoy with another vehicle carrying Samantha's body. James described the journey when he returned.

"What a nightmare! Ashley must wonder if she has come to hell on earth".

"When we arrived at the Coptic cemetery she looked totally bewildered. She asked, 'Is this it?' It is just a walled section of the desert with rough rocks to mark the graves, similar to those in Dahab for Muslims. If there had been horses instead of cars we could have been in a Wild West movie. I could hear the theme to *The Good, The Bad and Ugly* playing in my head. I think Samantha would have howled with laughter, but it didn't feel very funny. It was bizarre."

Diana's Grave

"The grave was already dug with sand slipping down the sides. I wondered if the coffin would fit. Some guy we didn't know started to drone on and would you believe it? The undertaker pulled out a can of air freshener! He sprayed it around as we stood in stunned silence. He even lifted the coffin lid and sprayed some inside. Samantha was laid to rest in the fumes of fake apple blossom! Ashley was in shock and quite out of her mind. It was quite a day."

We'd made sure Ashley was comfortable at Atelier Bohème before James accompanied the police and Farid to Samantha's apartment. The apartment had been locked up since they had discovered Samantha's dead body.

The apartment was then locked again and James was handed a key to give to Ashley. As they were leaving, they met a man in the stairwell. He politely introduced himself in well spoken English and explained that having heard about Samantha's death, he was interested in buying the apartment. Farid immediately quoted the man a very cheap price and James frowned. What were Farid's motives now? I called around some friends with apartments in the complex and they all told me it was worth much more. We couldn't figure out what he was up to, but no doubt all would be revealed.

Farid called Ashley that evening. "You must come to my office, now. There is a man who wants to buy the apartment. We need to make a sale contract. This will be best for you, to have it sold with no trouble."

She had just buried her favourite aunt and that creep of a lawyer was trying to bully her into selling the apartment for a low price. She refused, "No, no! This is all too fast. I haven't even seen the apartment yet. I will look at it tomorrow and then make a decision." Farid continued his whining but after such a hellish day Ashley told him all she wanted to do was rest. Her confidence was returning and she wasn't about to be bullied by some weasel of a lawyer.

Ashley told us of the call over a meal together in the early evening. After eating we left her resting at Atelier and drove to the apartment to clean it up, before she would view it the following day.

We both gagged and pulled our sleeves over our noses as soon as we opened the door. The stench hit us like a punch in the face. The apartment had been closed since they removed Samantha's body and nothing had been cleared out. James mustered his strength to deal with the bedroom while I opened every window, cleaned and cleared out rubbish. After some hours of scrubbing with disinfectant the apartment was somewhat presentable. As I sprayed the last air freshener James let out a sad sigh, "Poor Samantha to go with such lack of dignity. May she now rest in peace."

Next morning we again went to the apartment, this time with Ashley and a friend of Samantha's. Ashley was distraught. It was too much to be dealing with Samantha's death, the abysmal funeral, the cheating lawyer and then to see where Samantha had lived and died. Those of us living in Dahab had long ago accepted basic living conditions but to a novice visitor, the crumbling buildings must have looked only fit for squatting. She sobbed and cried in grief, trying to choose what mementos she should keep of her aunt. What remained, would go to the second hand shop. She had been told by Farid that the apartment should be emptied that day.

James's phone rang. It was the well spoken man telling him that he was still interested in purchasing the apartment but he had since been approached by Samantha's caretaker-come-driver, claiming he owned all the furniture and he required a commission from the proposed sale. These people were just ghouls! The potential buyer who was of Swedish Egyptian parentage, wanted to clarify with whom he should be negotiating. James told him Ashley was now the owner and she would be in touch.

We scheduled a meeting later that day for Ashley, Noah, Farid and the prospective owner, with me tagging along for support. The sale went well and both Ashley and the new owner were satisfied with the reasonable price, more than was suggested by Farid. We were still wondering why he had quoted such a low price.

However, then came the discussion of how much Farid was owed for his services. The supposed caretaker friend was also hanging around for his commission and "his" furniture. Farid presented a huge account for taxi rides, preparing papers, arranging the funeral plus one thousand US dollars per day for his time. Strange that the amount he was asking for was remarkably similar to the amount he had quoted for the sale of the apartment. Maybe that had been his game; a quick sale of the cheap apartment equal to the cost of his services and if it hadn't sold, maybe he was hoping Ashley would just give him the apartment for his 'efforts'.

By this time I was furious at their antics and angry that they were just out to exploit Samantha's death. I told Farid he was essentially a liar and a cheat. We knew that the funeral had been paid for by an old friend of Samantha's; but when offering condolences to Ashley he told her he had taken care of the funeral costs. Farid looked only slightly embarrassed at being caught out but continued to be offended that he had to accept a much lower amount. Noah got a commission as Samantha's real estate partner and the caretaker got nothing.

Farid was still smug enough to tell us that it would be impossible for Ashley to access Samantha's bank accounts without him. I was glad James wasn't there at that point, as I was sure he would have smacked him in the jaw, regardless of a recently operated collarbone. I told Ashley, "Don't worry. Just gather all the papers. We will manage it with the bank."

The following morning Ashley and I went to the bank, which happened to be the same one that I had used for many years. I had actually been their very first customer when their Dahab branch opened and prior to that I had banked with them in Sharm el Sheikh. They knew me well and it didn't take long before Ashley could access what money there was in Samantha's accounts.

Then we could all relax and pay our proper respects to the Samantha. I was happy that Ashley got to spend a few quiet days in Dahab, seeing and experiencing the life that her aunt had led there. Forcing me to focus on someone else's problems had helped to remind me that life isn't easy for anybody. In Samantha's case, even her death created issues others had to deal with.

After saying good-bye to Ashley, I once again went back to real life, with all of its ups and downs. And finally, on the last day of June, Luna returned to Dahab. My wonderful, tiny girl had flown all the way from Los Angeles to Sharm el Sheikh all by herself! I had missed her so much. I knew I would take over managing Leila's the next day but that was the last thing on my mind. It felt so great to be able to hug her again.

I was still also sorting out Leila's bakery and preparing to wrap things up before Dirk left. I still had to communicate to him via Sophia, so told her I was offering Dirk 10,000 Egyptian pounds towards the renovation. It was time to move on from negative attitudes and arguments.

Dirk's day to move out came soon enough. When I arrived I saw that he had baked overnight and they were still removing things when I got there. When I stepped into the kitchen I was shocked to see they had removed practically everything, leaving only the major items that had been itemised on the contract. I stared in disbelief at the bare kitchen.

When Sophia came later to take the money, I stalled, telling her I had to check everything first. "You can see for yourself there is practically nothing left. You know, when Dirk first took over the bakery, I provided a working business right down to crockery and cutlery, not to mention all the staff. He has left me with nothing. I want to check against the original contract. You will have to come back later."

She returned later carrying a crate of small items, plates and knives which didn't amount to much. I was sure Dirk knew he had taken more than he was entitled to but I just wanted to move on from all the bad energy. I gave Sophia the 10,000 pounds and it was done.

Leila's was finally mine again but as I took stock, I realised how much was missing and also how much of what was left was actually damaged. Even the oven was broken with parts missing. There was no way I could reopen for business the following morning, with what Dirk had left me.

I also discovered the whole place was crawling with cockroaches. There were hundreds breeding under the fridge, with baby cockroaches creeping through the warped door seals. They were even creeping out of the light sockets and other tiny cracks. I was horrified. No wonder Dirk had refused to let me see inside the kitchen. He actually came the following day in person to try to bully me for the outstanding four thousand pounds but I refused to pay it. He spat at me and left. 'Good bye and good riddance!', I thought.

I figured that I couldn't produce any food in that kitchen for at least a month. I immediately called the ice cream supplier in Sharm and delayed the delivery of the ice cream display counter. I sent the oven and fridges off to Cairo for repair and set about fumigating the whole place. Every night for weeks we sprayed for cockroaches and every morning we found more corpses to clear. Finally there were none left, so we set about sealing off every orifice we could find.

I also discovered that the last two electricity accounts remained unpaid. Electricity accounts were one of many difficult things to deal with in Egypt, changing them into a tenants name was out of the question, so my name was on the account. I knew there was no way Dirk would accept responsibility for them. So that was another few thousand I was out of pocket. I had been well and truly ripped off but at least he was out of my hair and I didn't have to listen to his complaining any more.

Chapter 9

Rebuilding Leila's

Over the next weeks we worked on Leila's every day to continue fumigating and renovating. I have always tried to be positive and look forwards in my life and all my energy went into revamping Leila's. I was already moving on in my mind from the fights I had been having with Dirk and Sherif. Over the weeks, every inch of the bakery was cleaned, scrubbed and redecorated.

Everything was moving along, although we had promised our friends at Rocksea in Nuweiba, that we would manage their camp while they took a break in Europe. We didn't want to let them down as they were so looking forward to their holiday. From the end of July, James and I took turns to travel to Rocksea to look after the camp. We would stay there for changeovers at the weekends, then one of us would return to Dahab to oversee Leila's.

All Together at Rocksea

Tom at Rocksea, Flying a Kite

After four weeks, Leila's ovens and refrigerators returned from being repaired in Cairo and nothing crawled anymore in the kitchen. While in Nuweiba, I experimented with sourdough bread and we designed a new menu. I rearranged delivery of the ice cream counter and planned to have it displayed just outside Leila's front entrance. I was pleased with how it was all coming together.

On the day before our official reopening I walked outside to see water splashing onto the ice cream counter. "What the...?", I frowned while looking up. Sherif had decided to rearrange the condensation hose from an upstairs air conditioning unit so that the dripping hose would splash onto our ice cream counter. Unbelievable!

Alf Leila Bakery

It was the holy month of Ramadan and he was sitting upstairs with some of his friends, enjoying the evening meal to break his fast. I asked him, "Why are you doing this? Don't you ever give up with your negative behaviour?"

"And why do you build ugly walls?" he retorted.

"Well beauty is in the eye of the beholder. I don't see my wall, which is effective for sheltering my courtyard, as ugly. You have built a useless expensive wall on my area, so I still had to make sure my area is sheltered! You must like wasting money."

Sherif had rebuilt another wooden wall completely on my side of the front entrance. Built like a trellis with spaces so wide, the predominant wind howled through it and it offered no shelter to my either my terrace or the ice cream counter. I had reattached the bamboo as a windbreak on Leila's side of the wall.

Sherif continued berating me for the fence, then started hurling insults at James, "Fuck you, you fucking American who has been fucking every woman in town...", screaming abuse out over the road. We refused to stoop to his level and just replied, "Ramadan Kareem," as we walked inside the bakery.

After a few more minutes of Sherif's tirade, I went next door to see Sherif's manager (with whom I could still communicate) and told him if Sherif didn't stop his bad behaviour, I would call the police. Their involvement couldn't make the scene any worse in my view. The manager did convince him to stop and had the condensation pipe moved it away to prevent it from splashing onto our ice cream counter.

Omar at Leila's Bakery

An uneasy truce was again declared. "Would these guys ever stop?" I asked myself. "No," was the obvious answer. In September, Dirk decided to stop by on his motorbike and insult Leila's guests who were eating breakfast in the garden. He harangued them with, "What are you doing eating here? The food at my bakery is much better," implying they should only eat in his bakery further down the road. Heaven knows what our customers actually thought of him but James was furious. It was all just too much to take on the chin any longer, as there were also vicious rumours flying around that I had kicked Dirk out without discussion, among other slanderous gossip.

James wrote an explanation of what had been happening, concerning the changes of contract and how we hadn't wanted any of these problems or gossip. He felt Dirk had had it all his own way with stories and gossip and it was time for some revelations and our side of the story. This was James's way of showing there was more than one version to the story.

James learned the hard way that most people are not really interested in the truth or even capable of discerning that there are two sides to a story and found himself being ridiculed for even trying. Remarks and comments made on social media were rude and insulting and most of the time, completely untrue. It seemed like everyone had an opinion yet hardly anybody even bothered to read James's explanation. Someone even suggested that we had stolen recipes from Dirk, a ridiculous idea given that everything had been passed on to him. How does that saying go? "Never explain and never complain. Your enemies won't listen and your friends already understand."

The most vigorous and demoralising reaction was from Kurt. The children were staying with him for a month and James and I decided to take a short holiday in Rome before we became busy at Christmas. On the day of our departure Kurt called and told me, "Are you completely crazy? Are you insane? How could you think that distributing a letter like that would make any difference? That people are interested?" Out of everyone, Kurt knew just how much

I had tried to make peace with both Sherif and Dirk, by changing as much as possible to keep them happy. Yet they were the ones who still weren't happy and hated the fact I was successful and had a positive life.

Kurt continued by telling me that James would no longer be welcome at Rush, that he was banned. Seriously? Banned from the nightclub where he had previously been a partner and where Kurt was now manager? I personally couldn't care less if I never stepped foot back in the place but to ban James who socialised there three times a week, was vindictive and purely personal. I asked him why he always sided with the men who were opposing me but I didn't really expect a reasonable answer. Kurt always had that attitude, that the other men were always right.

It just so happened that the actual owner of Rush walked into Leila's just minutes after my conversation with Kurt and when I told him what he'd said, he just laughed and said, "Don't take Kurt's threats seriously. James is an old friend since a long time ago and there is no way he is banned. I'm the owner and I will decide that."

Later that day, James and I drove to Cairo to fly to Rome, where we arrived early in the morning at Antonio's house. Antonio (being the successful fashion designer he is) was still in Riyadh attending to the whims of Saudi princesses, so we had the place to ourselves for the first few days. I was back on relatively familiar ground from my student days but Rome was new to James and I intended to enjoy playing my tour guide role again.

On Saturday afternoon we were taking in the sights at the Forum Romanum, when we noticed streets were being blocked off and there was a heavy police presence. We wanted to move on to the Colosseum but it was impossible to get past the police block. We were told a huge demonstration would be passing through and there would be no way to get past, so we decided to hang around for a while and see what was happening. It was a huge, peaceful demonstration about economic inequality in Europe. Apparently there were nearly a quarter of a million people protesting that day. At the beginning it was orderly but the police wouldn't allow citizens to join from the sidewalk.

As we decided to make our way home, the police kept closing streets forcing us to move further away from Antonio's house. At Santa Maria Maggiore we finally pushed through and everything looked peaceful again, as we strolled higher to Emmanuelle Philiberto where people were partying and celebrating on the in cafes and on the street. However as we rounded the corner into Viale Manzoni we stepped straight into a full blown riot, with smoke billowing along the street and whiffs of tear gas making it difficult to breathe. There were helicopters hovering overhead and people were running to escape, screaming in fear. This action was literally on our doorstep so we held hands as we sidled along the pavement and into the calm of Antonio's house. It was a surreal experience.

Later we watched on television as the peaceful demonstration had degenerated into a riot, with burning cars, smashed windows and many people were wounded. We sat incredulous to think we had left supposedly dangerous Sinai to find ourselves living in the middle of a revolution of sorts in Italy. The next day as we walked the streets, we saw the damage with our own eyes, thankful and unbelieving that no one had died.

We hired a small convertible and set off to visit friends and explore beautiful Tuscany for three days, cruising through Florence, Sienna and the autumn countryside. It was magical with James at my side, sharing glorious food and sampling wonderful wine.

When we returned to Rome, Antonio was back, entertaining us with his stories from the world of fashion and anecdotes of Saudi Princesses' behaviour. It was a world that I had once been so familiar with, yet it seemed a world away from my life in Dahab. We enjoyed our last days shopping and sightseeing in Rome, before packing our by then bulging luggage to return via Cairo.

Back in Dahab, the daily grind began again and the children returned to live with us after their month with Kurt. Luna started another private school in the hope that we could get her to focus and learn. I had initially started the home schooling from the American system that she was enrolled in, but our relationship was difficult and she paid little attention to my efforts. Kurt had tried too but had no better success, so we enrolled her with a German teacher at a private school where they would continue to follow the American system as closely as possible. We hoped for more concentrated behaviour from Luna at that small school.

We began working back at Leila's in earnest and everything had settled back into a relatively normal routine for the whole family. I had my new ideas to develop for the bakery, one of which was cakes decorated for special occasions. The previous year when Katherine had been staying with us, she had taught me the rudiments of working with fondant. I was looking forward to creating again.

With not even Sherif causing any problems, I dared to hope that we could have a quiet few months to build up the business and maybe sell it. Not to mention a few quiet peaceful months before we would finally leave Dahab for a new life in the United States of America. At that point we had the bakery, my Villa Bohème and the new addition of Atelier Bohème and James's rental Palm Beach Villa apartments. We had already given up previous holiday rentals as demand for them lessened.

We decided to see if we could sell the lease on Palm Beach Villa, as it bookings were a concern, as was helping Abdul to have a continuous income. However, we didn't manage to find many interested parties. The only serious inquirer was Madison, a foreigner married to an Egyptian hotel manager who was renting one of the Palm Beach apartments for six months. She had expressed interest in taking over both Palm Beach apartments, so we gave her a list of improvements and investments we had made which she could purchase to continue as a business. She kept stalling and wouldn't commit and her six month rental contract ended, so we stopped promoting the Palm Beach apartments.

At the end of November, we informed Salma, Abdul's wife, that we would be giving up the lease of Palm Beach Villas at the end of January. We told her we had been trying to find someone interested in taking over the lease to continue in a similar arrangement but had found no one. I asked Salma how they would like to handle the return of the bond of 5,000 Egyptian pounds. It was relatively normal in Egypt to actually use the bond as the final rent payment, as it's very difficult to get landlords to actually repay any cash. She told me she didn't know about that and she would have to ask Abdul.

The ubiquitous Dahab rumour mill started grumbling, as James heard from friends of Abdul, that he apparently, owed Abdul money. This was supposedly regarding the 500 Egyptian pound reduction per month that Abdul had allowed James, to compensate for the improvements James paid for when remodelling the apartments (back when James and I had begun our relationship). Abdul apparently now said that James owed him back rent ... of which nothing had been mentioned during four years!

For sure, the property on the beach front was valuable, but when James had first moved in, it wasn't maintained and not useful for tourist rentals, with broken and unattractive decor and furniture. By the time we were leaving, it had been greatly improved and was a sought after, prime property.

James was devastated that his long term friend was behaving as if James had cheated him. He was on the same emotional roller coaster that I had ridden, learning that someone he considered a close confidante, was capable of behaving so badly. Abdul then refused to speak directly to James, sending messages via his various friends. I knew exactly how James was feeling. After all these years of being so close, helping us when we had the car accident (especially James with his injuries) and organising summer holidays so we could stay next door to Abdul and his family. It was as if he hated us but maybe he just had a bad conscience and didn't want to deal with James directly.

Although James was hurt inside, he quickly realised that we had to start thinking ahead to all the things they might try enforce on us and how we could salvage as much as possible from the situation, before it was stolen from beneath our feet. Madison had moved out and we had holiday bookings in both apartments over Christmas, so we hoped everything would run smoothly until at least January.

Our minds were now in two places, the present in Dahab, Egypt and the future in California, USA. On the 6th of December, we all flew to Germany to meet up with James's relatives who were on a cruise along the Danube River. His wealthy uncle had chartered an entire boat to where the cruise ended in Nuremberg. James's family had offered to carry some luggage back to the States for us and his parents travelled back to Kaiserslautern to meet up with my parents and discuss our move to California. It was so reassuring that both of our families were in agreement about our future move and willing to help us as much as possible.

When we returned to Dahab, Madison approached us again about her concerns in relation to taking over Palm Beach Villas. I told her that I had to be honest and couldn't recommend she actually do that, because Abdul was no longer behaving in an honest and open manner. I advised her that she should carefully consider what dealings she would have with him in the future. I also told her that I had stopped marketing the Villas from the end of November, as we had no future in them beyond the end of January.

When I relayed this to James he was sceptical about her motives. He said, "She has no intention of taking over Palm Beach from us. She was just "fishing" to see what you would say. She is probably already dealing with Abdul behind our backs." James usually has great instinct for these sorts of things, honed after years of travel and living in the Middle East.

When the last booked guests left after New Year, we started to quietly remove all our furniture and decoration from the two apartments. Then, as luck would have it we received a booking for Villa Two and Abdul relayed that he had prospective tenants who would like to view Villa One. We had to turn around and sneak everything back in to the apartments again. It was almost comical and a little exciting to be playing our game, to beat them at their game.

On the 20th January, Madison told us that her Egyptian husband had contacted Abdul and they had arranged a new contract to take over Palm Beach as it was, just as we suspected. She said that we could get our 5,000 Egyptian pounds deposit back and she would take over the business. We doubted very much that we would get any money back, so I just told her it was too late for that as we had to hand the keys back at the end of January anyway.

The following day a friend of Abdul's called to let us know he would arrive to Dahab two days later on the 23rd January to "wrap everything up". We told him we had guests until the 25th and besides that, our rent was paid until the 31st of January so we would finish everything then.

We knew our plan was running out of time, so that night we made furtive trips back and forth to remove as many of our belongings as possible from the uninhabited apartment. Whatever would fit in our car was packed in, until there was hardly any room to drive in it. I also arranged for a man to come and remove our air conditioning unit the following day too, as well as an open pick-up truck for the larger pieces of furniture. Our Bedouin friend, Yasser, came to collect a cabinet we had given to him. Just as Yasser was leaving, Abdul's Bedouin friend, Ibrahim, entered the front garden as the last of the furniture was being loaded into the truck. He told me to stop what we were doing and accused me of stealing Abdul's property, "How can you just take Abdul's things like this? You are a thief!"

I stood my ground and told Yasser to drive off with the furniture despite the tense situation. I also called the police and said they should come straight away to the beach front. The air conditioning man stopped what he was doing and quietly disappeared, as more and more of Ibrahim's Bedouin friends arrived and started to hassle me.

I let out a quiet sigh when the police finally arrived. I was determined the group were not going to force me to leave but they certainly weren't being friendly. I explained to the police that I was only moving *our* belongings and showed them that in fact, Abdul's furniture was still in the apartment. I agreed I would stop removing our things until Abdul arrived, so long as the Bedouin consented to not disturb our guests in the other apartment.

As we drove away I remarked, "You know what? I'll bet that Abdul even tries to claim that our Avanza is his car!" By now I was getting to know how these people operated. Sure enough within a couple of hours, Mohamed, another friend of Abdul's, called to threaten us that Abdul would cause problems over the ownership of our car. Abdul mistakenly believed that James had used an invalid driver's license to register the Avanza. It wasn't the case of course, we didn't owe him any explanation but it confirmed just how low Abdul was prepared to stoop. Mohamed also told us our guests had to move out of the apartment immediately, despite our paid up lease not expiring for another week.

Of course we couldn't trust anyone to do what they had agreed to do in front of the police, so I went to find our guests who had just finished diving and took them initially to our trusted friend, Yasser. We all returned to Palm Beach to find the Bedouin group had broken down the door into the other Villa and were milling about in the garden and the beach front, essentially spoiling for a fight. Fortunately, I had taken the guests to the property so they could collect their luggage and I also tried to remove our towels, bed linen, pictures and other household items. I knew it would most likely be the last chance to take what was rightfully ours.

The Bedouin abused me verbally and I hurled it right back, accusing them of not adhering to the Koran and helping Abdul steal these things from us. It was a tense situation but I was angry enough to stand up to all of them. They were already labelling me as a "crazy white women" and I wasn't unhappy to play the part. When they started to demand I give them the keys I refused, saying I would only give them to Abdul as he was the owner, then we left.

James and I discussed the situation and decided the best form of defence was attack. Not literally of course, but we decided it was best if we went to the police station that night to lay a complaint against Abdul. He was most likely about to do the same against us and it was best to have our side of the story reported first. Abdul was well known in the community so we would be on the back foot defending ourselves. We already knew the hard way, that anything could be twisted and turned in Egypt. We rehearsed our claim, gathering what evidence we could. Fortuitously, James had photographed all his renovations in progress, so there was a record of all the improvements he had made. Just before ten at night we made our way to the police station in Medina.

The officers politely listened to our claim taking down our report. When we opened the laptop to corroborate our claim with photographs and videos, they seemed very surprised and attentive to our situation. I asked them what would happen from there and they assured me that "everything would be fine", that I "should not be worried" and that "Abdul couldn't harm us". I quietly rolled my eyes, wondering how true that would prove to be.

Late afternoon on the following day we received a call from Abdul's friend, demanding that we immediately return the keys to the apartments. I just told him I would come later, that I was in a meeting. "Besides," I said, "they have already broken into the apartments so what do you need keys for? And our contract still has another week so they are breaking the law."

Yasser decided he would make a last attempt at mediation. He returned to us with the demand that, "Ella should apologise for all the evil things she said before anything can go any further." My eyebrows raised in mock surprise, "Really? Seriously? This is the demand from someone who has called me an asshole hundreds of times on the phone? The answer to that is, 'I don't think so'."

We decided to return to the police station, this time with a lawyer. We end up waiting for hours in the now familiar, grimy building with policemen constantly coming and going. After explaining our story again to three different officers (repeatedly showing each of them our photo documentation) someone finally decided that Abdul would have to come in to explain his side of the story. Abdul was summoned to the police station which must have been somewhat embarrassing, as he knew many of the officers personally. He greeted them like old friends, shaking hands, slapping shoulders in hugs, kissing cheeks. Where we were concerned however, he was prepared for a fight and remained stubborn, refusing to accept our claim for our belongings that remained in the apartments. He didn't want to give in, under any circumstances.

We were tired and fed up with whole situation but were just as adamant that we wanted our belongings, including two expensive air conditioners. We were prepared to give up the 5,000 Egyptian pounds security deposit, as we knew the likelihood of getting cash returned would been more difficult than getting blood from a stone. Abdul wouldn't even accept that deal so we agreed that we would let the court in Nuweiba decide. Both parties would have to prepare written statements and travel to Nuweiba for the following morning's court session.

James had had enough! He threw himself on the ground, kneeling in front of Abdul and kissing his feet. Everybody's mouths gaped wide open and their eyes popped out at the sight of James on the floor, myself included. James pleaded, "Abdul, I hereby thank you with my life! You helped me so much when we had the car accident. But that does not mean you can try to rip me off as much as you like." Abdul was flustered but didn't know how to react as he sat there with what may have been a look of repulsion on his face. I grabbed James aside to have a quiet discussion. I suggested maybe we should just accept one air conditioner and be done with the whole debacle. James agreed so we put it to Abdul – one air conditioner returned and he could keep the rest. Abdul still refused!

So at eight the following morning, all the parties met at the police station in preparation to travel to Nuweiba for the court session. Just as we preparing to leave, at the 'eleventh hour' Abdul decided he would accept our offer; we could have one air conditioner. Our final demand was that they should deliver it to our house. So within one hour of us returning home the debacle and any relationship were both finished, including an important friendship of some years. Just sad, no winners.

James and I looked at each other in relief but also with some trepidation. It wasn't a comfortable feeling knowing that we had just won a small battle against an influential enemy. The police said that he could no longer do us any harm but we weren't prepared to trust their word for it. "Let's go to Rocksea for a few days. We were ready to go to Nuweiba anyway," I suggested. "Great idea!" agreed James so we disappeared for a few days to let the dust settle over the gossip that would be sure to be flying around Dahab.

We mulled over another end of what we thought was a good relationship, with a person we had trusted as a friend in Egypt. We had never in a million years expected that from someone who had literally lived next door at times and with whom we had fun summer holidays. We were fairly sure that Madison (and especially her husband), had their hands in the game and they quietly took over the holiday rentals, along with what was left of our interior decoration and remaining air conditioner.

It was the however, the motivation we needed to continue planning our exodus from Egypt. We couldn't be sure that America would indeed be our promised land but we knew that our years in Sinai were coming to an end. We advertised our things for sale and made tough decisions about what to keep and what had to go.

What to do with our dog was a constant worry. There was no way we were going to abandon him to Dahab's streets as some people resorted to in the end. Eventually, a friend in Ras Abu Galum offered to give him a new home and I was so relieved.

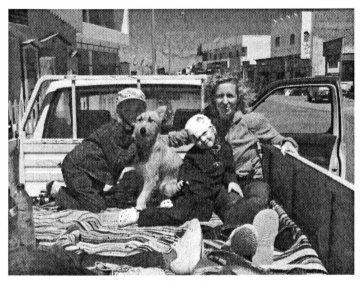

Us and our Dog

I suggested to my friends that we do a final camel trek up the coast as we had often done with our guests. At first they agreed to the idea but as the day approached, they all pulled out preferring to spend their day in Dahab for various reasons. It was left to me to go with the children and our Bedouin friend, Yasser

We left Dahab by pickup at about 8 o'clock in the morning, to drive to the Blue Hole where we were to join the Bedouins waiting with their camels. We tumbled out of the vehicle and the children scrambled on to the couched camels. The children had nothing to fear from riding camels as they had ridden so many times before. Two Bedouin boys were handling the camels and for sure they had been working with camels their whole lives. It isn't an uncommon sight, to see tiny toddlers grabbing the camels and bossing them around even though the boys hardly reached the camels' knees.

Yasser drove to park the pickup back at the south end as was required. I was happy to walk with our dog, so with just the two Bedouin boys in attendance, we started off up the steep track towards the tiny Bedouin settlement of Ras Abu Galum.

The first part of the track climbs up over a steep promontory before dropping down again to the water's edge, a trek which usually takes just over an hour at an easy pace. As we started to descend the steep zig zag, I went ahead with our dog to make sure we were out of the camels' way. I could see over the track edge to the swirling water fifty metres below. I remembered when I first came to Dahab there had been no guiding wall along that edge and it made my stomach lurch to remember a story of a camel falling over to its death. I called to the dog to stay close to me.

Suddenly I heard loose stones flying as one of the camels behind me stumbled down the track. It was Tom's camel and I was shocked to see him clinging onto the wooden saddle horn. One of the boys had given the camel a slap on its rump to keep it moving but it had reacted by taking off down the steep slope. A fast moving camel throws a lot of energy through its body and tiny Tom was being thrown about on top like a rag doll! Everything happened in slow motion in front of my terrified eyes, as adrenalin pulsed through me. I raced back toward the bouncing camel with my arms up trying to slow it down.

Tom held on for dear life but I could see he was losing his grip as I launched myself towards him. Too late! Tom flew in a high arc towards the boulders and stones that lined the track. In horror and panic, I reached him a split second too late. He landed head first and lay in a crumpled heap slumped on the ground. He was alive, but it wasn't seconds before blood began to seep from his head.

He started to babble in three languages while he lay limp and moaning in my arms. It seemed his entire skull was cut open and I didn't know how to stop the blood flow. The Bedouin boys just looked on in horror unsure of what to do either. Yasser had almost caught up with us by the time the camel had bolted and rushed down the slope. He quickly gathered Tom in his arms and we scrambled back up the steep track back towards the Blue Hole. It seemed like adrenalin gave us power, as it wasn't minutes before we arrived back at the pick-up.

Tom's wound was still bleeding profusely as head wounds are apt to do. We clambered into the pickup with our now very excited dog on the deck in the back. There was no way he would stay there alone and we had no rope to tie him up, so he too was squashed into the front. There wasn't much room for two adults, two children and a dog in an area designed for two people maximum. Yasser still managed to change gears and drive efficiently for the twenty minutes it took to return to Dahab.

We unloaded Luna with the dog at home then rushed on to our saviour, Dr Rumi, at his clinic. I had called him while en route and he arrived at the clinic within five minutes of us. Hospitals were able to take emergencies but care was unreliable and erratic, so it was better to just deal directly with a local doctor first.

Dr Rumi was an oasis of calm as he administered medication to sedate Tom and prepared to attend to the still bleeding wound. All the while Tom was screaming and I came very close to fainting as it took some time to shave the hair around the long wound and clean the area. It's a sound no mother wants to hear from her child. Dr Rumi skilfully managed to apply stitches but by the time he had finished, so was I, both physically and mentally.

It wasn't until some hours later that we got to go home. By then Tom seemed totally normal but the rest of us were completely exhausted. Delivery of our dog would have to happen another day. We had planned my birthday celebration at our favourite Tarboush House, so dragged ourselves along to keep the date but none of us were in any mood to party. It was a rather tired, sad affair when I celebrated my last birthday in Dahab.

Dr Rumi recommended that I watch Tom constantly through the night and wake him regularly to make sure he wasn't drifting off into a concussion while sleeping. Dr Rumi was relatively sure there was no skull fracture but waking him was a necessary check for the first few hours. Tom made it through the night fine and literally bounced back the following day like any healthy child. So much for the our lovely last camel trip!

By April, we had sold most of our furniture and household items and lived on call. It was a bonus that we were still in Dahab to enjoy a fun and well organised Dahab Festival. The children had a great time taking part in their last Circ Bonboni performances.

We enjoyed the countdown until we would finally leave Sinai, ticking off the final sales and finding homes for pets. Work at Leila's had settled down and we were happy with the loyal staff being able to run the place without us. However, there were still a few crazy situations to deal with. No surprises there!

Directly after the revolution, many buildings were erected in Dahab without papers or control. One of these was directly to the west of Alf Leila, blocking off any view of the beautiful mountains with its ugly concrete walls. It had been built while I was away exploring the United States, in spite of Sherif having papers to say we had originally owned that corner section with a building permit. Up until that time, with the help of the government and police, we had been able destroy any attempt to put up walls and build on that section.

With Alf Leila no longer being any concern of mine, my real Estate friend, Hamza, had negotiated with the Bedouin builder that so long as the wall facing Leila's was finished to a good standard and painted well, there would be no problems from me. We made the most of the situation, creating a shaded, private garden for guests to sit in.

Sherif however wasn't at all happy, as the two storey building blocked off the west view of the setting sun over the mountains. The same view we had looked over from the balcony during the Dahab bombing several years earlier. In May, military troops arrived in Dahab to attempt to bring law and order back to the illegal building situation and Sherif drew hope as the whole area was cordoned off with one hundred and fifty soldiers and a hundred police on stand by, so the bulldozers could start demolition.

In opposition, a group of Bedouin were occupying the building as well as the land, so there was shouting and heated discussion. Suddenly the bulldozers stopped work, but not before some of the structure had been destroyed. The situation was very tense as spectators wondered what would happen. The Bedouin owner produced a piece of paper showing he was the legal owner with title to the land. It must have been a shock to Sherif that he had been outplayed at his own game.

I had a good relationship with the Bedouin owner and I continued to develop Leila's garden into a cosy, sheltered place. He had even helped me when Dirk was abusing my guests and staff, so there had been few problems over the previous year after that. Nonetheless, one day Mohamed called me to report that the neighbours had built a wall between their building and my fence. He was probably happy to stir up problems. Upon investigation, I discovered a freshly cemented, badly finished wall was being built on my property. It reached up higher than my fence and was very ugly. "Stop building this wall! Now!" I said.

No one responded in the slightest. I was so incensed that I didn't say one more word and started to kick the wall down with my feet. That finally produced some action as many people swarmed to the properties. It always astounds me how quickly men mobilise to any sign of physical fighting. Like flies to crap.

There was a lot of noise (or '*dousha*') but the final discussion came down to the Bedouin owner and our friend Yasser. We had signed the ownership of the bakery over to Yasser sometime before, to avoid the possibility of Sherif trying to steal it from me as there were difficulties concerning foreign ownership. That was the first time anybody else became aware of this change of ownership. With Bedouin negotiating with Bedouin, it became a matter for much discussion and resulted in the agreement that they could build a wall to a height of three feet on our border.

It was hardly a month later, one evening during the festival when we were returning some gear to the bakery, that Luna noticed they were once again rebuilding the wall. The workers were working at night, to rebuild a six foot wall against the fish restaurant. I was furious! This time I didn't bother with words, just picked up the bricks and started throwing them. James came to help, despite being dressed in dressy white clothes from the festival event. There was much yelling from the workers and Bedouin who had been sitting at the neighbour's coffee shop. Again it wasn't minutes before other young men arrive spoiling for a fight and began to hit James with sticks. Our staff and others on our side, were trying to stop the whole debacle as the police turned up and the crowd scattered.

The two Bedouin owners finally arrived too and everything calmed down again. No one wanted to press any charges with the police who went away somewhat disappointed that they hadn't anything further to do. With the battle lines well and truly drawn, the building of the wall stopped and it remained at three feet high.

Luna

Chapter 10

New Beginnings

It took months to gather everything together for our Green Card applications so that we could apply for permanent residency in the United States. Bureaucracy is the same all over the world; unwieldy, time consuming and so nonsensical in many respects. As if one good original idea, gets bounced around in the dirt gathering all sorts of unnecessary layers of manipulation. But the power is in the paper pushers' hands and it has to be done. My Egyptian training at least left me well qualified for that.

Luckily James's cousin was an immigration lawyer in the States, who was able to tell me exactly what I needed to do. One thing about applying for a Green Card, is that if you apply when you are in the States you have to stay there until a decision is made. If you apply from outside the country, you cannot enter the USA until you have the card. In or out, you wait.

Another requirement was to request papers from the police authorities of all the countries I had lived in (to prove I had no criminal records in those countries), including Germany, Italy and Egypt. I contacted my Egyptian lawyer, and asked him to help me deal with it. I had always lived in Egypt with legal visas, but never permanent residence. Most foreigners in Egypt do the same, unless they are married to Egyptians. It meant applying for a visa every year but the process was relatively simple. But that was one of the reasons I was applying for the Green Card from Germany and not Egypt. As my American lawyer pointed out, the US immigration service wouldn't understand how that was possible.

My Egyptian lawyer said I would have to go to Cairo. He also said that I should make sure I was fully covered with a *hijab*; scarf and arms, legs. In other words, dress like a Muslim Egyptian woman. There wasn't a huge risk he said, but we would have to through some heavily guarded areas to get to the offices and it would just make life easier. I was all for that.

He was right about the guarded areas. There were military personnel everywhere; troop carriers, guns and it looked like lock down, even though the revolution had been well over a year before. It wasn't that pleasant but strange how quickly one adapts to seeing soldiers and police with guns loitering about. After a few questions, they just let us go about our business to access the offices I needed. Of course, once it was explained what I needed, there were some extra unofficial fees to be paid. I was well used to that. Bribery in hand, I had the piece of paper I needed.

The requests from the US often came without warning. I had just left Italy from our short holiday when I learnt I needed Italian papers, so I decided to try via the Italian Embassy in Cairo while I was there. The staff there just shrugged their shoulders, telling me they had no clue what I needed. It was pretty obvious they had no intention of finding out either. In the end I called an Italian friend and asked for their help. I gave her power of attorney in Italy so she could apply on my behalf for the papers. Obtaining the German papers was relatively straight forward, thankfully!

Well before the end of 2012, I had gathered everything and sent off my Green Card application. The processing of the application should usually take six to nine months maximum, so by the beginning of 2012 we were expecting some notification from the immigration office in Germany. There wasn't anything more we could do, but wait.

By April, we had sold most of our possessions and decided that we may as well give up the rent on our beloved house in the palms and move into Villa Bohème. That forced us to really take stock of what was left and decide what we should take and leave at Villa Bohème. What remained could be left in Villa Bohème or given away. I even started a social media page called, "Gifts and Wishes" so people could find homes for stuff that they wanted to give away. Moving house made me feel so nostalgic but it was good to clear out baggage, both physical and mental. The school year finished in Egypt in May, so we decided that we would fly to Germany by the middle of June anyway. Flights were getting more expensive by the day as European summer holidays approached and there was no point hanging around in Dahab over the melting summer.

The notification of our interview finally arrived! The interview would be at the end of June in Frankfurt. Finally we could feel our plans falling into place! Villa Bohème was booked for some days before we left too, so we decided to move out of there as well. Kurt would have the children for a few days, while James and I would take a short holiday. We would base ourselves at Rocksea in Nuweiba to enjoy our last days in Sinai on the beach. We packed our bags and made plans to spend a week in Israel, Jerusalem especially. I knew that I would regret having spent so much time in the Middle East, so close to those ancient cities, if I had never visited Jerusalem. Naturally, I loved it. Jerusalem was iconic and fascinating, but bittersweet too with all the ongoing ethnic tensions in Israel. We hired a car and explored up the Dead Sea and took in as much of the history as we could.

My friend Ingrid was keeping touch with Kurt concerning Luna and Tom. I wasn't feeling that confident about Kurt's behaviour. All of a sudden, he seemed to be so protective. My instinct told me that he might make trouble but I hoped he would put the children first. I had arranged with Ingrid, that she would have the children for two nights then come to meet James and I in Eilat. We could then all go together to the amazing Dolphin Reef. I was factoring the extra night with Ingrid in Dahab in case Kurt didn't take them to Ingrid's as arranged.

Kurt had also told me he wanted to take Luna, an 8 year old, scuba diving. This was the same guy who had previously stated only a few years before that children of 14 years shouldn't scuba dive! I told him that I didn't agree. No, he wasn't to take her scuba diving.

They all arrived in Eilat, excited to be going to Dolphin reef. But Ingrid had some disturbing news for me. Kurt had taken the children on the day as arranged, but the following day he had collected Luna again and taken her scuba diving after all. He had told Ingrid that I agreed. In the end, no harm was done but that surely indicated what he was capable of at the last minute. Anyhow, Dolphin Reef was magical. We all had such a great day.

Back in Nuweiba we just relaxed at Rocksea, spending time on the beach to make the last days in Sinai count. Kurt was calling the children all the time, sometimes two to three times a day. His behaviour was making me increasingly nervous and Luna and Tom could sense all the tension. I knew I was taking them away from their birth home and although they were looking forward to new adventures, they were also unsettled. It was going to be difficult enough for them and Kurt's behaviour was just what we didn't need or want, before leaving Egypt. In Kurt's mind, I was taking his children away from him and he had no say in the matter. Yet from the very beginning he had taken so little responsibility for them. I remembered the day I had arrived to live in Dahab and told him I was pregnant. I remembered how he had reacted, accusing me of trapping him and cutting his freedom. Well now he had his freedom and he was still complaining. He was still paying nothing towards their lives. I told him he would always be welcome to visit them anytime, that he could bring them back to Egypt for holidays. But all I could see was him was sulking and petulant about us going.

As for myself, I was just pleased to be moving forward to a place where I felt we had a future and could build a life and perhaps a business. In Egypt, I felt that the sands were always shifting. I now knew that was how many people (especially those with some success) liked to keep it. With everyone else on shifting sands they could have power. When something was shady or illegal, they could sneak up behind and pull everything out from under others, just when it suited them. That is what Sherif had done to me over the hotel and what Abdul had done to James over the apartments. So long as there was chaos and corruption, people like that could keep things moving their way.

I had agreed to go via Dahab on our way to the airport so the children could say goodbye to Kurt. But I changed my mind. I had visions of him making a huge scene, upsetting the children, myself and possibly even making us miss our flight to Germany.

We all said our own personal imaginary goodbyes as we were waved through the Dahab check point and turned right towards Sharm. I didn't allow myself any nostalgia. At that point I only felt a sense of "good bye and good riddance!". I called Kurt and said I was sorry but we didn't have time to call in at Dahab and we were going straight to the airport. I was thinking far ahead. Each mile towards the airport was a mile brighter for our future.

James wasn't flying with us as he was staying another three weeks to tidy up the last of our gear and prepare Bohème without us being around. Once we had done at the check in we turned around and could see Kurt. He waived and shouted to make the kids see him. I was mortified! He began showing me his middle finger and swearing at me making a huge scene in front of everybody but I was more concerned about Luna and Tom. Kurt was doing just what I was trying to avoid. I grabbed Luna and Tom and rushed back over to the security gate. Luckily the guards let them back through. At least once we showed up Kurt stopped cussing and yelling but I was so angry with him. Everything calmed down and he stormed out of the airport with everyone staring at us. James and I agreed that he should stay in the airport for half an hour or more to let Kurt calm down.

All I could do was go back to check in counter and hope everything would be OK. The children were very quiet and looked a little stunned. Despite any problems James and I had experienced in Dahab, we had managed to keep the children out of them. We eventually made our way to the next security check and went through. I made one last call to James who was still waiting in the airport and told him I would remove my Egyptian SIM so there would be no more calls until I got to Germany.

As we sat waiting to board the flight, I heard a phone ringing. At first I thought, 'it can't be mine. I've just turned my phone off!' But I looked in my bag and realised it was my German number! I had put my German SIM card in and by mistake, hadn't switched the phone off. It was James. "Kurt was waiting outside all this time. The police are here separating us but I don't trust what this madman will do in the desert between here and Dahab. Can you talk to him and tell him to pull his head in!" I was furious at Kurt. I told him to stop behaving like a madman. He knew why we leaving and one of the main reasons was to give Luna and Tom, his children, opportunities to go to good schools. I said he had time all these years to contribute and now he would just have to accept they were going. The children could hear my whole conversation, telling him to leave James alone, to grow up and stop fighting.

"Oh, Mama. They won't hurt each other will they? I love them both." Luna was crying. "Tell them to stop fighting." Tom was wide eyed and staring into space.

"Luna, I hope that they will both behave like the adults they are meant to be." I knew James was smart enough not provoke Kurt but he would also defend himself if he had to.

As far as I was concerned Kurt, had well and truly done his dash with that episode. If he disrespected me enough to cause so much trouble, when I was trying to do the best for the children and their future, he could go screw himself. He had never really given a rat's ass up until that point. I decided that was last time I would have anything personal to do with Kurt. I would communicate with him concerning the children but apart from that, he would no longer exist for me.

I spent a tense trip trying to distract the children and trying to look forward to seeing my parents, family and friends in Germany. Each mile away from Dahab and Egypt was a mile closer to beginning our new American life.

The weeks we waited for James to finally join us in Germany weren't easy ones. I worried about James being in Dahab for the next weeks with Kurt and his cronies about. Egypt can be a spiteful place when friends in high places turn a blind eye or even collude to create a problem. James kept a very low profile and just went about tidying up loose ends and preparing Bohème for his final departure. Everything went as planned and without a hitch.

James had one request before we left Europe for the United States and that was to spend time in Ibiza where he had partied and DJ'd during his misspent youth. He still loved music and wanted to go for a few days. I found him a ticket flying from Cologne, so we both drove up there to spend a night together before he flew out to Ibiza. It was a relief to know the children were happy with their grandparents and we could finally relax with Dahab days behind us.

I returned to Kaiserslautern to prepare for the interview at the immigration office which was for about three days away. James would still be in Ibiza. I wasn't feeling nervous at all, confident in fact. I felt I had all the correct paperwork and our lawyer, James's cousin, assured me everything would be a formality. I was so wrong.

Turned out the interviewer was a complete creep, a complete and utter asshole actually. Where do they find these people? He was arrogant, accusatory, and mean which added up to a very ugly attitude. Even in Egypt, where men can be dominating and arrogant, in general public life, they aren't rude. I was totally taken aback by his outright hostility and aggression. I thought to myself, 'This isn't going to plan at all.'

"Why isn't your husband with you?" he barked.

"There was no indication that he should be with me," I replied with some confusion. "Where did it say he should be with me?"

The grilling continued "What is his job in the United States?"

"He doesn't have a job. He hasn't lived there for twenty years."

"How will you live there then?"

"We will look for employment immediately." I felt like adding, 'which is why I am applying to live there legally and work.'

After some time he sat back and gloated smugly, "Besides your sponsors don't qualify." I was flabbergasted! James's parents, John and Katherine, were acting as our sponsors which meant they guaranteed to support us for home and money in the event we had initial problems. I had seen the mountain of paperwork that they had supplied concerning their income, assets, bank statements and so on. After all that time and effort I was told our sponsors didn't qualify! If we had been told there was any problem we could have asked another of James close relations, many of whom were very wealthy. Not that we planned to rely on them apart from the initial home at James's uncle's place until we found more permanent work. I left the office dejected, demoralised and angry at such revolting treatment. When I spoke to James's cousin, my immigration lawyer, he assured me not to worry. It would be sorted. I hoped he was right but I lost confidence from that interview on. It was a lonely couple of days until James returned from Ibiza.

We waited to hear the final decision and after some time we got an email saying we could collect our passports and our Green Cards. Phew! Finally we could plan our next steps.

But the emotional rollercoaster never let up... Why is there is always a "but"? I took a closer look at our Green cards and realised there was a mistake. They had spelt Luna's name wrong on her Green Card! Unbelievable! Fortunately, it was corrected very quickly. *'El hamdo la Allah!'* I said to myself. I knew Arabic sayings would stay in my head, even after I left Egypt.

I had been checking flight prices every day and could see they were getting more and more expensive as summer rolled on and with the holidays approaching. As soon as we had our Green Cards, I booked flights for us to leave within ten days. Woohoo! it was all happening! All of us started to feel very excited and the energy in the air was electric.

Three days before we were due to leave, James got a phone call from the United States. It was from his mother. Her cousin, the daughter of the uncle whose property we were going to lend while working for him, had called her. I didn't take any notice until I heard James's voice starting to rise. He was yelling within moments and slammed the phone down so hard I thought it would break. I looked at him, eyes wide with unspoken questions.

"You just wouldn't fucking believe it! That fucking family of mine! No wonder I left the place for 20 years! Fucking assholes everywhere!" He was bellowing and I hoped the children downstairs couldn't hear all he was saying.

All I could ask was, "What's happened?"

"Apparently we can't live in the house because of insurance cover. Insurance cover! Americans and their fucking insurance excuses! Bullshit! We have nowhere to live and no jobs!"

I was speechless. "Oh my god...bloody hell." We had flight tickets for three days time. Our plans for a new beginning were seeping down the drain. If life is a game of "Snakes and Ladders", we had certainly just slipped down a boa constrictor.

Gradually James stopped yelling, but went to the other extreme of not talking. He was devastated. I too, was numb with shock. With one phone call, it was like our plans and our world disintegrated. Over the next few days I had to explain to my parents what had happened and that everything was again up in the air. I told the children to give James some space. He needed time alone.

James took to drinking whisky and sleeping outside on the balcony on the cold tiles. He kept repeating, "I don't want to go. I don't want to go. It was your idea to go live in the United fucking States. You go."

"I don't want to go without you. We'll think of something." I sounded pathetic, as I had no idea. I understood he needed to be by himself in his depression but I pleaded with him to come back inside. The balcony was too cold and he would get ill.

We did manage to discuss our options. They were simple on the face of it: stay in Germany, go back to Dahab or fly to the Unites States. We had no dreams of living in Germany and I wasn't keen on that idea at all. In Dahab we still had a house and a bakery but we had sold all our things and were leaving for real reasons. In the end, we decided it was still best to get on that plane and fly to Las Vegas where we still had happy memories about our crazy, happy wedding. It sure wasn't going to be plain sailing and we didn't even know where we would start our new life. I kept telling myself, "Don't worry. Everything will be fine. Living in Egypt has given us grit."

James was furious with his family. They had let him down so badly at the last minute. He was even angry at Katherine and John because they hadn't approached the uncle, Katherine's wealthy brother, at all. James felt she should have stood up to his uncle, her brother, on our behalf. He felt betrayed that after promising us a place to live and some work and then pulling out, they could have at least found us a place to live for a few months until we could find jobs. If insurance was really the problem he'd had months, years in fact to tell us. Not three days before we were to arrive!

As we boarded the airplane for Las Vegas I couldn't decide whether I was excited or fearful. Both, if truth be known. I was worried about finances more than ever. Our money from Egypt wouldn't go nearly as far in the U.S. We had literally banked on being able to stay at James's uncle's place to find our feet. But there was no use more crying over that lost opportunity.

When we got Las Vegas, James went to rent a car. It had to be a huge car for two adults, two children and sixteen pieces of heavy luggage. We sure were loaded up as we squashed into the vehicle to drive to James's brother's house in Palm Springs. They had offered that we share their small place until we found a place to live.

Exhaustion began to really hit after a twelve hour flight, plus travel time, plus the three to four hour drive ahead. James was driving and I was fighting dozing off. Eventually I realised we were lost. James wasn't letting on but I could tell. Neither of us had a working mobile phone to call for directions. Eventually we arrived in Palm Springs exhausted and disorientated.

So there we were, in the middle of the desert, in summer, sharing a house with another family of 4 and we needed to get some transport, find a place to live, find a house to live, find some way of making income. Just small stuff really...

The priority was to buy a vehicle large enough for all of us so that we could go exploring for a place to live. James had his mind and heart set on a Volvo station wagon but there weren't so many Swedish Volvo station wagons for sale. His choice did seem slightly crazy in the US, where there is a wide choice of cars and they are so much easier to come by than Egypt.

"Why do we need a Volvo station wagon?" I asked. "Surely there are other cars that will do just as well?"

"We have a family. We need a station wagon for all the stuff we need to carry around sometimes. And Volvos are extremely reliable and very safe. We will find one."

I had every confidence that if he wanted a Volvo station wagon, he would find one. I always admired the way James could be so free in his heart, yet at other times be so totally focused when he wanted something. Like when he had pursued me despite my initial misgivings. I was also aware that his injuries from the desert road accident probably reminded him every day about the importance of safety in vehicles.

Even though we were used to desert heat, it was stupidly hot in Palm Springs. In Dahab there were usually cooling breezes off the sea but that inland heat in Palm Springs was a killer. If we wanted any service from the car yards we had to go during the day. We traipsed around car sale yards looking for a car in 40°C heat at midday, with no shade. Our car hunting escapades in Sharm el

Sheikh in the cool of the night, now seemed so much more sensible. I was melting and exhausted from jet lag and heat. There were no Volvo station wagons.

We scoured Craigslist looking for anything that would be of interest and for information on jobs, places, rents. After a few days James found a Volvo station wagon for sale. It was a few hours drive away but it sounded perfect. Turned out, it was perfect, so we ticked one thing off the list. We had "wheels" to explore further.

We already knew the places where we thought we shouldn't live; for being too expensive, too crowded, too urban, too cold, or too dry. We would just have to do more exploring. We had mended some bridges with Katherine and John and they offered to look after the children so James and I could concentrate on the search. We poured over maps and searched the internet for possibilities, then just got in the Volvo and went driving. Money was always an issue in the back of our minds so we planned to sleep in the back of the Volvo where possible. The windows were shaded at the back and being a station wagon there was room to lie down.

We decided to head for the coast through San Bernadino which was close to Katherine and John's Crestline, then head north of Los Angeles, then towards Santa Barbara. We were both comfortable on the coast but knew that chances of finding a place we could afford were slim. And the Pacific Coast was much colder than we were used to.

In Ventura County we drove off the highway to explore inland a little, inland where James remembered driving many years before. A small valley opened out in front of us and as I looked around at the orchards, the green hills, the quiet streets and my heart made a little leap of excitement.

"James, this place looks interesting. What do you think?"

"Yes, I remember this place I think. Ojai."

"You've been here? It looks like a small place."

"It was a long time ago. Like 20 years ago! I did some deliveries here for some work I was doing."

"Well I think it looks great. Let's look around. Maybe there's a Real Estate shop somewhere." I was thinking that Real Estate companies would handle rental properties as well. We could look at properties in the window and ask to view them. It didn't take us long to find one but all the houses were for sale. We called the phone number anyway but the person explained that Real Estate companies only handled properties for sale. They told me the best place to look for rental properties was on the internet, on Craigslist. We pulled out our laptop and searched for rental properties in the area. To our mind everything looked so expensive, even a two bedroom apartment was $1500 to $1700 a month, which made us cringe when thinking of our house with palm trees back in Dahab. But there was no point stopping and looking back.

"Let's just see what we can find. Let's not worry about the price at the moment." I was thinking back to my days in the Black Forest, about learning not to put up barriers in my mind. "Let's just dream and decide what will be perfect for us. What are the things we would really like in our new house?"

James at first shook his head, "What good will that do? We are not going to find something that is perfect and that we can afford."

"Look, if we don't know what we want we will never find it. Let's just dream. It can't hurt."

So we sat in the car thinking over the things that would be important to us; three bedrooms, a garden to grow vegetables and spend time outdoors, a room for James to do massage therapy, and so on. Our dream list became more detailed as we worked out what our perfect house would be like.

Then we looked again on Craigslist. "These look interesting. Let's call." Not one of our calls was answered by a person, only answering machines. Our enthusiasm dropped as we sat in silence thinking where we should go from there. But just as James suggested we call it a day, the phone rang. It was the owner of a rental property that we really liked the sound of. She explained, "I'm at the property right now. If you like you can come and look now."

"Great! Yes, we would like to for sure. Can you give us directions?" as James explained where we were.

"Oh!" she said. "That is just around the corner form the house! You can be here in two minutes."

At first we missed the street we were looking for but drove past a pretty looking school. "Oh this would be perfect for Luna and Tom." The whole area felt great, vibrant with fruit trees and gardens.

The actual house was just a block away from the school. I felt a magical moment as we stepped onto the property - three bedrooms, garden, alternative entrance for a room for James's massage clients. The garden had grown fruit trees, apples, avocado, peach and a laid out vegetable garden. We were in love.

The owner explained that she actually had someone very interested in signing a contract but she hadn't decided yet. My heart skipped a beat. It sounded like she would rather not rent it to them. We talked about our situation, that we wanted a place as soon as possible so the children could start school in a few weeks. We told her we planned to live long term in one place and that we loved her house. The only problem was finances as we had recently arrived from Egypt with no cash flow and no jobs. We really loved the house but needed a little time to arrange finances. We asked if we could have a day to think it over. We got back in the car with a mixture of excitement and depression. How could we rent that place with so little cash? The owner wanted $10,000 contract up front and the rent was way over what we could afford each month.

We had planned to spend the night in the area anyway, sleeping in the back of the car at the parking lot of the Santa Barbara University. We were like two old hippy students parking up.

"We have to find a way James. This is too perfect to pass up."

"I agree. But how? We really can't put all our money into the bond and rent up front. Not until we have some income."

"Look. Let's see if we can just get the owner to give us a few days to work something out. I really feel this place is right for us. Let's call her back right now and tell her we want the place. James, we want this house!"

He took a deep breath and said, "OK. We want this house. I have no idea how we will get it. But, yes. Let's call her and tell her, 'We want the house.'"

seemed pleased that we wanted it. It had been her family's home where she had raised five children and she now had grand children. I think she liked the idea that it would continue as a family home. She was prepared to take a chance with us.

I also called John and Katherine and told them we had found a place but we had no idea how we were going to pay for it. Minor detail! I asked if they could bring Luna and Tom up the following day so everyone could see how perfect this home was. I think it helped when the owner met Katherine and John as they were obviously well established in the California and lived nearby. Luna and Tom loved it too. I could feel the owner wanted us to have the house, as much as we wanted to find a way. In my heart I knew we would find a way to make this happen. We signed the contract that day for the $10,000 bond and start of the rental. I had faith. Everything would work out one way or another. We were moving forward.

With school starting in a few days, I wanted to move in straight away so Luna would be settled for her first days. It turned out the school was a public school with 300 hundred pupils up to Grade 8 and the kindergarten started at 5 years old, so Tom would be able to attend too. The classes were small and would give Luna a good opportunity to adjust to life in the States. We moved in on the 15th of August and school started on the 20th, so everything was going to plan. What was even better was a Boys and Girls Club where the children could go after school until 6pm. That meant I could start looking for work immediately in North Los Angeles, which was only about an hours drive away. We would need funds immediately to pay the rent.

Just when everything was coming together, I started to feel unwell. I wasn't really ill but I wondered if the stress of moving and the immediate house hunting had driven my stress levels too high. Another possible alternative was also pushing its way into my consciousness. I had missed my period. A little voice kept whispering in my head, 'You're pregnant', but I just ignored it. I had missed periods before so just I told myself it was because of the stress, leaving Egypt, waiting for the immigration interview. My body had enough excuses to shut down in some way.

Then I missed a second period. I told James. "I feel a little unwell. Odd really. Not exactly sick."

"Oh, what do you think you have?"

I took a deep breath and blurted out, "I think I'm pregnant."

"Oh! His eyes popped. Slowly, "Wow! Really?" Have you done a test?"

"No. But I know this feeling from before. I feel weird, not ill. I don't know how this will work..." We both looked at each other, not quite sure what an extra complication would mean to our already stretched lives. I hadn't used any contraception for many months, since we had been officially married actually, but I hadn't got pregnant. I just thought after some time that it wasn't going to happen again. James wasn't interested in doing any fertility tests either. He had just said he would accept whatever happened. Luna and Tom were his children too.

"So you better get a test then." James was matter of fact about it. "Then we will have a better idea of what we do from here."

Soon after I walked past a sign in Ventura that said 'Pregnancy Centre' and thought, this looks like a good place to start. I turned back and entered the pleasant office. The woman behind the counter looked up, "Can I help you?"

"Yes, hopefully," I said. "I wonder if you can answer some questions for me."

"Sure, sure. What would you like know?"

"Well, I already have two children. And I think I'm pregnant. We've just moved to the United States and we are living in Ojai. I have no idea how it works here with pregnancy and birth."

The woman smiled kindly, "Have you done a pregnancy test?"

"No," I shook my head. "Not yet."

"Well, let's do that then and we'll know where to start. Everything will be just fine." The test was positive. I was pregnant with my third child. She immediately allocated me to a Doctor and made an appointment for me to see him as soon as possible to arrange more tests. I felt I was in the right place and she was right, everything would be fine, if not easy. I realised that the centre was from a religious order and aimed at younger women, maybe unmarried or teenagers but they were so calm and caring from the very beginning.

So there I was, recently arrived in the United States and already pregnant. I asked myself, Is my life repeating as it had done in Egypt? Every time I arrive in a new country to live I get pregnant? But that time I had partner, a husband who was with me in spirit and in body, willing to work to keep our family and our marriage together. In that respect, it was another world. Nonetheless, I also knew we would need some more help. There was no way I could contemplate looking for higher paid work in Los Angeles and would have to find something closer to home, maybe part time. I called my parents to tell them the news and to ask if they could help us out for a few months if we needed it to pay the rent. They agreed and wished us the best for my pregnancy.

James wanted to start work straight away as a massage therapist. It was something he knew well and had been doing professionally in top class hotels in Egypt. However for insurance purposes and Health and Safety reasons, he needed signed off certificates. Thatmeant he had to attend a school for six months before being signed off. It just had to be done. And paid for.

James started making jewellery again as well. He had been making jewellery all the time we were in Dahab on a small scale so he just put more energy into it again, looking for craft outlets and local markets. James also planned his garden, where he could grow our food in the rich fertile soil and the mild temperatures.

I looked for jobs in Ojai and started work as a receptionist at a small bed and breakfast. Ojai is a popular place for short breaks and long weekend guests. I told myself it's ridiculous that anyone might have a stigma towards a pregnant woman working but I wasn't sure how they would take my pregnancy so just didn't tell them. I was still healthy and fit so it wasn't long before I was also making and serving breakfasts. I realised that my pregnancy wasn't going to cause any negative issues. They were great people to work for.

I was aware that I had to be the rock in our family. It was difficult for everyone in their own ways. James was studying hard and focused on learning all he could for his course. The children settled into school but I knew they would be missing their very free life in sunny Dahab and the friends they had known all their short lives. I focused on being mindful, keeping up meditation every day, doing yoga and exercise.

I also started this book. I had so many negative feelings about my last few years in Egypt, that I knew I wanted to deal with them before our child was born. By having to remember, to lay it all out, to delve into my memories, my feelings, I had to deal with each issue as they came flooding back into my heart. I discovered there were many things I hadn't dealt with at all.

Writing cleared out a lot of pain and some confusion but I understood it would take time for healing to take place. Life in

Egypt had been good to me too but the chaos, the wilful confusion, the corruption make it so difficult for anyone, Egyptian or foreigner to build any lasting relationships there. Everything is built on shifting sands and you have to accept it to survive there.

I decided if I couldn't commit to extra employment then I would volunteer for a charity that cared for the homeless, by raising money and distributing meals and the like. I started unpaid work at a clothing shop. It meant sorting and selling clothes which was another nod to a layer of previous life in fashion, so long ago. There were no designs to draw and no production lines to check but it was lots of fun to see what would arrive in the donated bags.

A bonus of the volunteering was I got to choose and buy clothes for us at discounted rates. Clothes to wear were certainly not going to be an issue, except jeans for James – his long legs were more difficult to fit from donated clothing sacks. It wasn't long before we all had a great wardrobe. It also meant I got to know people in the community and started to make friends and settle in.

I was aware that I didn't want to accumulate as much stuff as I had before. I was consciously trying to keep things simple and be mindful about what we really needed. I became a specialist in wishful thinking. Whatever we needed, we wished for, literally. If we needed a piece of furniture, we wished for it and it would appear; in a garage sale, on Craigslist, or at the side of the road. There really is power in wishful thinking! I didn't question how it worked, but it did.

One evening as we relaxed outside in the valley of Ojai, we both stopped talking and just sat together. James had his arm around my shoulders and the other resting gently on my expanding tummy. We looked out over the valley at the Fall with leaves turning gold and copper. We were grateful to have found such a wonderful home where we could be together as a family. We had already come through so much but as a couple we got stronger every day. Those difficult times in Egypt made us tougher and softer at the same time. Regardless of where we were in the world, there would be issues to deal with, problems to overcome. In the end we get choices, even if it is only in the attitude we take. I decided there and then I would always try to make positive choices and be grateful for the good things in my life.

Luna and Tom

Epilogue

I sit here rereading my memoir, of some of the events that have happened in my life to date. I sit in a strong position in most respects, living a life I continue to choose, surrounded by my family and supported by friends all over the world. I know it has not been an easy road but I feel blessed and look forward to the future and what life brings.

After I left Dahab I really didn't want to look back over the past. I wanted to shut Dahab and the difficulties that I faced there completely out of my mind. I needed some time to heal the wounds and to feel stronger, before I could see many of those events through a rational perspective. Life in Egypt had been difficult but I knew that I was only seeing the hurt, like a patient recovering from an operation.

However, I was also aware that I was carrying the future of a new life that was growing daily inside me. I did not want the negativity of Egyptian life, to impact on our new life in the United States. I had to find a way to clear it from my mind.

That was when I decided to write this memoir. And I wanted to have it completed before our baby was born so I could treat those memories like a history, that could be filed away for a long time, if necessary. Once my story was on the pages, I felt I wouldn't have to remember it anymore. It was also written as a way of explanation for my children and family, so they could understand some of things that happened, both the dark and the bright days.

When I first started to remember, the writing was painful and raw. As I looked back everything seemed so negative in my painful memories, my Egyptian story seemed a lot more dark than light. Yet it is said, "flowers grow out of the dark". As painful as it was at times, I realised that darker moments made me lighter and stronger. Many people who have come before me, have discovered this.

I was determined to file everything away before the birth of our baby. James was to be a father for the first time. He for sure was a father to Luna and Tom but he had never been through a pregnancy with a partner, so he too was feeling different pressures and emotions. It was however, a blessing for me to have him by my side, both physically and mentally. That pregnancy was a completely different experience to my previous ones.

My second son was born in April. I worked right up until a few days before he was born, surrounded by warm loving people at work and at home. Over those months of my increasingly obvious pregnancy, we all came to know each other well. I was fit and active throughout the pregnancy too, so I didn't see the point in stopping working.

James actually took over my job for four weeks until I could go back to work with my baby beside me. I feel children are part of our lives and should be alongside whatever we do as much as possible. Life was going in a good direction and I was determined to keep it that way.

In August that year, I had to return to Dahab to check on our properties, Villa Bohème and Leila's Bakery. The latter was being managed by our very reliable Egyptian staff, who we were so lucky to have. Egypt was still suffering political changes and tourist numbers throughout the country were low. I found everything was fine as far as the businesses were concerned and running as well as could be expected, under the circumstances.

Everything was fine with the businesses, but I wasn't fine. Returning to Dahab after almost a year opened up many of the old wounds. I still felt very hurt and abused by my past and the people there. I was more aware of the pain on returning, than when I was going through the problems. It was like the stitches had been removed too soon and the cuts had not healed. At that time I was too busy dealing with the trauma, it was like the real pain came as the nerves were healing and growing back. During the actual events I needed to be constantly be alert and respond to the situation in hand, without time to feel the actual pain I felt inside.

When I returned that summer I didn't want to have anything to do with any of those people who had caused me pain or those memories. I realised I wasn't in any mood to approach people, let alone mend any bridges. I had already written them out of my life with this memoir. Luna and Tom spent their time with Kurt but I didn't want anything to do with him. I spent much of my time in Nuweiba at Rock Sea or when in Dahab , only spending time in with my trusted Italian friend, Francesca.

Beneath it all, I had a hard time trusting anyone anymore. I realised events in Egypt had eaten away at my confidence. The shifting sands kept me unbalanced and I still didn't trust the ground under my feet. I returned to the United States, understanding I still had more healing to do.

To help, I started doing things I was familiar with and knew I could do. I started baking again to sell at local markets. Some days the whole kitchen was full of bread and other foods to sell and happy memories of my grandmother would flood my mind. As we loaded up our utilitarian Volvo, I knew James had been so right about buying it. We were in flow.

I began to look for new interests and a new career. I was seeking something that I could be totally absorbed in, just as I had been absorbed in fashion as a teenager. I would become a Health Coach. I had been interested in health and fitness my entire life and it is natural for me to want to share my knowledge of how one can improve one's health and one's life. When I began to study for my new career, I felt positive energy flowing through me again. I was learning and building a passion again for something I loved. Finding that passion, healed my heart.

It actually took a couple more years before I fully got my confidence back. Leaving Egypt and moving to the United States helped me find my inner rock again and my strength started to replenish.. But it was not so much about which country I was in, it was also about the people that I surrounded myself with.

It was some years before I returned to Dahab again, this time from a position of new found strength and returned confidence. I only had a preschool aged son with me and it was easy to have him in the warm sunshine that Luna and Tom had so enjoyed. I always tell Kurt he is welcome to pay for their tickets to visit, but as yet, he has neither contributed or responded.

On reflection now, I find that I don't dislike Egypt. The Egyptian people can be fantastic. Some are so very generous in difficult situations; even offering to share their last meal with you if that were all they had. They live in and have to deal with, what I managed to leave - hustle and corruption. When I returned a second time, people in South Sinai were struggling even more than previously. Tourist numbers had continued to decline after the revolution and regime changes.

But even after those years away, people remembered me and genuinely said, "Welcome back" with big smiles. Even if I found I didn't have enough cash on me at the supermarket they just said, "No problem. *Bokra. Bokra* Just bring it tomorrow." It is a lesson in humility that, after all that can happen in Egypt, that they are still so trusting and helpful. Those memories, I never want to lose.

I wanted to meet up with Natasha so I called her up and arranged that we go to dinner together. In reality we had been quite good friends, so we relaxed into a familiar easiness. I think she felt it cathartic to be able to talk to someone who had known her from the very first time she came to Dahab. She opened her heart to me.

In those years of my absence, Sherif had died, succumbing after a period of time to throat cancer. Louise Hay would have something to say about that, no doubt. I wished her luck. In a twist of fate, it was lucky that I had been forced through the process of separating ownership from Sherif when I did. If he had kept the unsigned papers, I would have been dealing with his family too with even less hope than before. At least by then, the bakery ownership papers were clear.

Sherif had been right about some things though. My rental property had been consistently booked since it was built and continues to be a small source of income. James had returned to Dahab on a number of occasions and made sure maintenance was kept up and also added a few more features, such as a small plunge pool for visitors to cool down in the garden.

By the end of the evening Natasha and I had completely made our peace. I met up at her house after that and we even had a "girls' night" together with 2 other girl friends just like old times. Good times.

Dirk still had two branches of his bakery operating, despite the increasingly dire tourist travel difficulties for South Sinai, so I admired his tenacity. I didn't bear Dirk animosity anymore but I wasn't sure if I had the willpower to deal with meeting him. He could be so abrasive at times. I also knew how aggressive he could be and I had no idea what his reaction would be if he saw me.

One day I went to his bakery alone as my son was at a play group with other children. I had decided that meeting him would be a good thing. I had nothing to be ashamed of and I would deal with whatever the meeting bought. I personally had no intention of bringing up past issues. For me it was about acknowledgement. Acknowledgement that everything that was in the past stayed there and I lived my life looking forwards.

I went into the bakery and asked if Dirk was around. "No, he's not here at the moment." I thought, 'OK, the flow says I am not to meet him. Fine.' I was about to leave when I saw Dirk pull up in his car. I was pretty sure he saw me so I waited. He took ages to get out of the car so perhaps he was trying to ignore me. I kept waiting, feeling a little nervous but determined to carry the meeting through. Perhaps Dirk had the same feelings of trepidation I did. Finally Dirk had to admit he could see me and got out of his car.

At first he was quite rude with an attitude that was for sure unwelcoming and belligerent, just like in the old days. I said, "

Dirk, I'm not here for an argument. I'm way past that. The past is past. I just want us to be able to look each other in the eye and remember the good times we had together in Dahab. Because there were good times."

He relaxed visibly. "Oh! I am pleased to hear that." He paused, and looked at me as if a weight was lifted of his shoulders too. He gave me a brief hug and we could both feel the power of forgiveness. Really, forgiveness is so strong. "I'm so happy that you have said that. There were good times, for sure."

"Yes, yes, there were. And those are the times we should remember and celebrate." I was feeling a little choked up too.

He continued, "You know my wife and I were quite worried what might happen with you back in town."

I was surprised, "Really? But I have been away from Dahab now for years! I only want peace between us."

"Yes. But things were so difficult and nasty..."

I cut him off. "Dirk, I didn't come to talk about any of the past. For me it's gone and I don't even think about it anymore. So you don't have to either. Let's talk about what's happening now. What plans you have. How your family is. Only positive things." I was totally free and over the past.

I knew that he was planning to expand to open a bakery in Cairo so I wished him well. I could see he swelled with pride over that. We talked about our kids, our lives and it was a relaxed and happy conversation. By the end I walked away knowing that I had faced another challenge and I was stronger for it.

That is what I will continue to do. Seek out my challenges and face them with love and energy. Some of that had been dimmed by Egypt but I know it is not the people's fault. They are dealing with their lives as best they can in simple, tough ways.

I know for me it is important to keep the love and light shining. It is overcoming the tough times that keep us learning and appreciating the good. I now have three beautiful, loving children, a soulmate as well as a partner and a new career, which is already bringing me much joy. Long may they all prosper.

Glossary

abaya	a long black long sleeved robe worn by Muslim women in Arabic speaking countries
Bedouin	Arabic speaking nomadic peoples of the Middle East
Bedouin tattoos	an ancient tradition, traditionally on women's faces, symbolising heath and protection, beauty and spirituality
Bokra	an Arabic word meaning *"tomorrow"*
Dousha	an Arabic phrase which means *"a lot of shouting and big gestures"*
Egyptian Pound	the currency in Egypt. (Note: when I was living in Egypt 7-8 EGP was worth 1 Euro and $1 USD around 5 EGP)
El hamdo la Allah	an Arabic phrase meaning "Praise be to God"
jalabiya	a loose, full-length gown with wide sleeves, often decorated with embroidery along its hems—collar, sleeves and skirt.
habibi	Arabic word meaning *"love"*
hijab	a head covering worn in public by Muslim women.
iftar	a meal eaten after sunset during Ramadan by Muslims to break the fast
lassi	a cool drink made from yoghurt or fruit
Mafeesh mushkila	a phrase meaning *"No problem!"* in Palestinian, Jordanian and Egyptian dialect.

Magnus Medina	word in Egyptian Arabic for *"City Hall"*
marmaraya	a Bedouin tea, made from the Marmaraya plant which grows in the Sinai desert
mezze	a Persian word in origin meaning *'taste'*, mezze is used to describe a combination of small dishes, often served at the beginning of a meal
riyadh	Arabic word for an interior courtyard or garden
sha Allah	*an* Arabic expression for *"God willing"* or *"if God wills"*
souq	a typical street market or bazaar in Arabic speaking countries
tahina	an Egyptian sesame sauce
shalwar kameez	a traditional outfit worn by both men and women
ta'miya	the Egyptian Arabic word for *'falafel'*, one of Egypt's national dishes
Weihnachten	German word for 'Christmas'
Yallah	a common expression in Arabic, which means *"come on"*, *"let's get going"* or *"hurry up"*

About the Author

Originally from Germany, I moved to Italy to study and worked all over the world for 10 years as a fashion designer. I settled in Egypt started a family and lived there for nine years until we moved to California. In our new home, I have reinvented myself as a creative business woman, a mother of three, while continuing to manage our vacation rental properties in Dahab.

Even though we found a beautiful place to live in the Ojai Valley surrounded by organic farming, I was shocked to the depths of my soul about the food and lifestyle I saw around me. So, I decided to nurture my family in alternative ways and created the home based bakery *Eva's Traditional Bread.* Natural slow fermented Sourdough Whole Wheat bread is my main product which I deliver fresh to people's door and sell at the Ojai Farmer's Market.

I became determined to find a way of keeping myself healthy with dietary and lifestyle changes. I intrinsically knew that "food is medicine". Now, at 50, I feel great! I am the healthiest I have ever been in my life. I am proud of my family working daily together in our kitchen and vegetable garden, to provide nutrient rich meals for ourselves.

Through my experiences, I have developed a passion for health and wellness. I was so inspired about what I had learned and wanted to share it with other people. So I enrolled in the internationally recognized training program at the *Institute for Integrative Nutrition (IIN)* to become a certified health and lifestyle coach. My education has equipped me with extensive knowledge in holistic nutrition, health counselling, and the importance of preventive care. Now, I am really excited to be able to help other people (especially moms) to achieve their health goals. My biggest awakenings have been to accept and learn to love myself, as well as to grow as a person. Writing this book has helped me to do so.

I hope to inspire you in your own growth. Feel free to get in touch!

www.goodbreadojai.com

www.eva hoffmann.life